Art, Sustainability and Learning Communities

Artwork Scholarship: International Perspectives in Education

Series editors: Anita Sinner and Rita L. Irwin
Print ISSN: 2632-7872 | **Online ISSN:** 2632-9182

The aim of the Artwork Scholarship series is to invite debate on, and provide an essential resource for, transnational scholars engaged in creative research involving visual, literary and performative arts. Approaches may include arts-based, practice-based, a/r/tography, artistic, research creation and more, and explore pedagogical and experimental perspectives, reflective and evaluative assessments, methodological deliberations, and ethical issues and concerns in relation to a host of topic areas in education.

In this series:

Provoking the Field: International Perspectives on Visual Arts PhDs in Education, edited by Anita Sinner, Rita L. Irwin and Jeff Adams (2019)
Living Histories: Global Perspectives in Art Education, edited by Dustin Garnet and Anita Sinner (2022)
Community Arts Education: Transversal Global Perspectives, edited by Ching-Chiu Lin, Anita Sinner and Rita L. Irwin (2023)
A/r/tography: Essential Readings and Conversations, edited by Rita L. Irwin and Anita Sinner (2024)
Art, Sustainability and Learning Communities: Call to Action, edited by Raphael Vella and Victoria Pavlou (2024)

Art, Sustainability and Learning Communities

CALL TO ACTION

Edited by
Raphael Vella and Victoria Pavlou

Bristol, UK / Chicago, USA

First published in the UK in 2024 by
Intellect, The Mill, Parnall Road, Fishponds, Bristol, BS16 3JG, UK

First published in the USA in 2024 by
Intellect, The University of Chicago Press, 1427 E. 60th Street,
Chicago, IL 60637, USA

Copyright © 2024 Intellect Ltd

All rights reserved. No part of this publication may be reproduced, stored in a retrieval system or transmitted, in any form or by any means, electronic, mechanical, photocopying, recording or otherwise, without written permission.

A catalogue record for this book is available from the British Library.

Cover designer: Tanya Montefusco
Cover image: Charlene Galea performing Ħawwel żerriegħa ('Sow a Seed') during Debatable Land(s), October 2021. @ Photo Elisa von Brockdorff.
Production editor: Laura Christopher
Series: Artwork Scholarship
Series editors: Anita Sinner and Rita Irwin
Typesetting: MPS Limited

Hardback print ISBN: 978-1-78938-897-8
ePDF ISBN: 978-1-78938-899-2
ePUB ISBN: 978-1-78938-898-5
Series ISSN 2632-7872 / Online ISSN 2632-9182

Contents

Introduction	Learning Communities and Creative Actions for a More Sustainable Planet Raphael Vella and Victoria Pavlou	1
Part 1	**Call to Action: Theoretical Considerations** Victoria Pavlou and Raphael Vella	11
Chapter 1	Promises and Delivery: Teacher Education for ESD-Enhanced Visual Arts Education Chrysanthi Kadji-Beltran and Victoria Pavlou	17
Chapter 2	Voicing a Sustainable Future Through Visual Arts Education: Culture in Action Martha Ioannidou and Soula Mitakidou	35
Chapter 3	Aliens or Allies? Towards Symbiotic Relationships in Art Education Raphael Vella	51
Chapter 4	An Aesthoecological Approach to Professional Learning Communities: Analyzing With CARE Emese Hall and Chris Turner	67
Chapter 5	Bridging Theory and Practice: Evaluating and Developing Projects That Connect Visual Arts Education and Education for Sustainable Development Ernst Wagner	81
Part 2	**Call to Action: Real-World Propositions** Raphael Vella and Victoria Pavlou	95
Chapter 6	Peer-Mentoring at the Intersection of Education for Sustainable Development and Visual Arts Education Vincent Caruana	101

Chapter 7	Visual Arts for Inclusion in Diverse School Contexts: A Kaleidoscope of Learning Soula Mitakidou and Martha Ioannidou	113
Chapter 8	Envisioning Better Futures: Integrating Sustainability Practices Into Museum Education for Elementary Student Teachers Victoria Pavlou and Chrysanthi Kadji-Beltran	129
Chapter 9	Drawing and the Global Climate Emergency: Affective and Connective Explorations Chris Turner and Emese Hall	147
Part 3	**Sustaining Diverse Epistemological Frameworks Through the Arts** Raphael Vella and Victoria Pavlou	**163**
Chapter 10	Lyric Convergences: Bringing Together Art, Philosophy and Places We Can Love Bob Jickling	169
Chapter 11	THE TWO|FOUR|TWO Art Group: Can Contemporary Art Practice Act as a Vehicle for Sustainable Development? Costas Mantzalos	187
Chapter 12	'Now We Know': On Coming Together as an Artistic Practice Margerita Pulè and Maren Richter	197
Chapter 13	Cross-Cultural Dialogue: Searching Traces and the Mahalla Festival Sabine Küper-Büsch and Thomas Büsch	207
Chapter 14	Participatory Art With Trees: A Pedagogical Approach Maria Huhmarniemi	217
Chapter 15	'Ngen' Ancient Spirits of the Woods: Art-Based Environmental Education in Chiloé Archipelago Francisco Schwember, Felipe Palma, Antonia Condeza-Marmentini and Guillermo Marini	227
Chapter 16	Trash to Treasure: Sustaining and Preserving the Krobo Bead Culture Through Community Learning Felix Amofa Gyebi	237
Chapter 17	Changing Climate, Changing Communities Stephanie H. Danker, Shafkat Khan and Katie L. Feilen	247
Chapter 18	Reclaiming the Street: The Expanded Garden Eva Marín Peinado	257

Chapter 19	Diffractive Methodology as a Posthuman Approach to Engage With Human Equity Through Socially Engaged Artistic Practice Susan (Susie) Lachal	267
Chapter 20	Inviting Teacher Candidates in Art Education to Become Global Agents for Sustainability Kazuyo Nakamura and Anita Sinner	279
Chapter 21	Social Sculpture Perspective: Re-Sculpting or De-Sculpting Citizenship by Shaping Art as a Vehicle for Social Change Ana María Marqués Ibáñez	289

Notes on Contributors — 301

Introduction

Learning Communities and Creative Actions for a More Sustainable Planet

Raphael Vella and Victoria Pavlou

Mapping the field

As one hovers far above a continent or two on an online mapping platform like Google Maps, it's not difficult to assume a kind of abstract view of geographic space and human interaction. At that 'height', the world's shades of green, ochre and blue look and feel clean. The feeling is not without precedent. In 1972, when the famous *Blue Marble* image photographed by the crew of the Apollo 17 spacecraft spread quickly around the globe in newspapers, people were drawn to this picture which seemed to portray a sense of world unity (Mirzoeff, 2015). Of course, *Blue Marble* had no street view or route planning options so the image retained the striking, utopian appearance that would inspire environmentalists and generations of children depicting world peace. The flat geographies of traditional cartography, on the other hand, pull us directly back into the conflictual field of geopolitics, with the vast expanse of each continent conveniently presented in a concise format and carved into nation-states separated by borders represented by thin, black lines. As we know, the historical connections between mapping, colonialism and power cannot be overlooked.

Nowadays, mapping is a more corporate affair. As we zoom into the digital terrain of towns and streets in Google Maps or Google Earth, we are prompted with small, circular photos or icons indicating the nearest sights, restaurants, hotels, grocery stores, gas stations and other business listings. We are warned of bad traffic conditions ahead in real time by Google's Traffic feature, which collects data from its users. Technological utopia is offset by the platform's monitoring of our behaviour. Crucially, the platform's users are no longer passive beholders of a static representation of space. We can take in vertical perspectives and navigate freely … to some extent. Inaccessible areas and low-resolution imagery of specific regions show that the digital verticality of such platforms is still impacted by political and economic inequalities (Graham, 2018). No system of cartographic representation, land surveying or geotagging – indeed, no technology – is innocent.

Yet, we absolutely need to grasp some sense of the global nature of contemporary challenges that affect human and nonhuman interactions with their environment if we want to shape a better, more socially just and caring way of living on this Earth. Researching context-specific challenges and creative responses that support quality educational initiatives and build resilience through partnerships and learning communities can drive transformation in various important sectors. This book does not offer miracle remedies for the environmental and social upheavals the world is experiencing. Instead, it proposes three components – art, sustainability and learning communities – that we consider absolutely essential in reorienting priorities. As art transforms matter and modifies environments and settlements, it captures some of the difficulties in articulating divergent interests, inequalities, movements of groups of people across borders, ecological disasters, events that form or shake civic life, and so on. Art revolves around the possibility of change: not necessarily utopian change or the short-lived kick of stylistic innovation but the ability to explore and assess the interaction of a world and human as well as nonhuman life with fresh eyes. Sustainability is a long-term goal; it 'is a paradigm for thinking about the future' (UNESCO, n.d.). Learning communities can feed into this sustainable vision by helping to build relationships based on cooperation, care and interdependence. The shared goals, connections and challenges of learning communities in formal and informal settings, in fact, are frequently referenced in all three parts of this publication, particularly in relation to the enhancement of processes of sustainable development. Finally, the 'call to action' in the title is the network of threads that links these three components together and pulls them forward, making it possible to draft new artistic, ecological and community-based coordinates beyond the limitations of national territorial lines.

Like the mapping platforms described earlier, the book has an international perspective that weaves visual representations (art) into issues related to politics, social groups, economies and cultures. Unlike maps, however, many problems that are targeted by discussions on sustainable development are international in scope and cannot (or should not) be limited by a state-centric mindset that dissects land into political territories and focuses almost exclusively on national policies and interests. The well-known Brundtland report (World Commission on Environment and Development, 1987) already indicated how

> From space, we see a small and fragile ball dominated not by human activity and edifice but by a pattern of clouds, oceans, greenery, and soils. Humanity's inability to fit its activities into that pattern is changing planetary systems, fundamentally. Many such changes are accompanied by life-threatening hazards. This new reality, from which there is no escape, must be recognized – and managed.
>
> (n.p.)

It has become abundantly clear that national strategies need to be informed by global concerns, however, without losing touch with the particularities of the local. Likewise, the book's 'call to action' is supported by its engagement with the interactive nature of diverse learning communities and creative actions in different regions of the world. The publication proposes the idea that coordinated, creative action and an awareness of a plurality of epistemological orientations can promote a sense of connectivity, lifelong learning and confidence in the possibility of changing current conditions. By addressing educational goals and contemporary artistic practices, many of the contributors in this publication connect visual and other forms of communication with environmental obligations and social issues and seek to promote a sense of active citizenship. Several of the chapters in the book's different parts showcase international, empirical, artistic and curricular research which presents a case for strong learning communities and takes a clear political stand in favour of socially engaged pedagogies. The activist potential of art education and artistic practice are interpreted within the context of broader global goals informed by principles of Education for Sustainable Development (ESD).

At the same time, it should be noted that multidisciplinary strategies are often constrained by institutional or discipline-imposed limits. Some of these limits are ingrained within the field of art education itself; as Wilson and Snöbjörnsdóttir (2022) argue, some art educators still stick to conventional models that restrict the role of art education to technical rather than political goals, despite an expansion of the field in recent decades. However, the cross-curricular nature of ESD lends itself to pedagogical research and experimentation that can also feed into the building of new models and goals of art education. Shared spaces of exchange in the fields of art, ESD and continuous professional development reflect upon and inspire experimental approaches to collective responsibility and solidarity, which are more crucial than ever in today's world.

Criticisms of sustainable development

The meanings of terms like 'sustainability' and 'sustainable development' are contested and a variety of definitions are employed in different fields and by different experts. The word 'development' is open to several interpretations, varying from meanings associated with economic advancement to more socially oriented empowerments of disadvantaged groups. If we describe sustainable development simply as the long-term evolution and survival of systems combined with the provision of good living conditions for people, we find that it immediately becomes challenging to define more clearly what good living conditions, life expectancy and even survival actually mean (Borowy, 2014). Among the criticisms levelled at the concept of sustainable development, a few stand out: problems associated with the correctness of the term itself, the term's association with environmental (over all other) concerns, multiple definitions leading to implementation difficulties, the selective tendency to associate potential benefits only with certain parts of the world, the controversial nature of modelling tools developed to analyze the concept of sustainable development, different views on SDGs, and the absence of clear strategies for organizational and financial implementation (Planetary Project, n.d.).

Literature on sustainable development indicates that, as a global development policy, it addresses the improvement of living conditions and the conservation of ecosystems, while aiming for a balance between social progress and environmental and economic goals (Mensah & Casadevall, 2019). The Brundtland report provided an early model for integrating environmental objectives with goals associated with social and economic justice. The sustainable development goals (SDGs) continued to explain more specifically how these objectives could be integrated but have also been criticized by some for being too wide-ranging, hence impractical tools to achieve all that they set out to advocate for and implement. Critical evaluations of the SDGs have ranged from requests for more clarity of indicators of success to calls for firmer political action. For some critics working in the field of economics, the SDGs establish unquantifiable targets that are difficult to monitor, particularly in developing countries where data about environmental and social dimensions are not easily available or simply not rigorous enough (Swain, 2018). Others have been critical of the language of specific goals: SDG 1, for example, whose title refers to the ending of poverty in all its forms everywhere, but refers mainly to extreme poverty and argues for nationally determined benchmarks, leaving a lot of leeway for partial implementations (Sengupta, 2018). In the field of education, Target 4.7 has come under close scrutiny, because it seems to assume that everyone agrees about indicators of the knowledge and skills that are required by learners to promote sustainable development (Brockwell, Mochizuki, & Sprague, 2022). Jickling (2017) has argued that the language of this particular target reflects an outcomes-driven and market-oriented model that leans towards measurement and indicators of success rather than a truly transformative and caring education.

ESD and art education

This belief in the need for an education that addresses people's relationships with a world they *care* about is one of the foundational aspects of this publication and the key to understanding the link between ESD and the arts. ESD addresses lifestyles, focusing on holistic learning and changes in behaviours that can contribute to more sustainable societies. Culture and the arts address important aspects like intercultural dialogue and frequently push people to take action around the world. While the Brundtland Report established the three dimensions of economic growth, social inclusion and environment, culture was later introduced as the fourth pillar of sustainable development, because the arts 'are the unavoidable bases for dialogue for peace and progress as these values are intrinsically connected to human development and freedoms' (United Cities and Local Governments, 2010, n.p.). Apart from the 'usefulness' of culture in serving the needs of the three other pillars of sustainable development, it is also relevant to look into ways of sustaining culture itself (Sabatini, 2019).

While all the chapters were written specifically for the book, some of the research in this publication emerges from an EU-funded, Erasmus + project called 'Visual arts education in new times: Connecting Art with REal life issues' (CARE). The CARE project (2019–22[1]) invested in the training of pre-service and in-service teachers in visual arts education (VAE) as a vital link to bring about a change in education and really connect learning with contemporary life. There is a need for European and worldwide educational systems to develop attitudes, values and behaviours in young people that can serve to build sustainable societies. An education for real-life issues, as understood in this research, is an approach to integrating challenges associated with living in today's world and thinking about how these challenges affect us, people in other parts of the world, nonhuman species and tomorrow's generations. If education is not viewed through a sustainability lens that addresses meaningful engagements with current challenges, we would be missing crucial elements like interrelated environmental, social, and economic challenges, including peace, freedom, social justice, climate crisis and environmental degradation (Bell, 2016). VAE, with its focus on both the mind and the body, has the potential to develop positive self-perceptions and identity and promote a sense of community through a shared spirit. VAE enables learners to develop confidence and ownership of learning; it provides alternative ways of learning, addressing the needs of all learners and provides opportunities for different ways of participation in and outside school. When infused with elements of ESD, it provides learners with opportunities for authentic learning and meets affective aims, attitude development, awareness raising and offers opportunities for action, thus establishing connections between schools and the real world. The CARE project created and established learning communities among academics, artists, schools and teachers (Hall, 2022; Ioannidou, 2022), whose impact had a snowball effect on children, as teachers were empowered to implement art units that promoted critical thinking, systemic holistic thinking, collaborative problem solving and were founded on the sustainable development values of respect for human and nature, justice, democracy, solidarity and tolerance (Ioannidou & Mitakidou, 2022). Teacher training in art education was infused not only with ESD principles but also with contemporary art practices and opened up possibilities for teachers to incorporate these in their art units.

CARE's innovation lies both in the combination of the fields of VAE and ESD as well as in its orientation towards overcoming instrumental approaches and empowering teachers and teaching practice within authentic situations that combine global and local issues. The conception is closely linked to constructivist concepts of teaching and learning: situatedness, authenticity, a diversity of contexts and perspectives and social integration. The aim was to achieve a reflexive notion of education with educational targets such as self-determination and autonomy, education as a stimulus and not as an intrusion, mechanical transfer or even pressure (Ferreira, Ryan, & Tilbury, 2007). Meaningful contexts and knowledge should help us to tackle the current problems in order to understand, deal with and actively shape future life situations that have yet to be determined.

The image of a teacher participating in the Cyprus local teacher training as part of the CARE project offers a glimpse of the impact of the training on teachers. In a visual reflection produced halfway through the training, a teacher produced the image in Figure I.1. When asked to talk about it, she pointed out that she tried to capture the connection between humans and nature; the multiple lines on the face indicate that we cannot only think of ourselves but also of others and that 'we' – as a collective human being – need to act through our hearts to sustain a viable future for ourselves but also for the environment and the animals living with us.

Figure I.1: Visual reflection on teacher training.

The structure of the book

The structure of the book is divided into three parts. Parts One and Two bring together many of the researchers involved in CARE, Frederick University in Cyprus, University of Malta in Malta, University of Exeter in the UK, Aristotle University of Thessaloniki in Greece and Ernst Wagner, chair of the European Regional Council of the International Society of Education through Art. Part 1 is generally theory-oriented and focuses on literature in the field, discussing shared spaces in art education, contemporary art and real-world issues. It considers the interplay of theory and practice as well as the dynamic interrelation of different disciplines, in particular VAE and ESD. The chapters in Part 1 present frameworks for teacher education that develop both disciplines and the transformative aspect of adult education, critique anthropocentric approaches to art education, evaluate the goals and values of professional learning communities within the theoretical framework of aesthoecology and propose teachers as agents of change.

Part 2 provides more concrete examples of pedagogies and learning theories that can be used to enrich the field of art education by bringing in principles of ESD, and also making frequent references to research conducted in the project CARE. Different chapters offer insights into the ways existing sustainability challenges in different geographical and social contexts can be introduced into art education classes and cultural site visits. Linkages between futures thinking and the medium of drawing in issues-based art education are developed. The importance of fostering peer networks or communities of learning by bringing together teachers, educational administrators and others is presented as a central component of a call for change in sustainability discourse and the educational field: only by initiating or encouraging localized strategies of collaboration, mentoring, co-creation and shared action can we begin to think of a transformed model of education that transcends restricted notions of competitiveness, individualism and standardization.

Part 3 presents briefer and illustrated case studies or statements of scholars and contemporary artists from a broad range of cultural contexts. Following an open call in mid 2021, the authors were invited to elaborate on their works and ideas, which revolve around various issues of sustainability. The diversity of contexts stands out in these contributions, with chapters hailing from different continents and cultural backgrounds. Community projects that make use of various activities, such as gardening, filmmaking, eating, creating ethnographic toolboxes and participatory practices that involve nonhuman entities like trees, are described, offering creative perspectives on the viability of alternative worlds.

The different chapters in Parts One, Two and Three share a concern for the sustainability of connections that we have, or may have had, with places, other living things, communities and the value of environmental justice. While our view of the world through the satellite imagery of mapping platforms is obscured to some extent by the dominance of market-led data, it is important to keep in mind that these new interfaces also cater for the possibility of (and perhaps, the need for) change. High above the representation of national border regimes, pollution sweeps blindly across lands and seas. Yet, at that height, it might also be possible to get a glimpse of what global solidarity could mean in the twenty-first century.

Note

1. http://care.frederick.ac.cy/

References

Bell, D. (2016). Twenty-first century education: Transformative education for sustainability and responsible citizenship. *Journal of Teacher Education for Sustainability*, 18(1), 48–56.

Borowy, I. (2014). *Defining sustainable development for our common future*. London: Routledge.

Brockwell, A. J., Mochizuki, Y., & Sprague, T. (2022). Designing indicators and assessment tools for SDG Target 4.7: A critique of the current approach and a proposal for an 'Inside-Out' strategy, *Compare: A Journal of Comparative and International Education*. https://doi.org/10.1080/03057925.2022.2129957

Ferreira, J. A., Ryan, L., & Tilbury, D. (2007). Planning for success: Factors influencing change in teacher education. *Australian Journal of Environmental Education*, 23, 45–55.

Graham, S. (2018). *Vertical: The city from satellites to bunkers.* Brooklyn, NY: Verso.

Hall, E. (2022). *Professional learning communities in a project connecting primary art education for sustainable development.* Cyprus: Frederick University.

Ioannidou, M. (Ed.) (2022). *The touch of art: Teacher training for sustainability through the visual arts.* Cyprus: Frederick University.

Ioannidou, M., & Mitakidou, S. (Eds.) (2022). *Children and teachers at work: Facing sustainability challenges through the visual arts.* Cyprus: Frederick University.

Jickling, B. (2017). Education revisited: Creating educational experiences that are held, felt, and disruptive. In B. Jickling & S. Sterling (Eds.), *Post-sustainability and environmental education. Palgrave studies in education and the environment* (pp. 15–20). London: Palgrave. https://doi.org/10.1007/978-3-319-51322-5_2

Mensah, J., & Casadevall, S. R. (Rev. Ed.). (2019). Sustainable development: Meaning, history, principles, pillars, and implications for human action: Literature review, *Cogent Social Sciences*, 5(1). https://doi.org/10.1080/23311886.2019.1653531

Mirzoeff, N. (2015). *How to see the world.* London: Penguin Books.

Planetary Project. (n.d.). *Criticism of the concept of sustainable development.* http://planetaryproject.com/planet_project/critical/

Sabatini, F. (2019). Culture as fourth pillar of sustainable development: Perspectives for integration, paradigms of action. *European Journal of Sustainable Development*, 8(3), 31–40.

Sengupta, M. (2018). Transformational change or tenuous wish list? A critique of SDG 1 ('End Poverty in All Its Forms Everywhere'). *Social Alternatives*, 37(1), 12–17.

Swain, R. B. (2018). A critical analysis of the sustainable development goals. In W. Leal Filho (Ed.), *Handbook of sustainability science and research. World Sustainability Series.* Cham: Springer. https://doi.org/10.1007/978-3-319-63007-6_20

UNESCO. (n.d.). *Sustainable development.* https://en.unesco.org/themes/education-sustainable-development/what-is-esd/sd#:~:text=Sustainable%20development%20is%20the%20overarching%20paradigm%20of%20the%20United%20Nations.&text=Sustainability%20is%20a%20paradigm%20for,an%20improved%20quality%20of%20life

United Cities and Local Governments. (2010). *Culture: Fourth pillar of sustainable development.* https://www.agenda21culture.net/sites/default/files/files/documents/en/zz_culture4pillarsd_eng.pdf

Wilson, M., & Snæbjörnsdóttir, B. (2022). Art, belonging, and sense and to whom nonsense belongs. In M. Häggström & C. Schmidt (Eds.), *Relational and Critical Perspectives on Education for Sustainable Development* (pp. 19–32). New York, NY: Springer.

World Commission on Environment and Development. (1987). *Report of the World Commission on Environment and Development: Our common future.* file:///C:/Users/Prof%20Raphael%20Vella/Downloads/our_common_futurebrundtlandreport1987%20(1).pdf

Part 1

Call to Action: Theoretical Considerations

Victoria Pavlou and Raphael Vella

The potential of future generations to respond to the challenges of today and the future lies in education and specifically in how teachers today embrace shifts in teaching for the future. We want teachers and teachers-to-be to 'reimagine educative futures by forging new collaborations that promote greater cultural diversity, intercultural dialogues and social inclusion and cohesion with responsiveness and awareness' (Sinner, Nakamura, & Yazdanpanah, 2022, p. 1). To better prepare teachers and teachers-to-be, we, teacher educators, need to revitalize teacher education in art education and embrace the interdisciplinary nature of sustainability.

Part 1 invites readers to envision pedagogical possibilities in teacher education both during initial teacher training and continuous professional development training and thus to envision visual arts education futures. This part also offers broader theoretical reflections about the power of art in the context of the various socio-ecological problems that the world faces. While schools and higher education institutions have increasingly adopted sustainability and the United Nations Sustainable Development Goals (SDGs) in their curricula, it is not always clear why and how art education fits into their efforts to address sustainability issues.

The authors of Part 1 share their views concerning art, sustainability and learning communities and propose models and philosophical standpoints that should inform current teaching and learning in art education. These models and philosophical standpoints aim to encourage teachers to promote a change of unsustainable habits of mind, which will lead to artful action on sustainability issues that are prevalent in teachers' local areas (real-life issues) and thus achieve transformation.

'Promises and delivery: Teacher education for ESD-enhanced visual arts education' by Chrysanthi Kadji-Beltran and Victoria Pavlou discusses teacher education and professional development models within the context of an expansion of the visual arts into broader spheres inspired by competences in Education for Sustainable Development (ESD). Informed by transformative learning and competence-based theories, the chapter advocates for a holistic, transdisciplinary, output-oriented approach. Transformative pedagogies play a central role in adult education but are also valuable in ESD, promoting systemic and critical thinking, collaborative problem-solving and other values and attitudes. They also expand the goals of educational institutions, making them part of a wider call to action. In the history and theory of art education, this transformative dimension is developed in reconstructivist philosophies which, as the chapter explains, can be engaged by art educators to make contributions towards social and global issues, in particular the UN Agenda 2030. The chapter proposes a professional development framework that is based on principles of adult education, presents experiences in transformative learning, promotes competence-based learning and connects school-based practices with real-life needs. The framework is multi-layered and invites readers to consider many interrelated components that need to be simultaneously addressed when training teachers in an ESD-infused art education curriculum.

'Voicing a sustainable future through visual arts education: Culture in action' by Martha Ioannidou and Soula Mitakidou discusses interconnections between visual arts education (VAE) and education for sustainable development in the context of a holistic education that embraces sustainability as a fundamental component of the quality of life for the future citizens. The authors' arguments build on VAE's potential to promote social cohesion and thus transform educational settings into agents of sustainability. Starting with the need to re-centre education around humanistic values, respond to the current need for solidarity – especially in difficult times like the COVID-19 pandemic and never-ending issues related to refugees and immigrants – and overcome stereotypes of VAE's role in schools (not simply 'art for art's sake'), the authors argue why and how to interrelate the fields of VAE and ESD. Further, they acknowledge the important role of teachers as facilitators of change and propose an approach for training future teachers that will enable them to achieve the best possible results in their future classes. By consistently linking everyday challenges with an understanding of sustainability goals and visual arts lessons, children will be able to meaningfully form and express their cultural identities in contemporary school practice.

Raphael Vella's 'Aliens or allies? Towards symbiotic relationships in art education' draws inspiration from a collage produced by a 9-year-old child and reflects on human–nonhuman symbiotic relationships in various fields, especially contemporary art and art education. The chapter argues that anthropocentric and xenophobic narratives based on notions of defence and conflict could be replaced by narratives of coexistence informed by a participatory philosophy associated with socially engaged art. This ecologically engaged art and art education helps to develop new processes of solidarity and disrupts binary divisions between nature and culture. By exploring forms of cultural and technological production like bioart, biomimicry and social sculpture, the chapter concludes that art education can direct us towards new points of contact between humans and nonhumans.

'An aesthoecological approach to professional learning communities: Analyzing with CARE' by Emese Hall and Chris Turner deals with another form of symbiotic relationship – that between aesthetics and ecology. Aesthoecology is described as a re-evaluation of the relationship between aesthetics and ecology, which, in turn, leads the authors to relate this theory to their discussion about professional learning communities (PLCs). Such learning communities have both aesthetic and ecological dimensions, nurturing affective relations and simultaneously promoting connections between teachers, learners and others. The chapter evaluates PLCs within the context of the international research project CARE and analyzes the aesthoecological aspects of the project, in particular, its collaborations between teachers and academic partners involved in the project.

Introduction

The final chapter of Part 1 aims to bridge theory and practice and lead the readers into the second part of the book which focuses on examples of sustainable praxes. 'Bridging theory and practice: how to develop projects that connect visual arts education and education for sustainable development' by Ernst Wagner discusses ways of theory infusing praxis and the other way around. By studying specific examples of sustainable art projects, Wagner proposes theoretical models for developing new meaningful and artful sustainable projects.

Reference

Sinner, A., Nakamura, K., & Yazdanpanah, E. (2022). Transnational tomorrows today. *UNESCO Observatory multidisciplinary eJournal in the Arts*, *8*(1), 1–11. https://www.unescoejournal.com/wp-content/uploads/2022/05/1.0_2022_VOL8_1-Editorial_v2.pdf

Chapter 1

Promises and Delivery: Teacher Education for ESD-Enhanced Visual Arts Education

Chrysanthi Kadji-Beltran and Victoria Pavlou

Introduction

Although education is an important tool for individuals' social participation and contribution to a better future, it can also be part of the problem (Orr, 2004). Sterling (2011) stresses that 'a great deal of learning, both every day and through formal education, makes no positive difference to a sustainable future, and may indeed make that prospect "less, rather than more likely"' (p. 18). Limitations to education for sustainable development (ESD) and sustainability actions are also posed by existing policies or priority practices (e.g. assessment) at the microlevel, and at the macrolevel, leadership has failed to translate high-level agenda-setting declarations and commitments into meaningful action (Kwauk, 2020). The hazard with education is that, instead of supporting change, it can also perpetuate rooted unsustainable practices and old habits (Wals, 2015). This paradox was highlighted years ago by Schumacher in an article written in 1974 and published in 1997, in which he argues that:

> The volume of education has increased and continues to increase, yet so do pollution, exhaustion of resources, and the dangers of ecological catastrophe. If still more education is to save us, it would have to be education of a different kind: an education that takes us into the depth of things.
>
> (Schumacher, 1997 in Sterling, 2011, p. 17)

So, which are the possible ways forward? Following Schumacher's argument, the quality of such education needs to be 'of a different kind', the kind that takes us into the 'depth of things' through reflexivity on what we do, and reflexivity on how we act and why we learn, which according to Raskin (2008) would lead us to think and act differently.

> Arts education has an important role to play in the constructive transformation of educational systems that are struggling to meet the needs of learners in a rapidly changing world characterized by remarkable advances in technology on the one hand and intractable social and cultural injustices on the other.
>
> (UNESCO, 2010, p. 2)

The World Alliance for Arts Education (WAAE) and all their member associations and partners in the world recommend transformative action for arts education in order to become integral to sustaining communities and meeting the needs of all people in the face of critical global challenges (WAAE, 2019). For addressing this emerging challenge, we need to carefully consider how demanding these new teachers' roles are, and what can be done to better prepare them to respond successfully.

In the sections that follow, we discuss the relation of competence-based transformative ESD with the social–critical orientation of VAE and its reconstructive, postmodernist approach. We also consider how the resulting complexity can be addressed within professional development (PD), and borrow elements from ESD PD models to develop and propose a multilayer framework for PD in VAE. In this context, we seek to support teacher empowerment, and address ESD-enhanced VAE as an example of the so-needed 'education of a different kind'.

Competence-based, transformative ESD and VAE

Turning to learning theories and outcome-oriented, competence-based ESD models, we can argue that transformative learning (TL) and competence-based ESD are important elements of this 'different kind' of education, especially in PD for ESD. Imperative within TL is transformative experiences with which the learner identifies and feels compassion and solidarity. Challenging assumptions and beliefs embedded in adult behaviour along with the resulting pluralism and dissonance also require reflection, criticality and a holistic transdisciplinary approach. For this purpose, TL requires new spaces for collaborative and social learning (Schnitzler, 2019). Collaborative learning spaces in PD can be facilitated within professional learning communities (PLCs). Collective learning differs from traditional forms of PD that focus on transferring knowledge and skills outside the school settings and context (Kadji, Zachariou, Liarakou, & Flogaitis, 2014). Instead, it results in a practical, applied outcome that sums greater than the parts, as collective learning combines the individual strengths and capacities of the group's members and benefits all engaged parties: teachers, children, the school community and the broader community.

Competence-based education on the other hand shifts education from input to output orientation (Kadji-Beltran et al., 2017; Rieckmann, 2011, 2018) and bridges the gap between knowledge and action (Leicht, Heiss, & Byun, 2018). It maintains the transformative potential of ESD, as long as it embraces approaches and methods that promote reflection, criticality and transformative experiences (Lotz-Sisitka, Wals, Kronlid, & McGarry, 2015).

Transformative and emancipatory pedagogies that promote a different way of thinking are inherent to ESD: pedagogies that promote critical, systemic thinking; holistic and transdisciplinary learning; futures thinking; collaborative problem-solving; sustainability values and respect for humans and nature, justice, democracy, solidarity, tolerance; and a raised awareness of the urgency to act (Ferreira, Ryan, & Tilbury, 2006). This framework for radical changes permeates teaching and learning through the curriculum and encourages the school's opening to society. It establishes a whole new educational paradigm that infuses ESD in all school operations: curriculum – teaching and learning; school organization;

and school interaction and networking with society (Flogaitis, 2011). It seeks to empower learners individually and collectively, to become agents of change towards a sustainable future and demands new roles for teachers and learners that are aligned with the millennium goals for education (UNESCO, 2017, 2018a).

A transformative, social–critical orientation is also identified in VAE. One of the influential ideological streams with a strong presence in art education is the reconstructive stream. Reconstructivists (Barrett, 1979; Freedman & Stuhr, 2004; Read, 1948) embrace the notion that the primary aim of art education is to contribute to social transformation. Instead of 'art for art's sake' they perceive 'art as a means to an end', that is, social change. For them art is an instrument through which to conduct inquiry and thus facilitate learning across disciplines; a vehicle that should be used to create an equitable society (Efland, 1990, p. 10).

Reconstructivists believe that through art, students will be able to understand and appreciate cultural differences and build character and resilience (Kim, 2015). Schools, as social institutions, should contribute to the reconstruction of society (Ewing, 2011). The need to reconstruct society is presented today under different movements and demands, such as socially engaged art and sustainable development (SD) through the arts (Dieleman, 2008; Thompson, 2012). More and more art educators contribute to the debate that art needs to focus on big ideas (Kim, 2015; Walling, 2006), engage students with visual culture (Freedman & Stuhr, 2004), embrace new media and overall provide them with a space in which to understand their experiences and respond to the world around them. In other words, several art educators argue that visual arts enable students to gain access to the real world, make coherent meaning and order for themselves out of the storm of images, comprehend themselves, their relations and the world around them and respond creatively by producing images and artworks that express their ideas, thoughts, positions, etc. (Ewing, 2011). Nevertheless, such practices that prepare students for further education, careers, life and citizenship (Dawes, 2008; Dillon, 2012; Eisner, 2008; Winner & Hetland, 2009) are marginalized and VAE, within formal education, fails to reach its full potential.

The ESD infusion in VAE facilitates connections with urgent real-life issues and simultaneously promotes creative, critical and systemic thinking, development of skills, attitudes, reflection and values. VAE can also benefit from ESD in terms of PD, considering the shared goals, objectives and context between the two.

So, what can ESD PD offer to VAE? Which elements could better support teachers and what ESD-inspired PD models can enhance PD in VAE?

ESD PD models and VAE

The introduction of ESD in PD programmes, due to its complexity of content, goals and characteristics, puts in question the effectiveness of traditional models and demands the use of appropriate PD. The same restrictions apply to ESD-enhanced VAE. Traditional PD programmes are inadequate as their context is predetermined and learners do not participate in their development and elaboration; their needs and worries are not considered; the results are rarely evaluated and programmes lack conceptual and theoretical foundations for their development and implementation (Fullan, 1991; Zachariou, 2013). Ferreira, Ryan, and Tilbury (2007) propose three models for teachers' PD in the context of ESD: (a) the collaborative resource development and adaptation model; (b) the action research model and (c) the whole-of-system model.

The collaborative resource development and adaptation model supports that change results by providing programmes, educational tools and means, which trainees will use after adequate education and training. In many cases, this refers to training teachers to use an educational package in a specific context. An important characteristic of this model is the collaborative involvement of the educators in the development of the material. This model does not seek a broader reform of the educational system, so the change it brings is limited to the participants and their professional surroundings. According to Schalcross (2004), the produced material is not assessed for its effectiveness, is not reviewed and soon becomes outdated.

The action research model constitutes a continuum of processes that include critical exploration, design elaboration, action and reflection. This model requires the teachers' critical reflection on the practices and actions they apply in ways that promote innovation and amelioration of the teaching and learning process (Tilbury, Coleman, & Garlick, 2005). The PD is adjustable to the learners' needs, giving them a certain degree of control. Evaluation and reflection are vital elements of PD and feedback processes, innate in this model, ensure direct and continuous improvement. Difficulties of implementation may include time restrictions and continuous engagement of the participants; nevertheless, it is a dynamic model that can establish ESD as a social learning process in different contexts and organizations (Varga, Koszo, Mayer, & Sleurs, 2007).

The holistic model seeks change through whole-institution approaches, as it considers that the change towards SD will only be achieved when all the levels of organization of the institution align their operations with SD principles. PD in the holistic model framework is school-based (Hewton,1988) and schools as learning communities can identify and easily resolve specific problems that might arise during the training of the teachers. Its complexity, due to a large number of participants, with different roles, needs and responsibilities, constitutes a challenge for its implementation.

Each model serves different purposes and is appropriate under different conditions and PD needs. The collaborative resource development and adaptation model enables educators with a specific interest in ESD to focus on the development of high-quality educational programmes and resources for a specific community/case. The action research model engages educators and learners in in-depth processes in PD and develops the competences needed to achieve change. Finally, the holistic model seeks a more profound reform of teachers' PD in ESD through a holistic change of the system and the multilevel participation of all interested parties that have a role in supporting and maintaining school change in the direction of SD within and outside school units (Zachariou, 2013).

The promise: Expectations from PD in VAE

PD for VAE should create conditions that serve the 'Seoul Agenda', and fulfil its goals:

- 'Ensure that arts education is accessible as a fundamental and sustainable component of a high-quality educational reform'.
- 'Assure that arts education activities and programmes are of high quality in conception and delivery'.
- 'Apply arts education principles and practices to contribute to resolving social and cultural challenges today's world is facing' (UNESCO, 2010, pp. 3–10).

Imperative for the achievement of the Seoul goals are the core VAE competences, e.g. responding to artworks, producing artworks and reflecting on the processes of producing and responding (Pavlou & Kadji-Beltran, 2021).

All the ESD elements for teacher education analyzed in the previous section are aligned with the goals of the Seoul Agenda and the Core VAE competences. Competence-based TL enables high-quality educational reform and creates new learning spaces that can ensure high-quality arts education activities and programmes. Additionally, collaborative resource development and adaptation as well as the action research PD models (Tilbury, Coleman, & Garlick, 2005) address specific needs and circumstances of the community in critical and reflective ways, and can therefore contribute to resolving 'specific social and cultural challenges' using appropriate pedagogies.

Transferring the lessons learnt by ESD PD to the context of VAE we developed a framework to support teachers' PD and to promote quality in VAE. In particular, the framework, which is elaborated in the following section, brings together four different components that need to be addressed when developing a teacher PD programme:

1. build teachers' competences,
2. create collaborative learning spaces through establishing PLCs,
3. connect the training with real-life needs and
4. offer experiences that are transformative enough to bring a change.

The delivery: An ESD-enhanced PD framework for VAE teachers

In this section, we scrutinize the theoretical foundations upon which the PD framework was developed. The proposed framework creates new learning spaces for VAE teachers' PD and

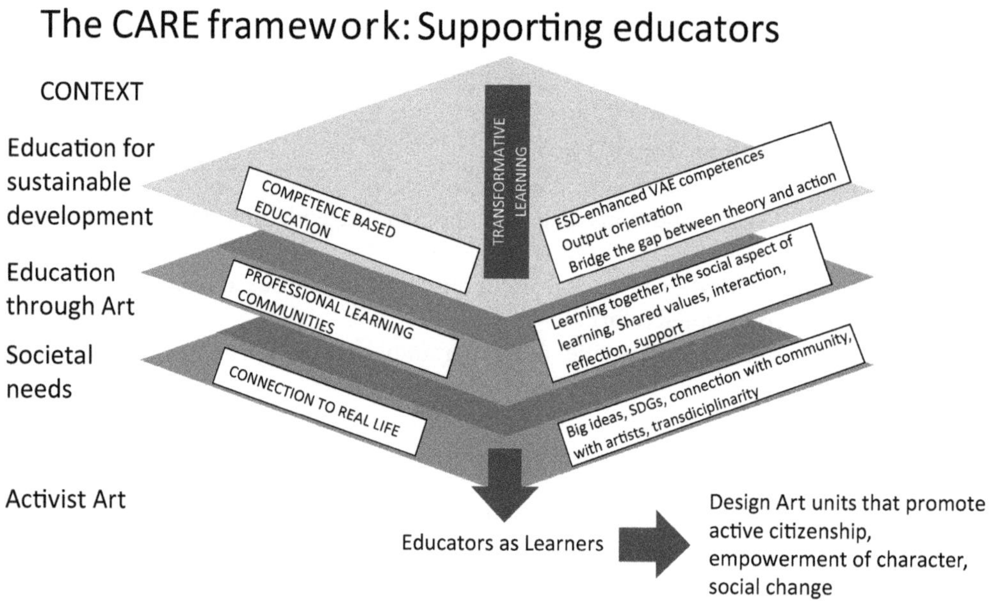

The CARE framework: Supporting educators

CONTEXT

- Education for sustainable development
- Education through Art
- Societal needs
- Activist Art

COMPETENCE BASED EDUCATION
PROFESSIONAL LEARNING COMMUNITIES
CONNECTION TO REAL LIFE

TRANSFORMATIVE LEARNING

ESD-enhanced VAE competences
Output orientation
Bridge the gap between theory and action

Learning together, the social aspect of learning, Shared values, interaction, reflection, support

Big ideas, SDGs, connection with community, with artists, transdiciplinarity

Educators as Learners → Design Art units that promote active citizenship, empowerment of character, social change

Figure 1.1: The ESD-enhanced PD framework for VAE teachers.

assembles important elements of PD approaches and methods (Figure 1.1). The framework was used by the Erasmus + Project CARE (http//care.frederick.ac.cy) for the development and delivery of a PD programme for VAE teachers. The CARE-PD programme addressed VAE teachers in primary schools, or student teachers and aspired to transform their experiences and knowledge and enable them to become agents of change.

The framework comprises four layers: on the first layer, the competence-based character of the training is depicted. PD is competence-based and seeks to help teachers develop the competences they need to effectively develop and deliver VAE in a real-life context with the help of ESD. 'New collaborative spaces for learning' constitutes the second layer of the framework, and transfers the training in schools, in the form of PLCs where participants will develop and elaborate their practice in a safe and supportive learning environment. The third layer represents the context in which teachers are asked to operate. VAE units should be based on big ideas, the sustainable development goals (SDG), connected to the school and surrounding community, in ways that bring a real-life dimension in education. An element of TL is infused in all layers of the PD framework (see Figure 1.1). Simultaneously different elements in the framework layers, indicate its connection to the Collaborative resource development and adaptation and the Action research PD models as the framework facilitates collaboration, learning together, and reflective processes. A detailed explanation of each layer/component of the framework follows.

The 'competence-based PD' layer

Pavlou and Kadji-Beltran (2021) have explored and mapped ESD competences with respect to VAE teacher competences and identified several convergences and overlaps between the competences pursued. The authors chose to use the rounder sense of purpose (RSP) model for ESD competences, since RSP was specifically designed for ESD educators (Vare et al., 2019; Zachariou, Kadji, Vare, & Milligan, 2019) distilled other ESD competences models (e.g. the CSCT model, Sleurs, 2008, and the UNECE model, UNECE, 2011) and reflected the four learning pillars of education for the twenty-first century (learning to know, learning to be, learning to do and learning to live together, Delors, 1996). The RSP model was then mapped with the core VAE competences: e.g. responding, producing and reflecting (Pavlou & Kadji-Beltran, 2021) (see Figure 1.2). The twelve RSP competences: systems and futures thinking; participation; attentiveness; empathy; engagement; innovation; action; criticality; transdisciplinarity; responsibility and decisiveness (Vare, Millican, & De Vries, 2018), placed in the context of VAE help teachers become competent to operate in complex conditions and promote through their

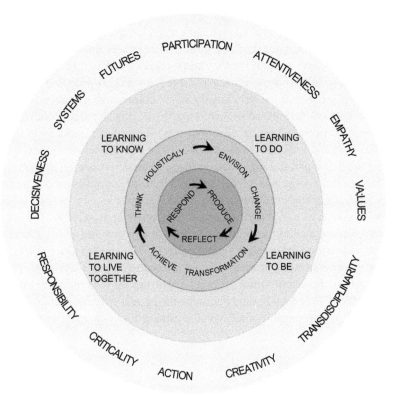

Figure 1.2: The framework of ESD-enhanced VAE educator competences (in Pavlou & Kadji-Beltran, 2021, p. 225).

teaching, sustainable practices and active participation in sociopolitical processes that re-orient society towards sustainability (Rieckmann, 2012; UNESCO, 2017).

The 'PLCs' layer

Another important component of the proposed framework is the creation of collaborative spaces for learning. PLCs have proven to be effective collaborative models of teachers' PD. They are formed when a group of professionals work together and critically interrogate their practice in an ongoing, reflective, collaborative, inclusive, learning-oriented and growth-promoting way (Stoll & Seashore-Lewis, 2007). Group members share a specific domain of interest (Simpson, 2011, p. 702) and are characterized by shared values and vision amongst collective responsibility, reflective personal inquiry and dialogue with peers, collaboration and focus on individual and group learning (DuFour, 2004; Vescio, Ross, & Adams, 2008). Stoll and Seashore-Lewis (2007) suggest that PLCs do not focus just on individual teachers' learning, 'but on professional learning, within the context of a cohesive group that focuses on collective knowledge and occurs within an ethic of interpersonal caring that permeates the lives of teachers, students and school leaders' (2007, p. 3). They are used in helping teachers reshape their professional knowledge and change their classroom practices (Feger & Arruda, 2008; Jita & Ndlalane, 2009) as they address issues of quality teaching and learning.

Two possible levels of PLCs organization, applicable to any PD, are proposed in our framework: (a) the 'plenary' group community, including the whole community that attends PD, facilitating interactions amongst all its members during training; (b) the smaller groups communities formed by a few members, who are expected to collaborate to perform specific tasks, for example develop and deliver ESD-oriented VAE units in their schools. The PLCs organization can be flexible and the tasks, although developed and supported by all group members, are not necessarily delivered by all group members. In both cases (plenary and smaller), communities need to receive support and feedback from the PD organizers (see Figure 1.3).

PLCs should be seen as a continuation of teachers' training, in schools. The opportunities for practical implementation of the theory learnt and interaction and collaboration within the community provide added value to the training offered. The smaller group interaction forms familiarity and closeness among its members and creates a safe and supportive context for the unit implementation. The community provides opportunities for reflection, interaction and personal and further PD and enables further networking and school opening as it encourages collaborations not only amongst teachers but also amongst schools and children.

The 'connecting PD to real-life needs' layer

PD programmes that aim to enable teachers to enrich their art teaching with SD issues inevitably need to facilitate connections with real life. Teachers need to embrace the

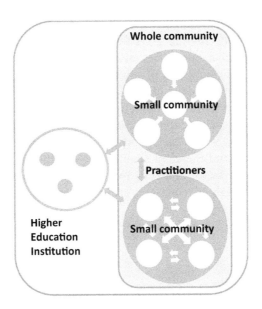

Figure 1.3: PLCs' levels of organization.

reconstructive role of art (learning through art; postmodernism; Freedman & Stuhr, 2004) and place special emphasis on the function of art in society. This does not mean that other roles of art, such as the expressive and discipline-based role and learning in and about art, cannot be acknowledged (Efland, 1990; Larrick, 2008).

The reconstructive role of art has many overlaps with the philosophy of ESD. Its basic position is the promotion of basic values through the visual arts with the aim of a more democratic and sustainable society (Emery, 2002). Thus, art units are expected to approach important issues, such as big ideas (e.g. freedom and justice) as well as SDG (e.g. SDG12 sustainable cities and communities) with a transdisciplinary lens (Nordén, 2018) and focus especially on those sustainability issues that are prevalent in students' local area. Further, the contribution of contemporary artworks is crucial in connecting art with real life. It is important for teachers to be informed about the political activism of many contemporary artists. This can be a first step in recognizing the importance of the Agenda for 2030 (UN, 2015), which presupposes our action not only at the level of national policy and funding but also at the grassroots level. From a pedagogical point of view, such artistic strategies function as models of social justice and promote decision-making skills that lead to improved equality in practice.

Connection with real-life issues enables teachers to recognize the importance of context and to realize that there are different cultures and different ways in which different issues can be documented, acknowledged and resolved. Postmodernism challenges teachers to consider how they can revise and break down stereotypes, study issues of identity, nationality and cultural heritage, recognize marginalized cultures and marginalized groups of people, recognize the active role of children as critical 'readers' of images and artworks, and promote the creation of art that emphasizes meaning rather than composition or technique (Hardy, 2006). In short, the complexity of contemporary society and the need to connect art with real life should be at the centre of their planning of lessons. Education in the visual arts should – especially nowadays – be directly linked to daily life and provide tools for children to understand and critically appreciate their world and contribute to the creation of a sustainable society. Art that is interested exclusively in itself ceases to attract older children and especially adolescents and therefore should be questioned (Campana, 2011). In our times, art should not solely focus on artistic techniques and processes in an abstract and restrictive model, but through art education art should lead children to a process of real participation and collaboration.

The 'TL' component

TL, being one of the most important theories in adult education, is the element that transgresses all layers in our framework (see Figure 1.1): the competence-based education layer, the PLCs layer and the authentic experiences of the real-life connections. TL is the process of effecting change in a frame of reference (habits of mind and a point of view); in other words, it is the process through which we come to recognize and modify the assumptions and beliefs that frame our tacit points of view and influence our understandings, our values and interpretations of the world, that determine our actions (Mezirow, 2009, 2000). Throughout their lives, adults acquire a coherent body of experience – associations, concepts, values, feelings, conditioned responses – frames of reference that define their personality. These frames of reference are the structures of assumptions through which we understand our experiences and can become barriers to acquiring new or modifying existing behaviours in adults. TL tackles inertia and rooted, resilient, unsustainable practices and assumptions, it enables the envisioning of new trajectories and futures and inculcates agency and a sense of purpose. Therefore, transformative theory is important in adult education and is infused in all dimensions of the proposed framework.

As has been observed, TL transverses all layers in our PD framework. Figure 1.4 highlights elements of TL that could apply within our PD framework.

The framework was applied to the development and delivery of a PD programme for VAE teachers in four countries as part of the Erasmus + Project CARE. In the implementation that took place in Cyprus, the training addressed generalist primary school teachers. It included 40 hours of training (18 in synchronous meetings and 22 in asynchronous activities) and a school-based practical phase. Teacher PD was participative and included scenarios and opportunities for reflection, followed by a cross-disciplinary approach, and used ESD methodologies also appropriate for VAE. During the school-based training, participants were expected to work in groups to develop ESD-enhanced VAE units and

TRANSFORMATIVE LEARNING RESULTS FROM:	PD ELEMENTS AND CONTEXT
Transformative experiences! Identification → Compassion → Solidarity	Scenarios Virtual tours Interactive activities around big ideas and the SDGs
Critical self-reflection on assumptions and critical discourse	Visual reflective diary, reflective interaction around big ideas and the SDGs through Art
Critical Pedagogy (awakening of critical consciousness to effect change through social critique and political action)	Interdisciplinarity Appropriate teaching strategies (e.g. debate, role play, brainstorming and concept mapping) that support learning through the arts
Social learning through interaction and dissonance that is created when different perspectives meet in socially favourable conditions	Addressing conflict issues for SD Interactive, collaborative learning Learning in Real life context
New spaces for collaborative and social learning	Professional learning communities Learning through the Art Learning in the Community Action in the Community Collaborations with artists

Figure 1.4: Mapping of TL elements in the PD framework.

teaching material and deliver these in their classes in schools. The teaching units developed had to draw their context from real-life issues and were translated into big ideas and connected to the SDGs through scenarios, virtual tours and exposure to artwork serving specific purposes, ideologies and politics. The real-life context provided by the ESD–VAE synergy enabled the school's opening (even during the pandemic) and the teaching units-projects were embraced by the local community, the school community, the community of learning, and provided new spaces for collaborative social learning that lead to action and change in the direction of sustainability.

The experiences acted as stimuli for critical self-reflection and self-reflection on unquestioned assumptions embedded in our way of thinking. The CARE project created conditions for teachers' reflection, through reflective diaries' recordings, as well as peer interaction enabling thus a TL process. Genuine transformation, in the case of Cyprus through a multidisciplinary approach to VAE, became the pinnacle of action and was expressed through the children's work and actions: a success indicator of the teachers' effectiveness. The outcomes of the PD implementation by the different partner-countries are presented in Hall (Ed.) (2022) (http://care.frederick.ac.cy/docs/CARE_IO5.pdf). Although our intention here is not to elaborate on the Cypriot PD experience, we can comment that high positive feelings and satisfaction were reported by the teacher participants.

Concluding remarks

Producing a PD framework that can respond to contemporary societal and educational needs and can empower VAE educators for this role, is a demanding, complicated process. Despite the challenges emerging from the multiple dimensions, we consider that the confluence of the competence-based, real-life, PLCs and TL elements, results in a promising framework for effective professional learning that can empower teachers to lead to change. The framework is suitable for practical curriculum subjects such as visual arts and also prepares teachers to enhance VAE with issues (such as sustainability issues) that require innovative, transformative and reflective approaches, as it transfers skills and competences that respond to modern challenges in education. It immediately puts theory into practice and allows for enhanced and critical, pedagogical content knowledge for the teacher.

These characteristics place our framework within the collaborative resource development and adaptation and the action research PD models (Ferreira, Ryan, & Tilbury, 2007). Change is obtained through the use of appropriate means and tools that are only possible after adequate training and supported by collaborative efforts. As a process, it is flexible: it is adjusted to the needs and interests of the group members and collaboration allows constant feedback and adjustment of the process by members of the group that are more advanced in the implementation. The impact of the specific PD models (collaborative resource development and adaptation and the action research professional development models) is targeted and can be most effective in the participants' specific educational settings. Teacher participation in the process ensures a sense of ownership, commits the teachers to the implementation of the material and motivates its further dissemination (Tilbury et al., 2005). Interaction amongst teachers also encourages critical reflection and actions that will enhance and raise the quality of their teaching.

The proposed PD framework, as the CARE project experience showed, can have a broader impact on the educational community, especially affecting the way in which we, teacher educators, should think about our courses. Our framework aspires to trigger discussion about emerging implications for VAE teacher education, as well as ESD-oriented PD, for other disciplines, that support and promote ESD.

References

Barrett, M. (1979). *Art education: A strategy for course design*. Portsmouth, NH: Heinemann Educational Books.

Campana, A. (2011). Agents of possibility: Examining the intersections of art, education, and activism in communities. *Studies in Art Education, 52*(4), 278–291. https://doi.org/10.1080/00393541.2011.11518841

Dawes, M. (2008). Beyond process: Art, empowerment and sustainability. In G. Coutts & T. Jokela (Eds.), *Art, community and environment. Educational perspectives* (pp. 65–76). Bristol: Intellect.

Delors, J. (1996). *Learning: The treasure within*. UNESCO of the International Commission on Education for the Twenty-first Century (highlights). International Commission on Education for the 21st Century. Paris: UNESCO. https://unesdoc.unesco.org/ark:/48223/pf0000109590?posInSet=12&queryId=f9897ad1-e31b-4acf-a2d8-e64997ad28ab

Dieleman, H. (2008). Sustainability, art and reflexivity: Why artists and designers may become key change agents in sustainability. In S. Kagan & V. Kirchberg (Eds.), *Sustainability: A new frontier for the arts and cultures* (pp. 108–146). Frankfurt am Main: Verlag für Akademische, Schrift en.

Dillon, P. (2012). Framing craft practice cultural ecologically: Tradition, change and emerging agendas. In M. Ferris (Ed.), *Making futures: The crafts as change-maker in sustainably aware cultures* (pp. 72–78). Plymouth: Plymouth College of Arts.

DuFour, R. (2004). What is a professional learning community? *Educational Leadership, 61*(8), 6–11.

Efland, A. D. (1990). *A history of art education*. New York, NY: Teachers College Press.

Eisner, E. (2008). What education can learn from the arts. *LEARNing Landscapes, 2*(1), 49–67.

Emery, L. (Ed.). (2002). *Teaching art in a postmodern world: Theories, teacher reflections and interpretive frameworks*. Champaign, IL: Common Ground.

Ewing, R. (2011). *The arts and Australian education: Realising potential*. Sydney: Australian Council for Educational Research.

Feger, S., & Arruda, E. (2008). *Professional learning communities: Key themes from the literature*. Providence, RI: Education Alliance, Brown University.

Ferreira, J., Ryan, L., & Tilbury, D. (2006). *Whole-school approaches to sustainability: A review of models for professional development in pre-service teacher education*. Australia: Australian Government Department of the Environment and Heritage and the Australian Research Institute in Education for Sustainability (ARIES).

Ferreira, J. A., Ryan, L., & Tilbury, D. (2007). Mainstreaming education for sustainable development in initial teacher education in Australia: A review of existing professional development models. *Journal of Education for Teaching, 33*(2), 225–239.

Flogaitis, E. (2011). *Education for the environment and sustainable development* [Εκπαίδευση για το Περιβάλλον και την Αειφορία]. Greece: Pedio Publications.

Frasz, A., & Sidford, H. (2017). *Mapping the landscape of socially engaged artistic practice*. Oakland, CA: Helicon Collaborative.

Freedman, K., & Stuhr, P. (2004). Curriculum change for the 21st century: Visual culture in art education. In *Handbook of research and policy in art education* (pp. 815–828). Milton Park: Routledge Handbooks.

Fullan, M. (1991). *The new meaning of educational change*. Toronto: Toronto Teachers College Press.
Hall, E. (Ed.) (2022). *Professional learning communities in a project connecting primary art education for sustainable development*. Frederick University, Cyprus. http://care.frederick.ac.cy/docs/CARE_IO5.pdf
Hardy, T. (Ed.). (2006). *Art education in a postmodern world: Collected essays*. Bristol: Intellect Books.
Hewton, E. (1988). *School focused staff development: Guidelines for policy makers*. London: Falmer Press.
Jita, L. C., & Ndlalane, T. C. (2009). Teacher Clusters in South Africa: Opportunities and constraints for teacher development and change. *Perspectives in Education, 27*(1), 58–68.
Jita, L. C., & Mokhele, M. L. (2012). Institutionalising teacher clusters in South Africa: Dilemmas and contradictions. *Perspectives in Education, 30*(2), 1–11. https://www.ajol.info/index.php/pie/article/view/81902
Kadji, C., Zachariou, A., Liarakou, G., & Flogaitis, E. (2014). Mentoring as a strategy for empowering education for sustainable development in schools. In *Professional development in education* (Vol. 40, pp. 717–739). Milton Park: Taylor and Francis.
Kadji-Beltran, C., Christodoulou, N., Zachariou, A., Lindemann-Matthies, P., Barker, S., & Kadis, C. (2017). An ESD pathway to quality education in the Cyprus Primary Education Context. *Environmental Education Research, 23*(7), 1015–1031. https://doi.org/10.1080/13504622.2016.1249459
Kim, H. (2015). Community and art: Creative education fostering resilience through art. *Asia Pacific Education Review, 16*(2), 193–201.
Kwauk, C. (2020). *Roadblocks to quality education in a time of climate change*. Brookings: Center for Universal Education at Brookings. https://www.brookings.edu/wp-content/uploads/2020/02/Roadblocks-to-quality-education-in-a-time-of-climate-change-FINAL.pdf
Larrick, P. (2008). *Perspectives on arts education and curriculum design*. Sacramento: Sacramento County Office of Education, CCSESA California.
Leicht, A., Heiss, J., & Byun, W. J. (Eds.). (2018), *Issues and trends in education for sustainable development*. London: UNESCO.
Lotz-Sisitka, H., Wals, A. E., Kronlid, D., & McGarry, D. (2015). Transformative, transgressive social learning: Rethinking higher education pedagogy in times of systemic global dysfunction. *Current Opinion in Environmental Sustainability, 16*, 73–80.
Mezirow, J. (2009). An overview on transformative learning. In K. Illeris (Ed.), *Contemporary theories of learning: Learning theories in their own words* (pp. 90–105). Milton Park: Routledge.
Mezirow, J. (2000). *Learning as transformation: Critical perspectives on a theory in progress. The Jossey-Bass higher and adult education series*. San Francisco, CA: Jossey Bass. https://www.ecolas.eu/eng/wp-content/uploads/2015/10/Mezirow-Transformative-Learning.pdf
Nordén, B. (2018). Transdisciplinary teaching for sustainable development in a whole school project. *Environmental Education Research, 24*(5), 663–677. https://doi.org/10.1080/13504622.2016.1266302
Orr, D. (2004). *Earth in mind – On education, environment and the human prospect*. Washington, DC: Island Press.
Pavlou, V., & Kadji-Beltran, C. (2021). Enhancing arts education with education for sustainable development competences: A proposed framework for visual arts education educators. In

E. Wagner, C. S. Nielsen, L. Veloso, T. Suominen, & N. Pachova (Eds.), *Arts. Sustainability. Education. ENO yearbook* (Vol. 2, pp. 217–235). Berlin: Springer Verlag.

Raskin, P. (2008). World lines: A framework for exploring global pathways. *Ecological Economics, 65,* 461–470.

Read, H. (1948). *Education through art*. London: Faber and Faber.

Rieckmann, M. (2011). *Developing key competencies for sustainable development.* Presentation for Summer School 'Implementation of Sustainability into Research and Teaching of Higher Education Institutions in Eastern Europe', Lüne burg. Leuphana, University of Lüneburg Institute for Environmental and Sustainability Communication. http://fox.leuphana.de/portal/files/1232787/Rieckmann_Competencies_and_Sustainability.pdf

Rieckmann, M. (2012). Future-oriented higher education: Which key competencies should be fostered through university teaching and learning? *Futures, 44,* 127–135.

Rieckmann, M. (2018). Learning to transform the world: Key competencies in education for sustainable development. In A. Leicht, J. Heiss, & W. J. Byun (Eds.), *Issues and trends in education for sustainable development* (pp. 39–59). Paris: UNESCO.

Shallcross, T. (Ed.) (2004). *School Development Through Whole School Approaches to Sustainability Education: The SEEPS (Sustainable Education in European Primary Schools) project*, Manchester, Manchester Metropolitan University.

Schnitzler, T. (2019). The bridge between education for sustainable development and transformative learning: Towards new collaborative learning spaces. *Journal of Education for Sustainable Development, 13*(2), 242–253.

Simpson, D. (2011). Reform inequalities of process and the transformative potential of communities of practice in the pre-school sector of England. *British Journal of Sociology of Education, 32*(5), 699–716.

Sleurs W. (Ed.) (2008). *Competencies for ESD (Education for Sustainable Development) teachers. A framework to integrate ESD in the curriculum of teacher training institutes*. Vienna: ENSI. https://www.ensi.org/global/downloads/Publications/303/CSCT%20Handbook_11_01_08.pdf

Sterling, S. (2011). Transformative learning and sustainability: Sketching the conceptual ground. *Learning and Teaching in Higher Education, 5,* 17–33.

Stoll, L., & Seashore-Lewis, K. (2007). *Professional learning communities, divergence, depth and dilemmas*. Buckingham: Open University Press.

Thompson, N. (2012). *Living as form: Socially engaged art from 1991–2011*. Cambridge, MA: MIT Press.

Tilbury, D., Coleman, V., & Garlick, D. (2005). *A national review of environmental education and its contribution to sustainability in Australia: School education*. Canberra: Australian Government Department of Environment and Heritage and Australian Research Institute in Education for Sustainability.

UNECE. (2011). *Learning for the future: Competences in education for sustainable development*. Geneva: UNECE. https://unece.org/fileadmin/DAM/env/esd/ESD_Publications/Competences_Publication.pdf

UNESCO. (2010). The Seoul agenda: Goals for the development of arts education. *World Conference on Arts Education*. https://unesdoc.unesco.org/ark:/48223/pf0000190692

UN. (2015). *Transforming our world. The 2030 Agenda for Sustainable Development*. Resolution adopted by the General Assembly, United Nations. https://documents-dds-ny.un.org/doc/UNDOC/GEN/N15/291/89/PDF/N1529189.pdf?OpenElement

UNESCO. (2017). *Education for sustainable development goals: Learning objectives*. Paris: United Nations Educational, Scientific and Cultural Organization. http://unesdoc.unesco.org/images/0024/002474/247444e.pdf

UNESCO. (2018a). *Issues and trends in education for sustainable development*. Paris: UNESCO.

Vare, P., Arro, G., de Hamer, A., Del Gobbo, G., de Vries, G., Farioli, F., ... Zachariou, A. (2019). Devising a competence-based training programme for educators of sustainable development: Lessons learned. *Sustainability, 11*, 1890.

Vare, P., Millican, R., & de Vries, G. (2018). A rounder sense of purpose: Towards a pedagogy for transformation. *Research in Action Special, (4),* 18–22.

Varga, A., Koszo, M., Mayer, M., & Sleurs, W. (2007). Developing teacher competences for education for sustainable development through reflection: The environment and school initiatives approach. *Journal of Education for Teaching: International Research and Pedagogy, 33*(2), 241–256.

Vescio, V., Ross, D., & Adams, A. (2008). A review of research on the impact of professional learning communities on teaching practice and student learning. *Teaching and Teacher Education, 24*(1), 80–91.

Walling, D. R. (2006). Brainstorming themes that connect art and ideas across the curriculum. *Art Education, 59*(1), 18–24.

Wals, A. J. (2015, 17 December). *Beyond unreasonable doubt. Education and Learning for Socioecological Sustainability in the Anthropocene* [Inaugural address held upon accepting the personal Chair of Transformative Learning for Socio-Ecological Sustainability], Wageningen University. https://arjenwals.files.wordpress.com/2016/02/8412100972_rvb_inauguratie-wals_oratieboekje_v02.pdf

Winner, E., & Hetland, L. (2009). Art for our sake: School art classes matter more than ever – But not for the reasons you think. *Colleagues, 4*(2), 2–5.

World Alliance for Arts Education. (2019, 28 October–1 November). *Frankfurt declaration for art education*. In WAAE 9th Global Conference, Frankfurt/Main, Germany. https://www.insea.org/wp-content/uploads/2021/08/WAAE-Frankfurt-declaration.pdf

Zachariou, A. (2013). Teachers' professional development and education for sustainable development. Orientation focal points. In C. Kadji-Beltran & A. Zachariou (Eds.), *Education for the environment and sustainable development as an educational framework in primary and preprimary education [in Greek]*. Nicosia: Frederick Research Center.

Zachariou, A., Kadji-Beltran, C., Vare, P., & Millican, R. (2019). Professional development and sustainability. In W. L. Filho (Ed.), *Encyclopaedia of sustainability in higher education*. Berlin: Springer.

Chapter 2

Voicing a Sustainable Future Through Visual Arts Education: Culture in Action

Martha Ioannidou and Soula Mitakidou

Through art alone are we able to emerge from ourselves, to know what another person sees of a universe which is not the same as our own and of which, without art, the landscapes would remain as unknown to us as those that may exist on the moon. Thanks to art, instead of seeing one world only, our own, we see that world multiply itself, and we have at our disposal as many worlds as there are original artists, worlds more different one from the other than those which revolve in infinite space, worlds which, centuries after the extinction of the fire from which their light first emanated, whether it is called Rembrandt or Vermeer, send us still each one its special radiance (Proust, 1996, p. 254).

A view of VAE today

Rapid social changes in recent years have fundamentally changed traditional perceptions in the field of education, paving the way for an ongoing dialogue over various issues, including how to modify existing curricula. However, within this discussion, stereotypical perceptions prevail and continue to focus on the skills and abilities children must acquire and cultivate to secure a successful career, ignoring their holistic development. Consequently, students enter formal learning often rife with restrictive preconceptions about what needs to be taught. Concerning the visual arts, as mandated by the formal curriculum, the students' limited exposure to them contributes to a widespread attitude of doubt and depreciation among parents and educators, rendering VAE 'a waste of time in an already burdened syllabus'. This perception can be likened to the forced domestication of the baby elephant;[1] similarly, limited exposure to VAE stifles the freedom of choice and the creative expression of children who, from the first day they enter formal education, are trapped in a strictly defined and rigid structure.

In the face of unprecedented developments sweeping through the twenty-first century at a dizzying pace, we are still desperately advocating for the arts and their educational value. Recent findings of the European research project CARE[2] highlight the prospects of a much-needed reconstruction. The project, which triggered a systematic investigation into the curricula of the partner countries[3] and performed field research on the premises of the schools themselves, showed that structural problems in schools are made worse when the hours dedicated to the arts are reduced or when an art infrastructure is lacking. Currently, existing educational models limit creative artistic expression to the use of visual arts for aesthetic purposes. However, this limited purpose is incompatible with society's purported intention to create a more sustainable future, build on its cultural continuity and educate its younger generations to make connections between knowledge, culture and quotidian life dilemmas, all within a context of holistic development.

Works of art often remain 'mute and distant' in school life, adorning – in the best case – textbooks' covers and inner pages. They may subconsciously imprint themselves in the students' archives of images and memories. Still, students are seldom encouraged to retrieve these images at will or connect them with other knowledge or experiences and thus apply them resourcefully in their daily lives. Better integrating the visual arts across facets of school life not only offers an alternative means for students to open their minds to new ideas and opinions and develop their creative self-expression, but it also enhances the aesthetics of the school space, promoting – among other things – the production of more sophisticated school functions.

Nevertheless, evidence of attempts to develop interdisciplinary connections (i.e. within courses such as literature or history) indicates that these arise from personal initiatives in the educational community rather than formal sources and remain isolated and ultimately unrewarding efforts (Bamford, 2013; Sotiropoulou-Zormpala, 2016). VAE has the power to convey culture critically by transcending the familiar optical visions, in a way that renders the arts a valuable learning toolkit. This fact points to the need for a meaningful and systematic interdisciplinary appreciation and approach to VAE in school curricula, exemplifying the variety of creative expression among people and cultures. Such an approach entails the integration of VAE within a holistic education scheme advancing sustainability (Ioannidou, 2018). Artistic creativity, a fundamental cultural principle, can serve as a pivotal bridging element between VAE and transform schools into agents of sustainability (Humphries & Pelletier, 2018). The objective of the modern school could be to facilitate students to locate, appreciate and critically interpret artworks and cultural assets they encounter in their daily lives across the curriculum. Students need to be encouraged to understand that artworks do not simply 'adorn' museum displays or illustrate books and magazines but are enduring links to human thought and creation, providing endless sources of inspiration, reflection and reconstruction that can lead to a sustainable future.

Subsequently, and through the presentation of critical arguments and dominant concepts, the importance of combining the two fields of VAE and ESD will be demonstrated, emphasizing the role of teachers as facilitators of such a change. Further, a proposed approach to curriculum planning for the effective use of visual arts in sustainable education will be succinctly described. Finally, by accepting museums as essential contributors to holistic formal education and targeting their core values and practices, the chapter will suggest ways to harness their power, mainly through museum education; this promises a sustainable future for all cultures by actively and uncompromisingly engaging teachers and children.

Breaking down walls, building bridges: VAE in collaboration with ESD

The relationship between sustainability and art goes back several centuries. In the past, the focus would either be the content or technique or even the clever use of materials.

Contemporary artistic practices tend to focus more explicitly on the most pressing topical issues, such as those related to the threats of the recent pandemic. This tendency is consistent with UNESCO's Sustainable Development Goals (SDGs[4]), which are also a reference point for artistic endeavours internationally. The Seoul Agenda, this crucial twenty-first-century text on the development of arts education, aspires to revise and transcend past dominant positions, such as 'art for art's sake', to instrumentalize art towards advancing an interdisciplinary education (Siegesmund, 1998, p. 203), thereby 'promoting within VAE the idea of active participation in a process of social, environmental, economic, and cultural shift, which is necessary for ensuring a sustainable present and future' (Vella, 2022, p. 3).

The correlation between the concept of sustainability and the visual arts is multi-dimensional. The objectives of both are harmoniously integrated, interacting and complementing each other directly or indirectly in formal and non-formal education (e.g. in museums and cultural spaces). Furthermore, the visual arts are a universal language, an expression of cultures and peoples worldwide, with the potential to unite all people. They provide concrete opportunities to generalist teachers and art educators dedicated to equitable education, to change students' perceptions and to motivate them to broaden their ideas creatively within the context of ESD activities (Hunter, Aprill, Hill, & Emery, 2018). According to the basic principles of sustainability, all children, regardless of age, race, sex, economic or social status, are entitled to full access to cultural facilities and activities and the opportunity to develop aesthetic skills. By engaging in the visual arts, children who are non-native speakers and children with learning difficulties or with disabilities can participate in and significantly contribute to their school and local communities and 'help extinguish old stereotypes and create a global culture truly representative of all people' (Goldberg, 2017, p. 29).

The visual arts discipline enables young people to delve into their personal feelings and thoughts and find ways to manage and express them appropriately. VAE also helps young people explore and redefine connections among values, consider the social changes around them and understand cultural ties and differences. On the other hand, ESD, fluidly and skilfully, embraces the visual arts through its involvement in positive hands-on practice, observation, analysis and evaluation. Artistic creations are an integral part of social tradition, and children need to experience social customs and traditions to understand the special significance of this procedure. In this framework, students' interactions with living, contemporary artists energize the educational process, cutting across the values and common goals of VAE and ESD while serving as an inspiration and challenge within the school environment. Artists hold a multi-dimensional role not purely as essential creators and interpreters of artworks but also as carriers of the practices of an era, clashing or interfering with the regimes of truth, as Foucault (1969) highlighted in his book *The Archaeology of Knowledge*.

In today's world, where globalization has contributed to cultural homogenization and a resulting reductionist way of thinking, the need to protect cultural heritage and preserve cultural diversity seems imperative. Cultural diversity has always been manifested through different languages, values, habits and practices. It is valuable to current and future generations because it creates direct and integral links with biological diversity (Higgins, 2013). Often, in the name of economic development and technological advancement, the role of the visual arts is diminished, and local traditions and cultural diversity are sacrificed. To avoid this, targeted partnerships between VAE and ESD can practically and emphatically highlight the uniqueness of each culture (Duxbury, Gillette, & Pepper, 2007). Multidisciplinary and collaborative projects embedded in a school's routine can free students from specific cultural constraints by helping them understand their cultural identity, encouraging them to preserve cultural diversity and values and promoting local traditions. Ultimately, cooperative efforts for a sustainable future are vital for promoting the peaceful coexistence of culturally pluralistic societies (Nurse, 2006).

Cultural heritage is a social asset to which everyone has an inalienable right; bestowing a system rich in cultural references to future generations provides a sense of historical continuity and confidence. This concept was the basis for developing a new course in the School of Primary Education (Aristotle University of Thessaloniki) launched in 2021, leading to an arts-rich, interdisciplinary, collaborative approach to learning. The proposed approach recognizes the importance of intercultural dialogue as a valuable tool for creating sustainable visions. Aiming to bridge the goals of VAE and ESD creatively, this approach contributes – among other things – to promote diverse cultural communities within and outside the educational environment (school, university or other). A decade earlier, Tilbury and Mulà (2009) attempted to demonstrate the interconnection between ESD and culture through a project that facilitated the exchange of valuable forms of knowledge and sustainable artistic practices that enhanced traditions, the financial strength of communities, acts of solidarity and social justice. Through their inspiring project, Mulà and Tilbury concluded that 'the challenge is to ensure that these initiatives do not remain in isolation, but instead cross-fertilise each other and feed into the ESD policy agenda' (Tilbury & Mulà, 2011, p. 5).

VAE offers young people the opportunity to participate in collective activities and learn to become active citizens. Our recent experience with the new course and the CARE project (Ioannidou, 2022) confirms the initial hypothesis for its development: when promoting the visual arts and their cultural, social, environmental and economic dimensions within a sustainability framework, you create an optimistic legacy and a viable perspective for the future. Guided by creativity and imagination and using reflective methods such as updating symbols and messages, the visual arts proved to have the transformative power to motivate students to actively collaborate in creating meanings for their own culture as well as participate in the culture of others, thereby shifting to the basic sustainable principle defining culture: we care, we share, we learn together (Higgins, 2013, pp. 23–24).

Thus, dynamic visual interventions are a vehicle for sustainability and, with the contribution of artists, can serve as an essential catalyst for creating new collaborations between schools and local communities while at the same time strengthening intergenerational learning. For example, the conceptual framework of cultural ecology can stimulate a discussion about the need to rethink the role of education, emphasizing the dynamic interaction between continuity and change, conservation and regeneration, all concepts fundamental to sustainability. The argument for a dynamic combination of VAE and ESD does not self-evidently stir positive views (Dunkley, 2015). Accordingly, Belfiore and Bennett (2007) argue that although art may have educational, cognitive, humanitarian or other purposes, the value of a work of art is firmly embedded in the aesthetic realm.

Teachers as facilitators of change

To transform learning into an active, engaging and dynamic endeavour through the visual arts, critical pedagogy embraces art and invites learners, regardless of age, to critically comment both on the works themselves and the setting in which they were created. Paulo Freire considered the visual arts a disarming method to achieve dialectical and liberating educational outcomes as their transformative character led to a more humane society (Freire, 1973; Morris, 1998). The visual arts facilitate diverse representations of life, providing opportunities for comparison, updating facts and dynamic intercultural dialogue. In this context, learners question the status quo while trying to understand how it emerged in the first place. They learn to recognize and shape their own identity, which usually leads to action. Thus versed, students make connections between art and their own experiences, develop critical thinking, and learn to see and think of themselves and society from varied angles and perspectives.

Artistically and culturally illiterate children may become future citizens with limited ability to question established 'normalities', claim their rights or pursue their sustainable future. VAE and ESD can contribute to the reconstruction of educational systems so that schools may provide children with the necessary abilities and knowledge to become active future citizens who can secure a sustainable future for themselves and the world.

It is true that generalist teachers, who are usually called upon to deliver art lessons, hardly receive the necessary instruction in the visual arts or sustainable development in their basic education, which makes them reluctant to use them in their teaching. Moreover, teachers' participation in educational programmes that motivate teachers to recognize and build on the connections between VAE and ESD in their practice remains a matter of personal choice rather than an official state policy or concern. Relevant research and certified training accessible to all, informed educational institutions and school counsellors, partnerships with research centres and universities aiming to establish networks of intergenerational learning support remain in the early stages of development (Pavlou, 2022).

Official institutions are responsible for educating teachers in these two fields, thereby supporting their professional growth and enabling them to support their students' learning and growth better. Knowledgeable and sensitized teachers are usually willing, at times eager, to experiment and take the risk of trying out innovative approaches, e.g., exploring the potential of the synergy of VAE and ESD (Tilbury & Mulà, 2011). Such interdisciplinary approaches to learning bring radical, inspiring changes in teachers' routines and practices.

They also engage students in a more meaningful and active way in appreciating all art forms and creations while developing their cognitive and critical skills.

Discussing changes in social norms and reacting to diverse social and political issues in life through VAE activates creative processes. When students are involved in such experiences, they enjoy deep satisfaction, increasing the likelihood of benefitting from a holistic, meaningful and valuable education. However, the concept of what is educationally valuable is foreign to current western pedagogical practices that seek to quickly stimulate and motivate students by using reward systems that have no intrinsic connection with students' experiences, culture, talents, preferences and inclinations.

Boosting curriculum planning

In the hands of trained and creative educators who respond enthusiastically to the challenge of creatively combining VAE and ESD systematically and daily, the visual arts can arguably become a 'driver' for change rather than just a 'vehicle'.

Group work on various interdisciplinary approaches and diverse conceptual frameworks can be drawn upon to introduce students through artworks to problem-based learning, enhance their understanding and motivate them to explore the links between environmental, social, economic and cultural issues. One sustainable function of the visual arts is the ability to enable us to participate empathetically in the lives of others. Through artworks and artistic practices, artists make it easier for students to viscerally recognize the experiences of others and thereby understand a world that would otherwise remain unknown to them. For example, a plain description of the frequency of destruction of children's recreational areas in densely populated urban centres may provide useful statistical information. However, it hardly evokes a sympathetic understanding of our identification with the conditions children live in and how their lives have changed, which can easily be brought to life through artistic creations. Consider the potential of such sources in teaching history, or, even more broadly, in social studies.

In the context of the new academic course in the School of Primary Education (Aristotle University of Thessaloniki), emphasis has been placed on the potential of the visual arts to facilitate student teachers' understanding, thus reorientating and enhancing the chief aims of VAE, which tend to focus more on production, performance skills and knowledge of the visual arts than on the quality of the student experience. In this vein, for example, a systematic attempt was made to introduce artworks from different historical periods to highlight and help future teachers understand, recognize and be able to exemplify and artistically engage with their students subsequently on the status of and the difference between an immigrant and a refugee. Thus, the small statuette of the *Refugee Child* (150 CE, National Archaeological Museum, Athens), *The Wreck of the Medusa* by Théodore Géricault (1818–19, Musée du Louvre, Paris), *What's North What's South* by Vlasis Caniaris (1988, Installation, Private collection, Athens), *The Ocean March: Homage à*

Delacroix I–III by Iannis Psychopedis (2016, Private collection), Jason deCaires Taylor's underwater sculpture *Raft of Lampedusa* (2016, courtesy of the artist), Vik Muniz's 'paper' Lampedusa (2015) exhibited at the 56th Venice Biennale, Kalliopi Lemos's *Pledges For a Safe Passage*, (2012) exhibited at the Third Çanakkale Biennial, a wooden boat covered with original votives and votives from tin obtained from soft drink cans carrying the names of illegal immigrants, and Alina Gavrielatos' baby shirts with the names of lost children exhibited at the Second Çanakkale Biennial (2010) were presented to students, together with performances and activist presentations by Wei Wei, Angeliki Avgitidou,[5] and other international and Greek contemporary artists. Along with exposure to these works, the students' research and artistic reflections led them to search for articles and books with accounts of uprooting and to critically evaluate current news as captured in social media. With our further encouragement and the support of their circles of families, friends and their local communities, they had the opportunity to listen to the language and music of migrants and refugees, to read and understand their myths and stories, to taste their food, to read excerpts from literary texts and not just 'see', but 'look deeply' at their art. The visual arts provided these student teachers with access to the timeline (past, present and future) that textbooks and lectures usually omit.

Given its broader sustainability perspective, VAE can engage with all the students' senses, feelings and ideas and help them develop their ability to understand the subtleties of remote experiences of others. This seems to be a primary goal for teachers, educational policy-makers and curriculum planners. A key feature of the value of introducing works of art into the curriculum is revealing the crucial role of art in expanding the scope of students' questions, bringing to the surface reflections on the repetitive nature of history that are 'taught but not learned', and updating our knowledge of the past. Thus, teachers and students are inspired and motivated to look critically, gain awareness of the issues discussed and gradually acquire strong voices to confront real-life problems and seek sustainable solutions for them.

Merely presenting the skills, talents and achievements of the visual arts over past centuries does not suffice for the holistic development of students. They must engage in dialogue, research and critique as active participants and gain awareness of the parallel evolution of artistic creativity among human beings throughout history, reflected in artworks, daily life, and the myths and traditions handed down to us. The ultimate goal is to recognize the need to value and protect cultural diversity, adopt empathy for all and respect everyone's right to difference, not just as lip service but actively. That means taking the initiative to manage better cultural, natural and human resources.

Applying ESD through VAE does not in any way devalue aesthetic pleasure or diminish the opportunities students have in an art class to express themselves artistically. On the contrary, it is an enhancing approach for forming students' personalities and cultural identities in contemporary school practice. Its value is raised by consistently linking everyday challenges with understanding sustainability goals. A concrete way to achieve this could be to transform the walls and corridors of school buildings or playgrounds into canvases that spark interest and invite students to be artistic. These artworks can serve as references to the status of children in society or to children's rights, thereby triggering artistic activism and dialogue with the broader society. Empowering students through the visual arts enables them to act, not merely as passive participants led by others, but as initiators of the life they envision as future citizens.

Through VAE, teachers can also address the poor performance of students, in line with one of the crucial sustainable development goals – inclusion in education. Students often experience a loss of curiosity, a sense of inadequacy in their ability to learn and a disharmony between the school curriculum and their present and future lives. The effectiveness of integrating the visual arts across the curriculum and engaging students in artistic activity as creative thinkers within a context based on collaboration and community building makes the core curriculum relevant and meaningful to them (Mitakidou & Tressou, 2017). Artistic projects capture the imagination and build the confidence of otherwise disengaged students by creating an enthusiastic atmosphere of active learning among students, teachers and collaborating artists. The opportunity for young learners to work with artists in their school environment or museums is invaluable. Along with offering specialist knowledge and assistance in developing students' creative and social skills, artists introduce different cultural traditions and capitalize on cross-cultural approaches in examining artefacts and social phenomena. Teachers join in, sharing the role of animators and facilitators of new knowledge, ensuring that engagement extends beyond the immediate experience that generated it, thus leading to a change of attitudes and behaviours of the participants (Ioannidou, 2017). A successful transformation is demonstrated when formerly disengaged students expend effort in learning, persist despite difficulties, find ways to express thoughts and feelings through the visual arts, take pride in producing quality artistic and other schoolwork, and exhibit enthusiasm, curiosity and interest. Thus, students get to see the big picture and understand school life as part of their whole life and knowledge as a holistic, ongoing process.

Bridging VAE and ESD in practice presents new possibilities to teachers: better rapport with students, a renewed commitment to their student's learning and a genuine willingness to become co-learners in the classroom, which contributes to enhanced personal and professional development, despite their limited knowledge of the two fields (VAE and ESD) and the practical difficulties they witness, with insufficient media and inappropriate infrastructure.

Towards a sustainable museum education

Museums and cultural spaces that display art are not merely venues that encourage informal, improvised creation and participation. They are also ideal places where education for sustainable development can be promoted; they are rewarding places for raising moral and ethical issues via discussions and collaborative action learning. Therefore, it is appropriate and wise for educational authorities to build on the power of museums to assist in shaping a sustainable future for all cultures and secure the well-being of societies by actively and consistently engaging educators and children (Janes & Sandell, 2019).

In their role as custodians of cultural wealth, museums have a significant role to play in suitably and equitably pursuing the multi-dimensional goals of VAE and ESD. Essentially, museums are institutions initially founded on the central ideas of sustainability: preservation and conservation, but also a regeneration of a world culture in the making.

As such, museums are 'open windows to the world', with western and non-western cultures represented, in whole or in part. Museums aspire to campaign the position that there is not one dominant art or culture but many artistic, historical and cultural narratives. These narratives reflect the differences, as well as the similarities among cultures, and emphasize the complexity of the visual arts by taking western audiences far afield from their comfort zones, their accustomed territories, incorporating a social focus and offering the potential to transform contemporary societies' ways of thinking by exposing them to unfamiliar, intriguing, open-minded, inclusive and sustainable perceptions about our planet and our living 'together' (Samis & Michaelson, 2016). Museums help inspire and facilitate a global conversation on promoting peace, reconciliation, civic pluralism and democratic citizenship.

'Cultural organisations can be instrumental in both practice and policy to support the arts programmes in their local schools. They can have a consistent presence in the advocacy, and partner with schools to provide additional resources' (Humphries & Pelletier, 2018, p. 459). Museum objects and artworks uniquely address inequalities, injustice and environmental challenges, enhancing respect and interest in cultural polymorphism inside and outside the school environment. 'Museums are in a position to invent a new future for themselves and their communities' (Janes, 2013, p. 13) and 'make room for a commitment to the durability and wellbeing of individuals, communities and the natural world' (Berry, 2000, p. 134).

In an effort to achieve social inclusion, it is high time that cultural organizations and museums played a key role in facilitating multicultural dialogue with equal representation of western and non-western, advanced and non-advanced countries. In addition, museums and the visual arts have a leading role in this campaign by welcoming the 'voice' or providing spaces to the cultures of non-privileged groups, who are often expected to blend into the mainstream context without voice or identity. Integrating into the dominant culture in the framework of sustainable development principles discourages the silencing or alienation of other cultural identities. A sustainable, truly inclusive society makes space for everyone and helps those who have lost their livelihoods and cultural assets to find a way to preserve their customs and traditions and promote their culture, thus highlighting the common threads that tie communities together.

To this end, in practical terms, museums, in collaboration with schools and universities that are implementing VAE and ESD within their local communities, can coordinate exhibitions displaying students' diverse cultures, thus encouraging the creation of smaller museums of everyone's 'world' within educational contexts. Museums should also take the additional step of including young people not just as visitors but as active participants in the creation, preservation and promotion of culture and can strengthen the meaning of cultural assets by adding objects, stories or enriching the existing traditions of their home countries. This act of recognition, a proof of allocating equal value and importance, becomes a conscious way of guaranteeing the sustainable future of societies and cultures.

Cultural heritage is not simply a world-renowned archive of sacred treasures. The purpose of museums and the visual arts is not merely to showcase cultural treasures but also to facilitate audiences to understand cultural diversity and encounter different cultures' perceptions and institutions. The emphasis on cultural diversity encourages educators and learners to compare their own cultural assumptions with other cultures. They can then focus on the evolutionary nature of culture and the potential for change, understand the value of cultural perspectives and draw connections between contemporary values and the historical forces that shaped them.

Given that we are nurturing the first generation of 'digital natives', i.e., children who feel as comfortable navigating the online realm as their neighbourhood streets (Merritt, 2012, p. 99), museums could use social media and other technological tools available in the museum itself. Alternatively, through their website, they challenge this generation of children to embrace the museum as a familiar, hospitable place where they can seek their cultural identity, artistic nature and other interests, and thus creatively face challenges and real-life issues. Conceptualizing and generating community building in the virtual realm demands 'sustained communication and interaction by staff to encourage growth' (Valone, 2011, p. 279) and could face resistance at the beginning among educators and learners. Considering how prominent and distinctive the virtual world has become in young people's lives, this process of forming interactive, online learning cultural communities could gain viability and status over time, eventually becoming an attractive and welcome option for many students and teachers (Ioannidou, 2004).

Concluding remarks

Nowadays, visual arts can radically contribute to upgrading the standard of social living. With its universality, solid activist presence and imaginative, dynamic symbolism, the language of art communicates powerfully with young and old worldwide. Perhaps future demands for sustainable development will take for granted the need to strengthen the aesthetic awareness of citizens at both a conscious and a practical level. Aesthetic awareness is a universal ecological value, as it reinforces mutual understanding and world peace and reduces human misery for all peoples of the world by abolishing the boundaries between developed and underdeveloped countries, the strong and the weak, the privileged and the underprivileged.

Educational systems are increasingly concerned about the consequences of rapidly increasing and significant divides between advantaged and disadvantaged children. The visual arts should not be considered a luxury or superficial commodity, accessible only to people with a higher level of education or a certain financial status. They exist for all those who seek to experience emotion and exuberance through the 'beautiful', a mirror to our society.

They reduce tensions, soothe, sensitize and teach people to understand better all that surrounds them. Human beings can get to know themselves better through art and discover their faults, limitations, possibilities and havens. Individuals learn to see through a different lens, understand problems and look for solutions through the humility and serenity that a work of art often disseminates. The arts, especially the visual arts, are created through humanity's lives, experiences and ideas; they merge the individual with a greater whole and socialize the latter in solidarity with others, nature and culture.

The visual arts can help create a steady pace in the lives of younger generations and their highly uncertain future. Through creative and consistent collaboration, teachers can encourage children's enthusiasm, expression and critical thought, and invite them into the procedure of social and cultural making as active participants.

The negative consequences of technological development point to lonely societies with lonely people, as evidenced by daily acts of cruelty, violence and alienation. Additionally, rapid social and economic changes and the recent experiences gained from the COVID-19 pandemic have dramatically increased the need to consolidate the highly efficient and intuitive bridge between the visual arts, cultural assets and the principles of sustainable development in education. Maintaining democratic vigour and multi-cultural respect in a multi-dimensional and rapidly shifting world depends mainly on educating and empowering people, both young and old, theoretically, and practically, to adapt to new conditions and remain resilient to exogenous challenges (Adams & Owens, 2015).

In the aftermath of the modern myth of progress, the politics of the future is culture. We can hope for a peaceful and fairer future by drawing on cultural theory and recruiting the visual arts as critical social signifiers to project sustainable development goals into everyday life and educational practice.

Notes

1. The newborn elephant is tied to a tree with a strong rope. Initially, the baby elephant is unable to uproot the tree. Later, when the elephant is fully grown, it no longer seeks freedom and will live in captivity forever. Essentially, what holds the elephant back is not the rope, but the habit. Something similar happens to people, whose decisions and actions are often part of 'automatic behaviours' that stem from habits and become a context function.
2. *CARE, Visual art education in new times: Connecting Art with REal life issues* is an EU-funded, Erasmus + KA203 project (2019–22). The overarching aim of CARE is to empower teachers to build on the interconnection between VAE and ESD to pursue SDGs through the arts and wider cultural products.

3. Frederick University in Cyprus, lead partner, University of Malta in Malta, Exeter University in the United Kingdom, and Aristotle University of Thessaloniki (AUTH) in Thessaloniki, Greece. http://care.frederick.ac.cy/
4. https://en.unesco.org/sustainabledevelopmentgoals
5. https://www.aiweiwei.com/; https://vimeo.com/67289839

References

Adams, J., & Owens, A. (2015). *Creativity and democracy in education: Practices and politics of learning through the arts*. New York, NY: Routledge.

Bamford, A. (2013). The WOW and what now? The challenges of implementation of arts education. In E. Liebau, E. Wagner, & M. Wyman (Eds.), *International yearbook for research in arts education* (Vol. 1, pp. 175–187). Münster: Waxmann Verlag.

Belfiore, E., & Bennett, O. (2007). Rethinking the social impacts of the arts. *International Journal of Cultural Policy*, *13*(2), 135–151. https://doi.org/10.1080/10286630701342741

Berry, W. (2000). *Life is a miracle*. Washington, DC: Counterpoint.

Dunkley, R. (2015). Reimagining a sustainable future through artistic events: A case study from Wales. In T. Pernecky & O. Moufakkir (Eds.), *Ideological, social and cultural aspects of events* (pp. 100–109). UK: CABI.

Duxbury, N., Gillette, E., & Pepper, K. (2007). *Exploring the cultural dimensions of sustainability*. Ottawa: Creative City Network of Canada. http://crossingstreet.files.worpress.com/2007/09/culutral_dimensions_of_sustainability.doc

Foucault, M. (1969). *L' archéologie du savoir*. Paris: Gallimard.

Freire, P. (1973). *Education for critical consciousness*. New York, NY: The Seabury Press.

Goldberg, M. (2017). *Arts integration*. London: Routledge.

Higgins, A. (2013). Culturing education for sustainability: Evaluating a tertiary case study. In *Conference Proceedings at the People and the Planet 2013 Conference Transforming the Future*, RMIT University Melbourne, Australia. https://silo.tips/download/series-url

Humphries, M. G., & Pelletier, L. Y. (2018). Arts integration in education: Teachers and teaching artists as agents of change. In *Theory, impact, practice* (pp. 435–459). Bristol: Intellect Books.

Hunter, M. A., Aprill, A., Hill, A., & Emery, S. (Eds.). (2018). *Education, arts, and sustainability: Emerging practice for a changing world*. New York, NY: Springer.

Ioannidou, M. (2004). Museum education: Enriching the learning experience. In *Proceedings of the European Conference on Educational Research (ECER), NETWORK 20: Research in Innovative Intercultural Learning Environments*. University of Crete, Crete. https://eera-ecer.de/ecer-programmes/conference/15/contribution/27107/

Ioannidou, M. (2017). Artists as inviting personalities for self-exploration and social learning at school. *European Journal of Social Sciences Education and Research*, *11*(2), 52–58.

Ioannidou, M. (2018). Μια εικόνα ισούται με χίλιες λεξεις. Χίλιες λέξεις ισούνται με μια εικόνα; Ο ρόλος των Μουσείων Λογοτεχνίας και Τέχνης στην ενδυνάμωση ήστην αποδυνάμωση της λογοτεχνικής ανάγνωσης. In Β. Αποστολίδου,

Δ. Κόκορης, Μ.Γ. Μπακογιάννης, Ε. Χοντολίδου (Eds.). Λογοτεχνική ανάγνωση στο σχολείο και στην κοινωνία (pp. 591-602). [A picture is worth a thousand words. Are a thousand words equal to a picture? The role of the Museums of Literature and Art in the empowerment or in the weakening of the literary reading. In V. Apostolidou, D. Kokoris, M. G. Bakoyannis, & E. Chontolidou (Eds.), *Literary reading in school and in society* (pp. 591-602). Salt Lake City, UT: Gutenberg].

Ioannidou, M. (Ed.) (2022). *The touch of art: Teacher training for sustainability through the visual arts*. Cyprus: Frederick University.

Janes, R. R. (2013). *Museums and the paradox of change*. New York, NY: Routledge

Janes, R. R., & Sandell, R. (Eds.). (2019). *Museum activism*. New York, NY: Routledge

Merritt, E. (2012). Exploring the educational future. *Journal of Museum Education, 37*(3), 99-106.

Mitakidou, S., & Tressou, E. (2017). The arts as a vehicle to school literacy. In *EDULEARN17 Proceedings of 9th International Conference on Education and New Learning Technologies. Empowering learners in a digital world* (pp. 1157-1161). Morocco: IATED Academy.

Morris, C. B. (1998). Paulo Freire: Community based arts education. *Journal of Social Theory in Art Education (JSTAE), 18*, 44-58. https://scholarscompass.vcu.edu/cgi/viewcontent.cgi?article=1223&context=jstae

Mulà, I., & Tilbury, D. (2011). *Linking culture, education and sustainability: Good practices around the world*. Paris, UNESCO. http://insight.glos.ac.uk/sustainability/Education/unescoculture/Pages/default.aspx

Nurse, K. (2006). Culture as the fourth pillar of sustainable development. *Paper prepared for Commonwealth Secretariat*, London, UK.

Pavlou, V. (Ed.). (2022). *What is really happening now? Connecting art education with real life issues*. Cyprus: Frederick University.

Proust, M. (1996). *In search of lost time, Vol. 6: Time regained and a guide to proust*. Orlando: Vintage Classics.

Samis, P., & Michaelson, M. (2016). *Creating the visitor-centered museum*. New York, NY: Routledge.

Siegesmund, R. (1998). Why do we teach art today? Conceptions of art education and their justification. *Studies in Art Education, 39*(3), 197-214.

Sotiropoulou-Zormpala, M. (2016). Seeking a higher level of arts integration across the curriculum. *Arts Education Policy Review, 117*(1), 43-53. https://doi.org/10.1080/10632913.2014.966288

Tilbury, D., & Mulà, I. (2009). *Review of education for sustainable development policies from a cultural diversity and intercultural dialogue: Gaps and opportunities for future action*. Paris: UNESCO.

Valone, L. (2011). Cooking up an online community. *Journal of Museum Education, 36*(3), 279-287.

Vella, R. (Ed.). (2022). *Integrating principles of education for sustainable development into visual art education in teacher education programmes*. Cyprus: Frederick University.

Chapter 3

Aliens or Allies? Towards Symbiotic Relationships in Art Education

Raphael Vella

Human puppets and alien plants

> The parasitic relation is intersubjective. It is the atomic form of our relations. Let us try to face it head-on, like death, like the sun. We are all attacked, together.
>
> (Serres, 1982, p. 8)

Creatures that combine human and non-human characteristics have been a source of fascination for millennia. Fauns, sirens, centaurs and other hybrids crop up in mythology, religion, magic, science-fiction, children's literature, cartoons and various other fields. Many artists in the past have used animals to portray themselves: Frida Kahlo's small painting *The Wounded Deer* (1946), for example, shows the artist's head topped by antlers and attached to a deer's body that is pierced by many arrows. Hybrids like these may lead us to ask whether one of their identities dominates the other: Is Walt Disney's Goofy a dog with a man's body and clothes or a man with a dog's head and clumsy demeanour? For some, such comic hybrids always end up adapting animals to social life, transforming them, as John Berger wrote, into 'human puppets' (2009, p. 15). However, the transplantation of human components into animal bodies (and vice versa) is not simply the stuff of movies and folklore. For many years, bioprosthetic valves from cows and pigs have been used as human heart valve replacements. In the fields of regenerative medicine and organ transplantation, Hiromitsu Nakauchi is leading teams at Stanford University and the University of Tokyo to research the possibility of injecting a person's stem cells into a mouse or rat embryo, which is then implanted into another surrogate animal in preparation for the eventual transplantation of an organ into the patient who originally donated the stem cells (Cyranoski, 2019). If Berger lamented how animals have been marginalized, made dependent on human support and reduced to a spectacle in captivity (2009), biomedical research that uses non-humans also raises questions about anthropocentrism and the moral status and welfare of sentient animals. While animal experimentation for research purposes and captive animals in zoos clearly have different uses, implications, short- and long-term impacts and benefits, both scenarios highlight shifting hierarchical relationships between humans and non-humans and make us aware of the possibility of expanding the notion of solidarity to include beings that are not members of our own species.

This chapter will outline instances of anthropocentrism as well as different theoretical positions that have sought to rethink 'art education beyond anthropocentrism' (Kallio-Tavin,

2020). It will also propose an ecologically aware approach to art education that is informed by contemporary artistic practices, including the principles and practices of socially engaged art. The chapter will also take account of implied hierarchies and relationships between humans and other species which have inspired the work of contemporary artists and art educators, as well as students in art classes.

As I was scrolling through children's artworks produced during a lesson on alien plants that formed part of a European Union-funded research project, I came across a collage by a 9-year-old girl (Figure 3.1) that I couldn't resist returning to.[1] Initially, I was not entirely sure why I found the image so compelling. Given that I also had access to the teacher's notes, I searched for more information. I read that the teacher had described invasive species and their effect on the conditions of specific habitats to the class. The teacher's examples of works by artists like Seán Hillen clearly sparked the student's imagination. Glued onto a bright yellow background, three humanoid figures form a bizarre group of human–plant hybrids of different sizes in the girl's collage. On the left, a figure holding a long spoon and spade grows out of a plant pot. In the centre of the image, a (male?) figure topped by a snake plant stands on two quadrilaterals, while a taller, faceless figure on the right stands beneath a red rose that seems to have sprouted out of its neck. After reading the teacher's notes, it seemed to me that the child was implying that if we do not care enough for the integrity of ecosystems, we risk altering our own environment to such an extent that life itself becomes

Figure 3.1: Collage dealing with the subject of invasive plants, by a 9-year-old girl.

unrecognizable. Rather than focus exclusively on the negative effects that invasive plants have on native species and surrounding vegetation, this image seems to want to draw our attention towards their impact on human life.

Looking at these composite beings in the student's image, we might remark, following philosopher Timothy Morton (2017):

> In symbiosis, it's unclear which is the top symbiont, and the relationship between the beings is jagged, incomplete. Am I simply a vehicle for the numerous bacteria that inhabit my microbiome? Or are they hosting me? Who is the host and who is the parasite? (Morton, 2017, p. 1)

In the student's colourful collage, which body parts belong to the host and which belong to the parasite? While Morton helpfully explains that the word 'host' 'stems from the Latin *hostis*, a word that can mean both 'friend' and 'enemy' (2017, pp. 12–13), scientific and popular discourse as well as national and international environmental policies related to invasion ecology are overwhelmingly negative, revolving around the degradation of the environment, soil erosion, harmful chemical deposits, and so on. In this context, an invasive species is undoubtedly an 'enemy' or threat to biodiversity. The child's image very likely follows this storyline by presenting plants as intruders or outsiders entering human life and metamorphosing it into something grotesque. Such an interpretation of the collage is rooted in a real concern with this threat in different regions of the world, including Europe, where invasive alien species (particularly terrestrial plants) adversely impact ecosystems and society and have led to changes in legislation (European Commission, 2014).

While the exposure of students to data, lessons and artworks related to conservation is clearly crucial, it may also be useful to be aware of the dangers of over-emphasizing the militaristic language that tends to characterize invasive species research, especially in basic science journals (Janovsky & Larson, 2019). While terms like 'attack' and 'enemy' often used in the literature are reminiscent of conflicts and wars, the 'invasion' narrative is also analogous to how political rhetoric sometimes alludes to national borders and how the language of racism frequently defines migration and identity. Xenophobic discourse frequently alludes to irregular migrants as predators, parasites and a general threat to local culture, employment, and so on. It is based on an inside/outside mentality that Morton (2018) calls the 'Uncanny Valley'. Full of various 'other' beings, this valley 'becomes an artefact of anthropocentrism, racism and speciesism – of xenophobia, a fear of the "other", which is, often, really a fear of what we have in common with the "other"' (p. 176). At the same time, this fear is increasingly dominated by ecological changes that mirror human migrations. As Latour (2017) has pointed out, the urge to build borders to 'defend' ourselves against human migrants is entirely useless against much larger migratory and unpredictable phenomena like erosion, climate change and pollution that do not respect borders and creep into everyone's lives and homes. Speaking of one's own land today is challenged by the porosity of borders.

A sensitivity to the use of language is not the same as a denial of the seriousness of the potential threat of non-native species in different ecosystems. What is being suggested in this chapter is that the student's collage could potentially be associated with an entirely different narrative, one based on symbiosis rather than invasion, foreignness or anthropocentrism. What if we were to see in this collage a symbiotic coexistence of species rather than a struggle for survival or disruption of 'normality'? Moreover, what if art were to be conceived as the path through which such a symbiosis built on a deeper understanding and solidarity with non-humans must travel to become possible? Could art education play a role in formulating a different approach to looking at non-humans – an approach that is characterized by the desire for a shared home which is analogous to the participatory discourse associated with socially engaged art?

If Berger (2009) writes that animals and human beings look at each other across an 'abyss of non-comprehension' (p. 5), art educators may ask how the human gaze can bridge this abyss and supersede the reduction of the non-human to economic employability by shifting towards a non-hierarchical gaze that does not set apart the human and the non-human. The binary separation of human and non-human that tends to form the basis of anthropocentric thought needs to be reconceptualized if we heed Berger's warning about an impoverished and alienated non-human domain.

Plant signatures and talking lions

An overview of historical relationships between humans and non-humans highlights the difficulty of unlearning anthropocentrism. Berger acknowledges that 'animals constituted the first circle' (2009, p. 3) around people before a rupture between human beings and nature occurred in the nineteenth century. While this circular image placed animals in proximity to people in the past, it also reflected a sense of centrality that is uniquely human. Berger's ancient sources include Aristotle's scientific study of the animal kingdom (1965), which explains how animals are endowed with human traits like fierceness and cunning, and form part of a hierarchical scale that leads upwards from lifeless things to plants, on to animals and finally ending with humans. For Aristotle, human beings (their internal organs, behaviour, different gender traits, and so on) provide a kind of model for all, or the majority of, other living things. For instance, he observed that male cuttlefish hang around to protect the female when approached by an enemy, which, in Aristotle's world, reflects a similar gender-specific attitude towards courage in humans. Similarly, the Greek philosopher projected the incest prohibition onto animals.

However, another ancient and even more explicitly anthropomorphic doctrine places non-human life at the service of humanity to the extent that the external appearance of the former seeks to provide the latter with a sign of its amenability to human use. The belief in a link between plant morphology and the medicinal use of plants has been popular in oral history and herbal medicine for a long time and is usually referred to as the doctrine of signatures. According to this doctrine, the resemblance of plant forms to human body parts is an indication of their curative powers; hence, the heart-shaped leaves of foxglove plants supply people with a clue of their use in the mitigation of cardiac problems, the intricate shape of walnuts mimic the brain and its ailments, and so on. While a handful of ancient sources for this idea exist, the chief proponents of the doctrine were sixteenth-century scholars like Paracelsus and Giambattista della Porta. The Swiss physician and philosopher Paracelsus, for instance, interpreted the doctrine in theological terms, indicating that God had moulded non-human life in a way that would help human beings 'read' its meaning and possible use in medicine (Bennett, 2007). In his *Phytognomonica* (1588), della Porta also provides readers with useful illustrations that compare plant features to human and even animal body parts. Images in his book place plant roots that resemble fingers adjacent to a human hand (Figure 3.2), Maidenhair fern adjacent to a head with thick hair, and so on. The doctrine's 'signature' refers to a physical attribute that acts as a kind of semiotic shorthand for a specific ailment while alluding to nature's provision of a cure for that very

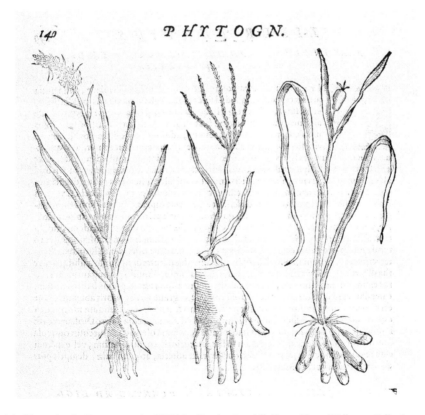

Figure 3.2: Illustration in *Phytognomonica* (1588) by Giambattista della Porta. Photo: Wellcome Collection.

ailment. Based on an analysis of natural design, the doctrine exposes human weaknesses as it evokes the ability of human beings to overcome such weaknesses. A human order of things counters biological disorder. The visual interpretation of forms – the backbone of art criticism and a common activity in art classes – is brought to bear on 'nature' to reveal hidden secrets that ultimately serve to place humans back at the centre of the circle.

What can we deduce from these various examples of human–non-human relationships, ranging from alien invaders to natural impersonators? First of all, they are always political relationships or power games. For example, contemporary political actors recognize troublesome links between the environment, issues like climate change, economic activity, resource management and elections. Second, Latour (2004) has argued that these preoccupations are not new challenges that only concern people living today:

> Never, since the Greeks' earliest discussions on the excellence of public life, have people spoken about politics without speaking of nature; or rather, never has anyone appealed to nature except to teach a political lesson. Not a single line has been written – at least in the Western tradition – in which the terms 'nature,' 'natural order,' 'natural law,' 'natural right,' 'Inflexible causality,' or 'imprescriptible laws,' have not been followed, a few lines, paragraphs, or pages later, by an affirmation concerning the way to reform public life.
>
> (2004, p. 28)

According to Latour (2004), this 'old' relationship between politics and 'nature' is comparable to the two sides of a seesaw, each of which is affected by the other's movement. There is an underlying unity between the two because human life cannot survive without non-human lifeforms like microorganisms which sustain countless natural processes. Yet, as we have seen in the doctrine of signatures, we can also conjure up stories about divine bonds or natural appropriations of human forms that do not really shake off an anthropocentric hierarchy of beings because they actually revolve around human interests. For Latour, the natural world's 'muteness' needs to be replaced by a more democratic collective enriched by 'the voices of nonhumans' (2004, p. 69). There can be no democracy without these voices, no collective without a real engagement with non-humans. Moreover, if we are to use militaristic language at all today, it needs to be couched in interdependent terms that 'fight' for the place of the non-human in human life rather than the human in non-human life.

This brings us to a second conclusion we can draw from our earlier discussion of human–non-human relationships: the need to imagine more entangled realities linking members of different species as well as social and posthumanist perspectives. Art, particularly contemporary art, helps us to visualize symbiotic relationships like these. Socially engaged art, for instance, focuses on immersive experiences that rely on collaborative and dialogic strategies like interactions, knowledge transfer and encounters that are employed to mould new social, learning or creative spaces and human relations. Conceiving a more ecologically engaged art would require us to imagine new forms of solidarity with non-human lifeforms, challenging exclusions and binary divisions between nature and culture in the same way as gendered or class-based divisions might be challenged by socially engaged art. It would require a deeper understanding of both visible and invisible interdependences between humans and non-humans that broaden our definition of the collective.

Nevertheless, if we really were to listen to the voices of non-humans, could we actually make sense of what they said? Wittgenstein famously wrote: 'If a lion could talk, we could not understand him' (1958, p. 225). And, assuming that animals were interested in making sense of human conversations, could a lion understand humans? In his award-winning documentary about the environmentalist Timothy Treadwell's encounters with bears and fatal mauling by a male bear (*Grizzly Man*, 2005), the director Werner Herzog describes his disagreement with Treadwell's sentimental view of nature, seeing – in contrast to Treadwell – no hint of understanding or kinship in the animals' blank faces. Others, however, are more critical of this belief in an 'abyss of non-comprehension' (Berger, 2009, p. 5) between people and animals. Morton (2017), for example, speaks of 'perforated worlds' (p. 90). We inhabit these plural, spectral worlds that flow into each other, just like noise. The blurry worlds of humans, bacteria and other things are not distinct entities with definite borders but run through each other's perforated fabric. In such perforated worlds, the roles of host and guest are interchangeable. To some extent, Morton writes, we *can* understand lions because our worlds are not mutually exclusive realities. The notion of symbiosis implies that neat boundaries are always exceeded by the worlds of lifeforms that we discriminately think of as utterly 'other'. Coral reefs, for instance, are formed of mutual relationships between coral and algae, providing the latter with shelter and the former with their amazing colours. However, coral reefs also need plenty of light to survive. These indeterminate systems of interconnections thrive on parasitism, which, following the thinking of Michel Serres (1982), is not to be interpreted as an indictment but can be seen as an expansion of our understanding of social systems based on operations that are at work in different living organisms. Serres gives an example based on a shift between 'sound' and 'noise':

> At the feast everyone is talking. At the door of the room there is a ringing noise, the telephone. Communication cuts conversation, the noise interrupting the messages. As soon as I start to talk with this new interlocutor, the sounds of the banquet become noise for the new 'us'. The system has shifted.
>
> (Serres, 1982, p. 66)

The systems that Serres refers to are relative and are punctuated by unexpected guests or 'parasites'. But an unexpected guest can host new conversations and turn one's 'normal' lifestyle into noise. In his narrative, the demeanour of the person who tries to make sense of the telephone conversation shifts as the sounds from the feast become a distraction. This interchange of guest and host, and flow of information and noise, forms the very basis of human as well as human–non-human exchange.

Bioart and biomimicry

How can art education engage with these perforated worlds and parasitic relations? It can engage at various levels: at the level of content, using arts-based pedagogies to explore the intersections of the human and non-human (Ward, 2013); at the level of experience, exposing students to natural environments like forests, farms, gardens, and so on; and at a more participatory advocacy level, integrating the arts and sciences to develop agency skills and work towards societal change (Trott, Even, & Frame, 2020). Often, these intersecting levels and interdisciplinary practices present creative learning in a broad curricular structure that incorporates sustainability principles like critical thinking, systems thinking and envisioning better futures (Hunter, Aprill, Hill, & Emery, 2018). Art educators can incorporate principles of education for sustainable development in their teaching by promoting social, environmental, economic and cultural transformation processes and integrating critical and creative thinking in collaborative, socially engaged problem-solving (Vella, Caruana, & Zammit, 2021). Arts pedagogies enriched with issues lifted from environmental, community-driven and other domains can lead to transformative learning and the exploration of innovative realities and futures.

Art education at different levels can counter the anthropocentrism analyzed by Berger (2009) and others who question classical humanist (Vitruvian, for instance) understandings of what constitutes a human being (Bayley, 2018). Some artists present symbiotic relationships through specific techniques that visually capture the relations of multispecies: for example, the cloudy, wet-on-wet watercolours of human and termite holobionts by Olga Lukyanova (Lukyanova, 2020). Integrating human–animal studies into art pedagogies can play a role in resisting the idea that animals are simply creatures tasked with fulfilling human needs. Dimke (2020) argues for an art pedagogy informed by animal ethics and the works of artists like Franz Marc, whose colourful paintings present animals' experiences as differentiated, individual experiences rather than generic ones. The ethical treatment of animals in contemporary artistic practices and broad parameters of posthumanism in art education can initiate beneficial dialogues with the non-human that transcend the notion of art-as-expression in art classes (Kallio-Tavin, 2020). The relationship between the exploitation of animals and the exploitation of groups of people in the history of capitalist expansion, for instance, can expand students' understanding of the normalization of the widespread oppressive treatment of non-humans (Hribal, 2007). Arts-based pedagogies can be combined to critique intersectional forms of oppression that relate animal issues to issues of race, class, gender, sexuality and ability (Fawcett & Johnson, 2019).

The critical potential of art and education is often thrown off balance by global capitalist agendas that drown out or domesticate principles of social justice or principles that deny that human agendas are inherently superior to others (Jagodzinski, 2019). However, educators who persist in searching for instances of symbiosis in artistic practice that work to blur binary distinctions like human–non-human can turn to relatively marginal yet richly interdisciplinary practices like Bioart (Jagodzinski, 2020a). Bioartists combine artistic and laboratory practices, manipulating biological processes and disseminating ideas about biotechnology and science as they inquire into areas generally overlooked by biology and engineering. Microbial art can be made by culturing microorganisms in agar plates to form patterns and images. Bioartists like Eduardo Kac also raise questions about genetically modified organisms or the exploitation of animals and 'challenge the boundaries between the human and the nonhuman, the living and the nonliving, the natural and the artificial' (Kac et al., 2017). Kac's work can also be interpreted as a denunciation of what Berger (2009) sees as a specifically human form of visual entertainment located in places like zoos which people visit to gaze at captive animals. According to Wolfe (2009), the artist's use of green fluorescent protein 'operates as a kind of feint or lure that trades on the very humanist centrality of vision that Kac's work ends up subverting' (p. 164).

Related developments in the arts and technology include biomimicry, which reverses the principle inherent in the doctrine of signatures by making human technology and design mimic natural forms and processes (e.g. by designing devices that generate power by imitating the movements of underwater plants or the structure of dolphin and whale flippers and tails). Literature on the possibilities of integrating biomimicry in science education (Coban & Coştu, 2021), design education (Stevens, Kopnina, Mulder, & de Vries, 2020) and other fields is growing. Inquiry-based learning that involves students in the principles and different levels of biomimicry can boost investigative processes essential in developing combinations of biological and design-related strategies. Even though biomimicry has also been critiqued for remaining entrenched in a capitalist system that is dependent on patents (Jagodzinski, 2020b), the idea of learning from non-human forms and behaviour to address issues like sustainability, conservation and challenges in various fields like architecture and the design of medical devices certainly holds great potential.

Coyote and artist

The pedagogical focus on a multiplicity of relations and partnerships described here can learn from the correspondence of biodiverse systems and socially diverse communities and networks as well as the complex responses to specific causes associated with these different systems and communities. An awareness of different kinds of discrimination and assumed hierarchies challenges humanist assumptions in education and underlines different kinds of knowledge. A valid entry point into such a discussion is Joseph Beuys' 1974 performance called *I like America and America likes me*, carried out by the German artist with a coyote for three consecutive days in a gallery in New York City. Isolated in a cage, his body covered in a felt blanket and holding a walking stick, Beuys tried to connect in various ways with the animal, a powerful symbol for Native Americans. Wolfe (2020) has written that Beuys's performance 'carries out a triple rebuke against the US: against its actions in Vietnam, its extirpation of native animal species seen to threaten or inconvenience its expansion of an extractive and/or agricultural economy, and its treatment of Native Americans' (p. 849).

As Wolfe suggests, the artist's conceptual linkages between human and non-human beings and oppressive conditions, as well as his preoccupation with a non-human dimension of democracy, highlight a biopolitical quality in his work that is often overlooked. Beuys, therefore, bypasses the persistent hesitancy in comparing human and non-human forms of oppression and refers to a schism between human and non-human, Indigenous groups and others. The coyote is presented as a resilient spirit animal which the artist tries to learn to coexist with. As the animal familiarizes itself cautiously with the man in the cage, new possibilities unfold.

> *I like America and America Likes Me* is a visual and dynamic encounter that shows interspecies communication – like all communication – is possible, albeit incomplete and rife with power imbalances and the distance inherent to a subject/object dichotomy if we project our human selves onto another, rather than receive the other as himself.
> (Sutton, 2017, p. 67)

The possibility of empathizing with these two beings' mutual isolation and interconnectedness creates a space in which the artist's notion of social sculpture can materialize. Beuys' hope for social transformation is coupled with a co-creation of meaning in the restricted space of the cage. This resonates with the goals of much socially engaged art. As an activist genre of artistic practice (or social practice, as it is sometimes called), socially engaged art moves away from author-centred interpretations and motivations and focuses instead on political engagement and the involvement of others, often non-professionals in performances, workshops and so on. Its many forms generally share a common distaste for social injustices, discrimination and other political or ecological issues like climate change. Socially engaged artists often cooperate with others to try to implement changes in social conditions, raise awareness about economic, cultural and other issues and/or create situations in which community members can influence policy and participate in cross-sectoral partnerships. Community-based collaborations in creating and maintaining sustainable gardens or green spaces, for instance, not only help to revitalize neighbourhoods in environmentally specific ways but enact a 'pedagogy of citizenship' (Garoian, 2019, p. 168).

While Beuys' central, authorial figure in his own performances may distinguish his position from that of many socially engaged artists working today (van den Berg, 2019), his belief in the need for political and ecological healing makes his ideas decisively relevant. Similarly, his ideas about the role of teacher–student exchange and an inclusive approach to creativity and social action have been compared to the ideas of Paulo Freire, theatre practitioner and theorist Augusto Boal and socially engaged artists like Rick Lowe (Finklpearl, 2013). Beuys' radical ideas about an ecological *Gesamtkunstwerk* that come into being through the revolutionary force of art (Adams, 1992) clearly resembles the philosophy of several artists and theorists associated with socially engaged art today and can undoubtedly inform an approach to an ecologically aware art pedagogy.

Dialogues and asymmetries

I Like America and America Likes Me confronts us with the shared vulnerabilities of man and animal in the confined space of a cage. Like the diminishing spaces and resources we share on our planet, the cage feels and looks like a hopeless place to be. We have two options: escape or coexistence. Like so many interactions between humans and non-humans, the relationship between the coyote and the artist is not a straightforward one, even though Morton (2018) reassures us that ecological awareness should, in theory, be easy because each one of us is 'already a symbiotic being entangled with other symbiotic beings' (p. 215). The human–non-human equilibrium we seek is unstable. Many people feel increasingly concerned because they cannot make sense of a natural environment that seems to be deteriorating fast and endangering their lives. Even though we know that extreme weather is linked to carbon pollution, we think of floods and wildfires as intrusions from the 'outside', like invasive species that barge into our family homes and businesses, causing irreparable damage to our properties and livelihoods. The strangeness of the world we inhabit today is akin to the strangeness of the hybrid beings in the girl's collage we started with. It is as though the figures in her image are no longer recognizable because they feel powerless at this stage of history in which the non-human no longer paces around passively in zoos. Extreme natural phenomena are hardly 'mute' phenomena; instead, they are high-pitched realities that throw human-induced chaos back in our faces.

Morton (2013) calls this stage of history an Age of Asymmetry, in which the general feeling is 'of the nonhuman out of control, withdrawn from total human access' (p. 172), an age in which art 'becomes a collaboration between humans and nonhumans' (p. 174). It is a collaboration with unpredictable results, as art should be. Its unpredictability arises from the very nature of symbiosis, whose immersive nature makes it difficult for us to separate host from parasite, conversation from noise, inside from outside and subject from object. Learning from socially engaged art practices and principles of symbiosis, art education can negotiate new ecological points of contact between humans and non-humans that are interdependent and hopeful, community-driven and simultaneously ecologically driven, uncertain yet structured around the possibility of solidarity. These points of contact will not necessarily be 'beautiful', like coral reefs tend to be, but they will foster dialogues that help to shape students' civic and ecological roles and the roles of nonhuman life in these asymmetrical times.

Note

1. The collage was produced in a class led by teacher Kamy Aquilina, as part of a project funded by Erasmus+, called 'Visual art education in new times: Connecting Art with REal life issues' (CARE – 2019-1-CY01-KA203-058258).

References

Adams, D. (1992). Joseph Beuys: Pioneer of a radical ecology. *Art Journal, 51*(2), 26–34.

Aristotle. (1965). *Historia animalium (A. L. Penk, Trans.)*. Cambridge, MA: Harvard University Press.

Bayley, A. (2018). *Posthuman pedagogies in practice: Arts based approaches for developing participatory futures*. Switzerland: Palgrave Macmillan.

Bennett, B. C. (2007). Doctrine of signatures: An explanation of medicinal plant discovery or dissemination of knowledge? *Economic Botany, 61*(3), 246–255. https://doi.org/10.1663/0013-0001(2007)61[246: DOSAEO]2.0.CO;2

Berger, J. (2009). Why look at animals? In J. Berger (Ed.), *About looking* (pp. 3–28). London: Bloomsbury.

Coban, M., & Coştu, B. (2021). Integration of biomimicry into science education: Biomimicry teaching approach. *Journal of Biological Education*, 1–25. https://doi.org/10.1080/00219266.2021.1877783

Cyranoski, D. (2019). Japan approves first human-animal embryo experiments. *Nature*. https://www.nature.com/articles/d41586-019-02275-3

Dimke, A. (2020). Art pedagogy and animal ethics. In C. P. Buschkühle, D. Atkinson, & R. Vella (Eds.), *Art – Ethics – Education* (pp. 298–322). Paderborn: Brill | Sense.

European Commission. (2014). *LIFE and invasive alien species*. Maastricht: European Union.

Fawcett, L., & Johnson, M. (2019). Coexisting entities in multispecies worlds: Arts-based methodologies for decolonial pedagogies. In T. Lloro-Bidart & V. S. Banschbach (Eds.), *Animals in environmental education* (pp. 175–193). London: Palgrave Macmillan.

Finklpearl, T. (2013). *What we made: Conversations on art and social cooperation*. Durham, NC: Duke University Press.

Garoian, C. R. (2019). Socially engaged art and its pedagogy of citizenship. *Studies in Art Education, 60*(3), 168–185. https://doi.org/10.1080/00393541.2019.1632601

Herzog, W. (2005). *Grizzly man*. Santa Monica, CA: Lions Gate Films.

Hribal, J. C. (2007). Animals, agency, and class: Writing the history of animals from below. *Human Ecology Review, 14*(1), 101–112.

Hunter, M. A., Aprill, A., Hill, A., & Emery, S. (2018). *Education, arts and sustainability: Emerging practice for a changing world*. New York, NY: Springer.

Jagodzinski, J. (2019). Artistic speculations and pedagogical challenges: Facing the Anthropocene. In J. Jagodzinski (Ed.), *Schizoanalytic ventures at the end of the world: Film, video, art and pedagogical challenges* (pp. 201–226). London: Palgrave Macmillan.

Jagodzinski, J. (2020a). Thinking 'The end of times': The significance of Bioart|BioArt for Art|Education. In J. Jagodzinski (Ed.), *Pedagogical explorations in a posthuman age: Essays on designer capitalism, eco-aestheticism, and visual and popular culture as West-East meet* (pp. 271–292). London: Palgrave Macmillan. https://doi.org/10.1007/978-3-030-48618-1_11

Jagodzinski, J. (2020b). Between the nonhuman and inhuman: The challenge of the posthuman for Art|Education in the twenty-first century. In J. Jagodzinski (Ed.), *Pedagogical explorations in a posthuman age: Essays on designer capitalism, eco-aestheticism, and visual and popular culture as West-East meet* (pp. 293–309). London: Palgrave Macmillan. https://doi.org/ 10.1007/978-3-030-48618-1_12

Janovsky, R. M., & Larson, E. R. (2019). Does invasive species research use more militaristic language than other ecology and conservation biology literature? *NeoBiota*, 44, 27–238. https://doi.org/10.3897/neobiota.44.32925

Kac, E., Laval-Jeantet, M., Mangin, B., de Menezes, M., Gessert, G., & Vanouse, P. (2017). *What bio art is: A manifesto*. http://www.ekac.org/manifesto_whatbioartis.html

Kallio-Tavin, M. (2020). Art education beyond anthropocentrism: The question of nonhuman animals in contemporary art and its education. *Studies in Art Education*, 61(4), 298–311. https://doi.org/10.1080/00393541.2020.1820832

Latour, B. (2004). *Politics of nature: How to bring the sciences into democracy*. Cambridge, MA: Harvard University Press.

Latour, B. (2017). *Down to earth: Politics in the new climatic regime*. Cambridge: Polity.

Lukyanova, O. (2020). Depicting holobionts. In B. Latour & P. Weibel (Eds.), *Critical zones: The science and politics of landing on Earth* (pp. 354–355). Karlsruhe:ZKM | Center for Art and Media Karlsruhe.

Morton, T. (2013). *Hyperobjects: Philosophy and ecology after the end of the world*. Minneapolis, MN: University of Minnesota Press.

Morton, T. (2017). *Humankind: Solidarity with nonhuman people*. London: Verso.

Morton, T. (2018). *Being ecological*. London: Pelican Books.

Porta, G. D. (1588). *Phytognomonica*. Neapoli: Apud H. Saluianum.

Serres, M. (1982). *The parasite*. Baltimore, MD: The Johns Hopkins University Press.

Stevens, L. L., Kopnina, H., Mulder, K. F., & de Vries, M. J. (2020). Biomimicry design thinking education: A base-line exercise in preconceptions of biological analogies. *International Journal of Technology and Design Education*, 31(4), 797–814.

Sutton, E. (2017). *Art, animals and experience: Relationships to Canines and the natural world*. London: Routledge.

Trott, C. D., Even, T. L., & Frame, S. M. (2020). Merging the arts and sciences for collaborative sustainability action: A methodological framework. *Sustainability Science*, 15, 1067–1085. https://doi.org/10.1007/s11625-020-00798-7

van den Berg, K. (2019). Socially engaged art and the fall of the spectator since Joseph Beuys and the Situationists. In K. van den Berg, C. M. Jordan, & P. Kleinmichel (Eds.), *The art of direct action: Social sculpture and beyond* (pp. 1–40). Berlin: Sternberg Press.

Vella, R., Caruana, C., & Zammit, C. (2021). It's about time: Re-imagining present and future times in art, education and sustainable development. In E. Wagner et al. (Eds.), *Arts, sustainability and education (Yearbook of the European Network of Observatories in the Field of Arts and Cultural Education (ENO))*. https://doi.org/10.1007/978-981-16-3452-9_6115

Ward, K. S. (2013). Creative arts-based pedagogies in early childhood education for sustainability (EfS): Challenges and possibilities. *Australian Journal of Environmental Education, 29*(2), 165–181.

Wittgenstein, L. (1958). *Philosophical investigations.* Oxford: Basil Blackwell.

Wolfe, C. (2009). *What is posthumanism?* Minneapolis, MN: University of Minnesota Press.

Wolfe, C. (2020). The biopolitical drama of Joseph Beuys. *New Literary History, 51*(4), 835–854.

Chapter 4

An Aesthoecological Approach to Professional Learning Communities: Analyzing With CARE

Emese Hall and Chris Turner

Introduction

This chapter seeks to offer both practical and theoretical perspectives on professional learning communities (PLCs) (Hord, 1997) in education, chiefly informed by the onto-epistemological theory of aesthoecology (Turner, 2019). We consider the synergy between aesthoecology and PLCs in general terms, before presenting a more detailed examination of the PLCs formed during an Erasmus+ research project: *Visual arts education in new times: Connecting Art with REal life issues* (CARE). Project CARE involves a partnership between four European higher education institutions, in Cyprus, Malta, Greece and England, supported by a quality assurance partner in Germany who represents the European Regional Council of the International Society of Education through Art. The research is aimed at exploring the connection between visual arts education and education for sustainable development in primary schools, a connection that has been previously under-researched. In this chapter, on a micro level, particular attention is given to the PLCs formed by the English partner at the University of Exeter, as one of the authors was the institutional research leader.

We now explain our theoretical positioning, to aid readers' understanding of the subsequent discussion. Aesthoecology is essentially a re-evaluation, in educational terms, of the relationship between aesthetics and ecology (Turner, 2019). It is envisaged that the relationship between the two is so close that it is interpreted as symbiotic, each element being enhanced by the other to such an extent that the dynamism of the relationship brings about a new conception of aesthetics and ecology (aesthoecology), which gives us deep insight into new ways of being and knowing. Consequently, the theory of aesthoecology gives rise to an onto-epistemology that has interesting and important implications for the ways in which educators, researchers and societies perceive education (Turner, 2019). Aesthoecology fits well with a critical discussion about PLCs for a number of reasons. For instance, aspects of connectivity link the work of teachers together to further the learning of pupils as well as themselves. The affective nature of listening and empathizing play a role in PLCs, as well as accepting vulnerability and the possibility of failing. Further, taking risks is a vital part of the learning process, and the language of aesthoecology – e.g. liminality and emergence – inherently can help to support and encourage professionals in the pursuit of new and untested ways of doing things.

Later, we will provide an expanded definition of aesthoecology. Next, we will discuss how aesthoecology can be broadly used to make sense of PLCs and will then explain the aims and objectives of Project CARE before looking in more detail at the CARE PLCs and the research findings related to those formed at the University of Exeter. Our argument throughout is that aesthoecology offers a rich language with which to understand the form and function of these PLCs.

Aesthoecology explained

The original definition of aesthoecology is as follows:

> the symbiotic and dynamic relationship between aesthetics and ecology, in which aesthetics represents the deep and often unconscious sensory awareness of being in the environment (our being in our environment), and the associated ecology, which represents a worldview as well as an intimate, unfolding and emergent understanding of the complexity, and immediacy, of our surroundings, which form our temporal landscape. Inherent in this, is the effect and affect that are predominant in the interaction between the two and the ways, often subtle, in which behaviours – actions, reactions – and consequences are elicited by the detection and emergence of individual and collective environmental changes.
>
> (Turner, 2019, p. 11)

As mentioned, aesthoecology is an onto-epistemology that represents a way of being in the world alongside a developing knowledge of the world. The two work together symbiotically, each bringing to the other something new and radical. This relationship has important implications that highlight some paradoxical questions between the culture of nature and the nature of culture. These paradoxes lie at the heart of many sociobiological questions and of some vexed interpretations of the meaning of education in a complex and troubled world.

Aesthoecology develops the view that, both somatically and intellectually, aesthetics and ecology are at the centre of the educational process: aesthetics because of the sensitivity and affectivity required to understand the world in which we live and its meaning; ecology because of the complex contexts in which we acquire this understanding. Education is, at the same time, both affective and connected.

Affectivity in this context might be defined as 'an acute and variously delicate sensitivity to the surroundings in which we find ourselves' (Turner, 2019, p. 98). This affective sensitivity determines our actions and has ethical, emotional and empathetic dimensions. This allows us to appreciate landscape, architecture, other organisms and material artefacts. Consequently, aesthoecology recognizes our connectedness to the animate and material world (Bennett, 2010; Braidotti, 2013) and this, in various spatial and temporal dimensions, affects our ways of being and sensitivities to becoming through the acquisition of knowledge. This provides a connectivity of existence.

We must emphasize that nothing exists in isolation. All living systems rely on interaction and the emergence and complexity of our developing cognitive landscape. The theory of aesthoecology argues that liminality is central to the way in which the new emerges. Liminality is a way of conceptualizing the transition from one state to another due to affective events in relation to ecological positioning and is an in-between space in which transition takes place. In geo-biological terms, it represents the transition from one state to another – land to water, shoreline to sea. This threshold between one state to another may be seen as both the entry and exit point between zones of experience or understanding. There is no linear trajectory but more of a multi-dimensionality to transition. This idea of liminality is valuable in educational discussions and in cultural interactions extending to relationships with all organisms and physical environments.

Liminality 'entails being on the edge of awareness and in sensitive anticipation of the next event' (Turner, 2019, p. 132). This represents a constant state of emergence, and consequently, this new materialist approach situates the aesthetic, the affective dimension, as a between relationship, thus representing the dynamic between the human and non-human (posthumanism), the material and the immaterial, and the social and the physical. Imagining the notion of liminality through the features of time, place and the future in a radical and dynamic fashion expands our understandings of nature that encapsulate 'the radical change toward the multiple, the temporal and the complex' (Prigogine & Stengers, 1984, p. 292). The temporal and the complex relate to an anticipatory mode of being that leads to an emergent future as opposed to one that extrapolates from the past (Osberg, 2018).

Having now shared a reasonably detailed explanation of the theory of aesthoecology, we will next illustrate its resonance with the general concept of a PLC.

PLCs: A general overview

A PLC is a type of community of practice (CoP) (Lave & Wenger, 1991), comprising a group of individuals who share the same interests and whose interaction helps them learn more about this interest. Learning is viewed as situated and socially constructed. However, a PLC differs from a CoP because a CoP does not have to include professionals and it does not have to place such strong emphasis on learning. This is a key distinction. Further, a CoP might be seen as a relatively loose network of participants, whereas a PLC, because of its greater intensity and its focus on learning, moves much more towards being a web or plasma in aesthoecological terms. It would be an exaggeration to say that this goes as far as being a hyperobject (Morton, 2013), but it would be reasonable and useful to interpret it as a complex assemblage (DeLanda, 2016) – an all-encompassing phenomenon, which connects us to something far greater and yet which impinges on us as humans in every way, much of the time not realized (Turner, 2019). Aesthoecology recognizes that the learning process can be messy and complex during the liminal phase and can therefore feel much more like a web than just a network of simple lines of connection. The significance of this point should not be underestimated. A PLC is not necessarily a neat and tidy entity; it is in a constant state of emergence.

A PLC places learning at its heart. It is helpful to make a clear distinction between what we mean by professional learning as opposed to professional development. Scherff (2018) usefully summarizes this distinction:

> Professional development, which 'happens to' teachers, is often associated with one-time workshops, seminars, or lectures, and is typically a one-size-fits all approach. In contrast, professional learning, when designed well, is typically interactive, sustained, and customized to teachers' needs. It encourages teachers to take responsibility for their own learning and to practice what they are learning in their own teaching contexts.
>
> (para. 3)

Crucially, although PLCs might include activities that singularly one could regard as professional development, together the activities support the long-term learning of the teacher. In terms of aesthoecology, there is a difference here between extrapolation – bringing forward already existing knowledge – and the formation and emergence of new knowledge through discourse and sharing experiences and feelings to facilitate future thinking (Facer, 2011). Having sight of the future is an interesting aspect of aesthoecology because it fits with the idea of affective anticipation and discussions on extrapolation. A one-off professional development event has a predetermined outcome. Professional learning is much more reflective and reflexive – less determined and more organic, leading to autopoiesis – i.e. the ability to relate to, and embrace, complexity. 'Autopoiesis refers to the minimal organization of a living system, which can both maintain itself in a closed circular process of self-production and interact with an environment in order to get nutrients and energy' (Žukauskaitė, 2020, p. 144). In aesthoecological terms, this means continued adaptation to emerging events, open to change, relating to changing environmental conditions. This is, in essence, affective anticipation – using the senses to 'feel' the future, intuition and imagination. This relates to the temporal, rhythmic nature of aesthoecology.

Professional learning has interesting connections with autoethnography. This may also further distinguish between professional development and professional learning. Denzin (2016), for example, suggests that experiences, as in any form of professional activity, can take two forms: a surface level in which the effects are unremarkable and a deeper level at which it cuts to the inner core of a person's life – an epiphany. Denzin draws on theories of liminality (Horvath, Thomassen, & Wydra, 2018), which rely on 'narratively structured, liminal, existential spaces in the culture' (Denzin, 2016, p. 131). In these spaces, there are dramas that exhibit 'complex temporal rhythms' and 'multiple and differing forms of and layers of meaningful experience' (Denzin, 2016, p. 131).

We now turn to a consideration of the required conditions to form successful PLCs (Hord, 1997), with reference to relevant principles of aesthoecology:

- *Supportive and shared leadership*: Aesthoecology supports the notion of leadership that requires a keen sense of creativity, future thinking and emergence. Leadership is also about transformation (critical change agenda) and transitional processes (liminality). Further, distributed leadership incorporates notions of support and sharing – these are functions of affectivity and connectivity, respectively.
- *Collective creativity*: The collective links to ecology (connectivity), and the creative element links to taking risks, as above. This approach negates linear approaches to problem-solving and instead values emergence and moving into the unknown.
- *Supportive conditions*: Empathy and connectivity are very much part of the theory of aesthoecology. Here we can see the value of strong relationships and communication, reflecting the symbiotic relationships between affect and ecology.
- *Physical conditions*: Material surroundings are part of, and an extension of, the individuals in the group. This new materialist (e.g. Braidotti, 2013), and posthumanist (e.g. MacCormack & Gardner, 2018) approach, which strongly informs aesthoecological principles, values the idea of space and place and highlights the more-than-human elements of the environment.
- *People capacities*: In aesthoecological terms, we see capacities as non-finite in that the expectation is that capacities are continually explored with no pre-supposition of outcomes at the outset. Aesthoecologically oriented practice assumes that risks are taken, and capacities are emergent.
- *Shared personal practice*: In sharing personal practice, commonality and difference enhance further the capacities of individuals and groups. This encourages the development of assemblages of practice – the formation of a web to capture good and less good practice and to tease out the critical differences between the two.

It is notable that Hord's (1997) definition and various examples of PLCs do not include any that exist in virtual form, probably because at the time of publication online communities were not commonplace. However, the connections to aesthoecology are nonetheless apparent to us and the fundamental principles of how to create and maintain a successful PLC are similar in real and virtual contexts.

Project CARE: Some further detail

As noted, the research project that is used as an illustrative case study in this chapter is called '*Visual arts education in new times: Connecting Art with REal life issues* (CARE)'. Visual art education (VAE) does perhaps not require further explanation. However, education for sustainable development (ESD) is defined by UNESCO (2021), thus:

> ESD empowers learners to take informed decisions and responsible actions for environmental integrity, economic viability and a just society, for present and future

generations, while respecting cultural diversity. It is about lifelong learning, and is an integral part of quality education.

(p. 1)

This definition holds numerous possibilities to connect with the principles of aesthoecology. Although ESD might appear to centre on real-world, practical concerns, the ways in which we conceive of these are naturally informed by our world-views that are ontological in nature. Again, both new materialism and posthumanism are particularly relevant to ESD because at their core are the ideas of equality and educational justice (Merry, 2020).

New materialism considers issues of matter, agency and posthumanism (e.g. Bennett, 2010). This is a recognition that the material world is not a fixed entity but is continually in flux, and its influence extends beyond that of humans. This should be inherent in educational practice – the melding of theory and practice – and should embed these characteristics of flux and dynamism (Turner, 2019). Issues such as climate change, global warming and the impact of plastics in the world are undoubtedly of significant ecological and social consequence and should be at the core of educational reorientation. These issues are just some of the many encompassed within UNESCO's (n.d.) SDGs, which were an integral aspect of the Project CARE training programmes.

There is a dearth of research that has examined the possibilities of linking VAE with ESD. Aesthoecology does exactly that. Although the aesthetic aspect of aesthoecology does not refer specifically to art, inevitably and inherently art is enmeshed with aesthoecology's ideas of affectivity, sensitivity and emergence (Turner & Hall, 2021). Aesthoecology does not explicitly distinguish between the aesthetic and the ecological, as it represents a symbiotic relationship embedded in posthuman and new materialist ontologies and examines our global presence from our micro-state, through our meso-state and to our meta-state.

Project CARE's main objectives are as follows:

- to research pre-service and in-service teachers' competences and needs in VAE and ESD,
- to use these findings to develop and deliver training programmes within each partner country,
- to support participants to implement teaching units in schools and assess pupils' learning,
- to create a culture of collaboration between educators (pre-service teachers, in-service teachers and the research partners) by fostering PLCs, and
- to research the training programmes, the impact of the teaching units, and the benefits and challenges of the PLCs.

All partners had responsibility for different aspects of the research. The University of Exeter coordinated the initial fostering of the PLCs and devising the research tools with which to investigate the PLCs' outcomes. The section below describes the CARE PLCs in further detail and, again, makes connections to aesthoecology.

PLCs within Project CARE

Project CARE has a spirit of collaborative learning at its heart, and, importantly, the CARE PLCs were intended to include both project participants (teachers) and project partners (researchers/trainers). Aesthoecology, because of its basis of posthumanism, recognizes that the way the world works is completely collaborative – that the interconnectivity in natural systems is the basis of sustainability. All partners had to rise to the challenges presented by the COVID-19 pandemic, as most PLC activities that would have taken place in person had to be hosted online. Each partner took their own approach to organizing PLCs, but all had the same research aim, which was to learn about how PLCs in VAE can develop as an important component of capacity building for sustainable improvement.

In carrying out data collection, each partner followed appropriate ethical guidelines. For example, at the University of Exeter, we adhered to the British Educational Research Association's [BERA] (2018) guidance on research ethics. For data collection, there was a target sample of 60 teacher questionnaires and twenty teacher interviews, divided evenly among the partners. We sought the following qualitative indicators: appropriateness and relevance of training, shared values and vision, teacher leadership, cooperation and trust. In constructing PLC case studies, the research focus was on determining the opportunities and challenges that the Project CARE's PLCs present: what social and physical factors foster or hinder communication, positive relationships, teacher confidence and competencies and perceptions of success. To ensure anonymity, reporting here will generalize the participants' responses and provide a holistic summary.

PLC facilitation and management at the University of Exeter

The University of Exeter CARE training programme began in January 2021. A fifteen-hour online study programme offered flexible involvement over a period of ten weeks. This training was non-accredited, and there were no formal points of assessment, but participation was designed to enable trainees to provide evidence of their progress towards meeting the Teachers' Standards for Qualified Teacher Status (DfE, 2012). The Exeter CARE PLC initially consisted of the 24 trainee teachers who signed up to participate in the training programme and the six researchers involved in the project. During the training programme stage, five mini-PLC groups were established with the aim of facilitating stronger connections (in terms of relationships), cooperation and communication. We have already noted the resonance of aesthoecology with this collaborative aim above, which has 'emergent properties' (Turner, 2019, p. 158). Each mini-PLC included one tutor and four trainees. According to the PLC formation advice from Arts Assessment for Learning (2019, para. 16): 'A group with too many members can't hear from everyone at every meeting. A group with too few lacks the diversity of perspective required to generate productive feedback discussions'.

The communication platform chosen was Microsoft Teams. There was one general CARE group for the wider PLC and each mini-PLC had its own group. To supplement the asynchronous Teams exchanges, 30-minute synchronous monthly online catch-up meetings were scheduled. The training programme phase of the research ended in line with the spring vacation at the end of March. As the six trainees who had chosen to continue with the project moved into the implementation phase, during which units of working fusing VAE and ESD were going to be taught in schools, the groups were amalgamated to form one large PLC, which met fortnightly, again online, due to both the pandemic restrictions and the geographical distance of the trainees whilst out on placement. The monthly synchronous 30-minute online catch-up meetings continued, but these were supplemented, at the participants' request, by fortnightly online catch-ups – also of 30 minutes in length – and individual tutor support via e-mail and Teams meetings. In addition, three Saturday transnational online VAE workshops were offered in June and July 2021. Hosted by UK-based art education charity, AccessArt, these were intended to promote inter-country communication and awareness of different participants' teaching contexts, pedagogical interests and professional learning. Those who attended the workshops appeared highly motivated and commented positively on their experiences. However, participant numbers were below what was anticipated because some partners/participants were already on their summer vacations.

The online discussions, activities and catch-ups were not recorded for data collection. This intention was not built into the proposal for institutional ethical consent and therefore only the questionnaire and interviews formally gathered participant feedback. This could be regarded as a valuable missed opportunity. However, to return to our aesthoecological connections, the linking of 'understanding and knowledge to ethics emphasises the idea that one cannot but ethically engage with the world, particularly within the contextual understanding that human and non-human beings intra-actively co-constitute the world' (Turner, 2019, p. 58).

All 24 training programme participants were invited to complete an online questionnaire at the official end of the training programme. The questionnaire findings (twelve respondents) suggested that the trainee teachers' experience in the PLC during the spring term could have been better. For example, participants reported that more emotional support could have been offered, and that collaboration had been difficult. However, they did not feel they were active members, and they seemed to understand that their colleagues were not active either. Comments concerning low levels of communication cited the pandemic as a key reason: generally, they did not find remote-study-supported collaboration or communication. Overall, sharing ideas was commonly identified as a key opportunity of the PLC, and lack of time to participate was the most cited negative aspect. In considering these findings in relation to the principles of aesthoecology, we can certainly see the significance of both aesthetics (regarding emotional support) and ecology (regarding collaboration/communication/participation). These observations will be expanded upon in due course.

Towards the end of the summer term, individual interviews were carried out with five of the six trainee teachers who participated in the implementation phase of Project CARE. These were conducted online using Teams, each time with the same interviewer (first co-author). Following transcription, qualitative constant comparative techniques were used for data analysis to arrive at key themes. Below a summary of findings is presented and connections to aesthoecology are drawn.

Opportunities of the PLCs

PLC participants appreciated feeling supported and affirmed by like-minded people, with shared beliefs and values. This finding demonstrates that affectivity is vital and almost more significant than effectivity, at least initially. Further, aesthoecology gives a possible basis for discussing beliefs and values, as these are the onto-epistemological underpinnings of the PLC. Regular communication enhanced this sense of community and brought the trainee teachers into contact with new people. Here we see a clear connection with ecology – i.e. connectivity. Another perceived opportunity of the PLC was that the trainees' contact with tutors was in a less hierarchical space (in contrast to, say, a lecture theatre environment). Participants reported benefiting from tutor expertise and guidance; they enjoyed sharing ideas and moving their thinking in different directions. This finding illustrates the importance of liminality and the idea of being constantly betwixt and between (Conroy, 2004). Further, the trainee PLC members appreciated the space and time to connect with, develop and nurture profoundly held personal philosophies regarding the purposes of education. There are strong connections here to understand the importance of both ontology and epistemology. Linking university-based learning with experiences on placement and continuing the dialogue between different concepts helped them to bridge theory and practice (liminality). Celebrating each other's successes and providing support for perceived failures was seen to be positive, and it was pleasing to see that emotional support notably improved between the questionnaire and interview stages. Here we draw attention to Addison's (2011) observation that 'affect profoundly conditions all social interactions, particularly those designed to construct dialogic exchanges' (p. 365). Indeed, in the PLC formation guidance written before the training programmes commenced, relationships and emotional considerations were included – see Hall (2022).

Challenges of the PLCs

The greatest challenge identified was remote communication, and all the trainees commented on the complications presented by engaging with online platforms. Microsoft Teams was generally disliked, and e-mail was greatly preferred. Notably, all the participants would have liked to be able to meet in person. This finding, in aesthoecological terms, seems to suggest that the participants felt more comfortable with the familiar hyperobject (Morton, 2013) of the university campus with its unique collection of spaces, objects, and individuals. There were likely to be more vibrant connections (Bennett, 2010) than in a virtual environment. Despite the PLCs providing emotional support, it was concerning that some participants described a sense of negativity about their school placements. The initial plan was that teachers could be invited to join some of the PLC activities, but this did not happen, and we had certainly not anticipated a lack of support for the CARE research by the schools. If 'the performative learning space affects learning in its own right' (Mäkelä & Löytönen, 2017, p. 255), then one wonders to what extent the outcomes of the study would have been different. First, if the PLCs had involved face-to-face interactions and, second, if the schools had been consistently supportive towards the trainee teachers and demonstrated the empathy and connectivity that are integral to aesthoecology. In terms of the physical conditions of the PLC (Hord, 1997), all participants commented on a lack of time to fully engage with the project. It is unfortunate that the PLC, and Project CARE more widely, could not have created a slowing down of pace, which would have been deeply in tune with the principles of aesthoecology (Hall & Turner, 2021).

Having discussed everything that was signposted in the introduction, we now consider our conclusion.

Conclusion

In this chapter, we have considered how the educational theory of aesthoecology (Turner, 2019) is relevant and useful in supporting the development of PLCs (Hord, 1997). Our argument is that aesthoecology offers a rich language with which to understand the form and function of PLCs, both in general terms and, more specifically, as illustrated above by reference to the Project CARE findings from the PLCs at the University of Exeter. Importantly, and as we have stated elsewhere, 'notions of affectivity, emergence, connectivity, liminality and anticipation are all present in the material world as well as in the world of ideas' (Turner & Hall, 2021, p. 17). In other words, aesthoecology has both practical and theoretical implications.

Because this book is a call to action, we stress the importance of aiming to make a positive difference and believe that PLCs have interesting potential in many different educational contexts. We warmly invite others to consider the relevance of aesthoecology to their future research. Here we have applied an understanding of aesthoecology to make sense of PLCs in Project CARE, but only once data were collected, analyzed and reported. We propose that it would be insightful to explore the potential of aesthoecology in a more integrated way, where this onto-epistemology informs research design and methodology from the outset.

Funding

The Project CARE research was made possible through a grant from Erasmus+ (ref: 2019-1-CY01-KA203-058258).

References

Addison, N. (2011). Moments of intensity: Affect and the making and teaching of art. *International Journal of Art and Design Education, 30*(3), 363–378. https://doi.org/10.1111/j.1476-8070.2011.01729.x

Arts Assessment for Learning. (2019). *Learning communities.* http://artsassessmentforlearning.org/communities/

Bennett, J. (2010). *Vibrant matter: A political ecology of things.* Durham, NC: Duke University Press.

Bennett, N., Harvey, J. A., Wise, C., & Woods, P. A. (2003). *Distributed leadership: A desk study.* Kingston: National College for School Leadership. https://oro.open.ac.uk/8534/1/bennett-distributed-leadership-full.pdf

Braidotti, R. (2013). *The posthuman.* UK: Reality Press.

British Educational Research Association [BERA]. (2018). *Ethical guidelines for educational research* (4thed.).BERA.https://www.bera.ac.uk/publication/ethical-guidelines-for-educational-research-2018-online

Conroy, J. C. (2004). *Betwixt and between: The liminal imagination, education and democracy.* Bern: Peter Lang.

DeLanda, M. (2016). *Assemblage theory.* Edinburgh: Edinburgh University Press.

Denzin, N. K. (2016). Interpretive autoethnography. In S. H. Jones, T. Adams, & C. Ellis (Eds.), *Handbook of autoethnography* (pp. 73–94). London: Routledge.

DfE. (2012). *Teacher standards.* https://www.gov.uk/government/publications/teachers-standards

Facer, K. (2011). *Learning futures: Education, technology and social change.* London: Routledge. https://doi.org/10.4324/9780203817308

Hall, E. (Ed.). (2022). *Professional learning communities in a project connecting primary art education with education for sustainable development. Report of intellectual output 5, project CARE.* Cyprus: Frederick University. http://care.frederick.ac.cy/docs/CARE_IO5.pdf

Hall, E., & Turner, C. (2021). Aesthoecology and its implications for art and design education: Examining the foundations. *International Journal of Art and Design Education, 40*(4), 761–772. https://doi.org/10.1111/jade.12387

Hord, S. M. (1997). *Professional learning communities: Communities of continuous inquiry and improvement.* Austin, TX: Southwest Educational Development Laboratory.

Horvath, A., Thomassen, B., & Wydra, H. (Eds.). (2018). *Breaking boundaries: Varieties of liminality.* Oxford: Bergahn Books.

Lave, J., & Wenger, E. (1991). *Situated learning: Legitimate peripheral participation.* Cambridge: Cambridge University Press.

MacCormack, P., & Gardner, C. (Eds.). (2018). *Ecosophical aesthetics: Arts, ethics and ecology with Guattari.* London: Bloomsbury Academic.

Mäkelä, M., & Löytönen, T. (2017). Rethinking materialities in higher education. *Art, Design and Communication in Higher Education, 16*(2), 241–258. https://doi.org/10.1386/adch.16.2.241_1

Merry, M. (2020). *Educational justice: Liberal ideals, persistent inequality, and the constructive uses of critique.* London: Palgrave Macmillan.

Morton, T. (2013). *Hyperobjects.* Minneapolis, MN: University of Minnesota Press.

Osberg, D. (2018). Education and the future. In R. Poli (Ed.), *Handbook of anticipation.* New York, NY: Springer. https://doi.org/10.1007/978-3-319-31737-3_88-1

Prigogine, I., & Stengers, I. (1984). *Order out of chaos: Man's new dialogue with nature.* New York, NY: Bantam Books.

Scherff, L. (2018, January 4). *Distinguishing professional learning from professional development.* Denver, CO: Institute of Education Sciences: Regional Educational Laboratory Program. https://ies.ed.gov/ncee/edlabs/regions/pacific/blogs/blog2_DistinguishingProfLearning.asp

Turner, C. (2019). *Education as aesthoecology* [Doctoral dissertation, University of Exeter]. Open Research Exeter. http://hdl.handle.net/10871/40105

Turner, C., & Hall, E. (2021). Transformation through aesthoecology: Affectivity, connectivity, and the role of art in promoting transdisciplinarity. In J. Power & C. Owen (Eds.), *Innovative practice in higher education. GLAD-HE special edition.* Staffordshire: The University of Staffordshire. http://journals.staffs.ac.uk/index.php/ipihe/article/view/219?fbclid=IwAR0Qt8ASHc9wEClYiGp6RzAfMFk84Dq9PtvDWs-N4ewnb47DFClP_tB6Enw

UNESCO. (2021). *SDG 4 Ensure inclusive and equitable quality education and promote lifelong learning opportunities for all.* https://tcg.uis.unesco.org/wp-content/uploads/sites/4/2020/09/Metadata-4.7.4.pdf

UNESCO. (n.d.). *UNESCO and sustainable development goals.* https://en.unesco.org/sustainabledevelopmentgoals

Žukauskaitė, A. (2020). Gaia theory: Between autopoiesis and sympoiesis. *Prolemos, 98,* 141–153. https://doi.org/10.15388/Problemos.98.13

Chapter 5

Bridging Theory and Practice: Evaluating and Developing Projects That Connect Visual Arts Education and Education for Sustainable Development

Ernst Wagner

Preliminary remark

In 2017, a team at the German *UNESCO Chair in Arts and Culture in Education* carried out an exploratory study on 'Arts Education and Education for Sustainable Development' (Wagner et al., 2021). Its first results were presented by the author at the World Summit on Arts Education held in Hangzhou and revolved around the observation that the *UN Agenda 2030 for Sustainable Development* fits together with the still most relevant policy document on arts education, UNESCO's *Seoul Agenda*[1] (UNESCO, 2010).

The exploratory study aimed to offer a model for practice and form a point of reference for the emerging discourse in art education and education for sustainable development (ESD). Based on a set of case studies, this approach is needed not only to examine basic theoretical assumptions but also to develop criteria and indicators for conclusions about how to shape practice and build a base for discussion. Additionally, exploring cases from different regions of the world helps to avoid a one-dimensional and Eurocentric perspective. A by-product of the following concepts comes in the form of an evaluation tool for teachers' daily practice that could also be used for assessing some examples presented in this book.

Methodology of the exploratory study

To get a deeper insight into the relationship between art education and ESD, fifteen stakeholders based in different countries were asked to contribute their observations and reflections through project reports from their respective countries or regions. As experts, they were invited to send a description and analysis of examples of good practices in arts education that address the topic of sustainable development. The respondents have all been members of the *International Network for Research in Arts Education*, founded by the UNESCO chairs in arts education, which was transformed into a UNITWIN network (UNITWIN, 2022) in the meantime. These respondents represented different world regions and different art forms such as contemporary and traditional visual arts, music, drama and dance. Eleven members of the network contributed.

In the second phase, the case studies were compared to a framework that uses 'Sustainable Development Goals' (SDGs), on the one hand, and a set of dimensions in arts education (Liebau & Wagner, 2017),[2] on the other. This framework for reflection was discussed with a group of experts.[3] Relating the case studies to the theoretical framework led – in a third stage – to a first and preliminary educational model that is based on the discourse about competencies in educational sciences (Weinert, 1999) and that was used to develop a model for visual literacy (Haanstra & Wagner, 2019).

The relationship between the case studies and the framework as well as the model was interpreted, and the observations made were sent back to the eleven contributors asking for their feedback. Following the revision of their manuscripts, the full final report was published at the Nanjing University in China while parts of it were published in Eça and Coutts (2019). Furthermore, an overview of the report is available in Wagner et al. (2021). Two of the examples from visual arts are discussed in this chapter in order to give a basis for the development of the criteria.

Two visual arts examples from the set of case studies

From India, Mousumi De sent an example about a non-formal setting in Thrissur, Kerala, developed by Jinan Kodapully. Jinan Kodapully, as De explains, preferred alternative approaches to teaching and learning rather than the essentialist paradigm often prevalent in such institutions. Instead, he encouraged progressive forms of education that are reminiscent of Dewey's experiential learning methods. Jinan Kodapully has facilitated several workshops on art and aesthetics (beauty) implemented in rural and natural surroundings. Children were encouraged to play and learn and/or make art in a free manner. Jinan Kodapully's approach played a vital role in the children's own learning process. Through this kind of art-making in an explorative and playful manner in a natural setting, children are sensitized to nature by observing and creating, similar to approaches proposed by Latour (2017) to overcome the dichotomy of culture and nature.

A video published by Jinan shows a boy standing in the rain, observing what happens in a puddle for several minutes.[4] It is a tranquil video, although we hear a lot of noise from the boy's friends in the background. The most critical issue in the clip is probably that, apart from observing the rain, 'nothing happens'. The experiences the boy has are experiences of nature, nature as an aesthetic and learning space. De explains that the main role of the adult or teacher was to provide a free and secure space for experiencing and learning, which is necessary for the development of this kind of contemplative observation of rain and earth, for example. The video shows how the boy is entirely focused and immersed in this experience, despite the background noise made by his friends. Here, the rain is part of a game for the boy – it is an aesthetic and sensory experience for learning, not a disturbance.

The discussion of this example led immediately to the question of whether the specific attitude of this child towards nature can be maintained by children even when they are teenagers or adults, meaning at an age in which they will take more and more responsibility for the environment. The risk is that the boy shown in the film, when grown up, will find fast cars or dangerous weapons as attractive as he found raindrops as a child and may declare his former attitude towards nature as childish. This means that educational models should be developed to ensure that valuable attitudes are sustained during a person's life. This may be achieved by supporting the development of metacognitive strategies. This discussion touches on one of the still controversial discourses in art education research, the debate about impact, measurement of impact and transfer effects.

Compared with the example from India, an example from New Zealand has a straighforward, distinct and directly addressed message. It was suggested by Ralph Buck, who wrote about this case study:

> Mark Harvey, a professional dancer, created this performance as part of the Maldives Exodus Caravan Show. The study focuses on the Maldives as climate issues are mainly affecting low-lying states such as the Maldives. 'Political Climate Wrestle', the name of his project, was a live dance performance. The 'Wrestle' was performed or presented by Mark. He defined an area in a park and invited members of the public to 'wrestle with him about climate issues': Mark explained to participants that as they wrestled, he would ask questions and give facts about climate change. He invited the co-wrestler to respond using his/her body and voice to agree or disagree. Each wrestle lasted for several minutes and attracted large audiences who would start to voice views and opinions about climate change. Mark managed the physical interchange expertly, ensuring that the wrestling was about ideas and not about the other person.
>
> (R. Buck, personal communication, 4 September 2017)

Later, during the discussion, Ralph Buck explained the link between the arts and sustainable development:

> The focus was on climate change and how members of the public interact with knowledge about climate change and their own consumption, production of goods and lifestyle that influences climate change. The event took language such as 'fight against climate

Figure 5.1: Still from Jinan's Video: http://www.backyardnature.net/jinan.htm

Figure 5.2: Stills from Harvey's Video: https://www.youtube.com/watch?v=BuEuSQ_m6o4

change' literally, raising awareness of the actual combat that is required. In this way, the performance addresses the question of what peace means in this context. The performance was very successful in raising awareness of climate issues.

(R. Buck, personal communication, 4 September 2017)

Observations

The first thing that is striking about these two examples is that they do not show what we would expect when we think of traditional approaches to art education. There is no painting or drawing, no handicrafts or clay modelling and no visit to a museum or an artist's studio. This fits with the observation that convincing examples of art education and ESD often use experimental forms of practice. The examples illustrate how non-traditional media and playful experiential teaching approaches have the potential to tackle aspects of sustainability in a possibly more sufficient and convincing way than traditional methods. The examples also demonstrate the vital contribution of art education to ESD.

However, we can also see a specific difference between the two examples: The target group shifts from children to adults and thus, the methods of educational 'intervention' change. In the second case, the environmental dimension is addressed in a very direct way by an artist – because adults can contradict each other since they already have their own position that can be negotiated.

Thus, the audiences are immersed in specific experiences, each in different ways. In the first example, the child perceives nature not from a distant point of view (like taking a picture at a photo stop in a tourist bus), but he is experiencing nature through being in it, being part of it. In the other example, the wrestle, the participant is part of an avant-garde art form, an interactive performance. This performance addresses conflict, not harmony, in the 'unprotected' open space.

Nevertheless, in both cases between contemplation and activism, the educational outcome is unclear, unsupervised and perhaps cannot be assessed. The experts who sent the two examples assumed or hoped that these efforts would lead to a change in attitudes that form the basis for a specific kind of behaviour.

Bridging Theory and Practice

Possible systematic categories of interpretations for a comparative approach

Reviewing all the case studies sent by the experts, different approaches to describing, categorizing and interpreting them were developed. The first one starts from the concept of semantic differential (Hofstätter, 1971) with respect to the character or qualitative profile of the educational setting. The second one discusses the case studies against the normative framework of SDGs, and the third one uses a general competence model.

The first approach was used mainly in a descriptive way.[5] The first set of polarities had been: contemplation vs. agitation; individuals vs. communities; skills and knowledge vs. attitudes, habits and motivation; cultural heritage vs. contemporary art forms; and economic empowerment vs. sustainable consumption. Informed by the semantic differential method, the polarities can also be expressed by adjectives like (see Figure 5.3):

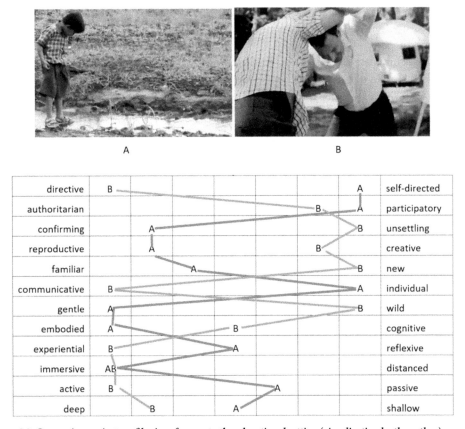

Figure 5.3: Comparing project profiles in reference to the educational setting (visualization by the author).

87

- At the pedagogical instruction/teaching level: directive vs. self-directed; authoritarian vs. participatory.
- At the pedagogical settings level: confirming vs. unsettling; creative vs. reproductive; new vs. familiar; communicative vs. individual; wild vs. gentle.
- At the learning process level: embodied vs. cognitive; reflexive vs. experiential; distanced vs. immersive; passive vs. active; shallow vs. deep.

This attempt offers a possibility to reflect on processes of learning in a transparent way and thus answers the question of how to evaluate practice against theory. In Figure 5.3, the two examples discussed earlier (the child in the rain and 'Political Climate Wrestle') are classified against all different levels.

The second approach differs from the first attempt and thus delivers new insights. It is based on an interpretation of the SDGs in order to link sustainable development and arts/culture. It uses a set of four dimensions in arts education: the environmental, sociopolitical, economic and cultural dimensions (Liebau & Wagner, 2017). Three out of the four dimensions already represent the broadly accepted dimensions of ESD as developed by UNESCO, for example in the Roadmap for ESD:[6] the environmental, the social and the economic dimension. Only the cultural dimension is missing in the latter and many other UNESCO documents.[7] Nevertheless, in the context of arts education, it is not only useful but necessary to include this fourth dimension.

This approach leads to a selection of SDGs that is more relevant for arts education than others, like SDG #3 (well-being), SDG #4 (education), SDG #5 (gender equality), SDG #8 (decent work), SDG #9 (innovation), SDG #10 (reduced inequalities), SDG #11 (sustainable cities), SDG #12 (consumption) and SDG #16 (peace). It also allows for the interpretation of the SDGs, referring to the four dimensions: Sustainable consumption, production and settlements have a strong link with the ***environmental dimension***. The inclusion of the

Figure 5.4: The SDGs.

Bridging Theory and Practice

SDGs – diversity, equality and peace – can be referred to as the ***sociopolitical dimension***. We have '***cultural SDGs***' – education, diversity, heritage and lifestyle. And last but not least, work, tourism and innovation are ***economic dimensions***. It seems important to emphasize that the SDGs are of course interwoven; they cannot be divided and they can be referred to in more than one dimension (for instance, diversity).

All case studies collected for the study (Wagner, 2017) were nominated by the experts because they considered them good practice examples. Examining them in respect of their link to the SDGs can lead us to compare the examples in relation to their content.

Figure 5.5 shows that the two presented projects have similarities and differences, for example, by addressing the cultural aspect of lifestyle but not the economic dimension. The categorization also demonstrates the possibility of clarifying the examples' specific profiles. Complex artistic interventions like the 'wrestling performance' can address many different aspects whereas a focused educational project like the Indian one is more selective. Thus, we can use a framework based on the above approach to evaluate measures related to the content. People responsible for particular projects can also use this to decide on their focus. But we can also use such a framework to examine other case studies or reports but also daily practice or the projects presented in this book. The application of the framework to the example from New Zealand above has led to the observation that nearly all SDGs chosen in the beginning through a theoretical reflection can be addressed in visual arts education (VAE). Only one is missing, and that is the economic dimension. This is an interesting omission, perhaps a blind spot for art education.

In the following section, the third approach is discussed.

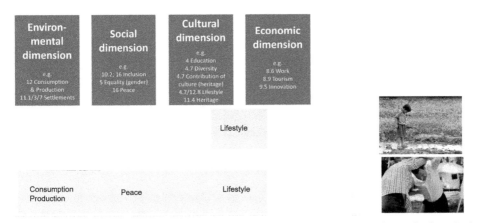

Figure 5.5: Comparing project profiles in reference to SDGs, relevant to arts education (visualization by the author).

Application of an educational model

A third approach in evaluating existing projects or discussing projects to be developed can be carried out by using educational or competence models. The very first example from India made it evident that experiences alone will probably not be enough to bring forth a sustainable change of attitudes in the further course of life. It can only be the first step and needs to be followed by further steps. Other examples from the set[8] can give us a blueprint for this. In light of this, we can state that the pedagogical process that is required could perhaps be characterized in the following way, addressing the following aspects (see also Figure 5.6):

- The VAE project refers to a situation or an experience that is relevant to the educational goal.
- Additionally, the influence of concurrent and contra-productive but often attractive experiences and the power of negative values have to be reflected and negotiated in a participative process using metacognitive methods.
- In a complex process, the reflection of the (relevant) experiences enables a value-driven attitude to be shaped. This process creates knowledge about the importance of the specific attitude and thus delivers an incentive to act.
- Skills are developed, such as being able to communicate, create, understand and critique. An awareness of the transferability of these skills to other situations is fostered.
- Knowledge about the field in which the learner should act cannot be missed in the learning process.

Figure 5.6: Educational model (visualization by the author).

Bridging Theory and Practice

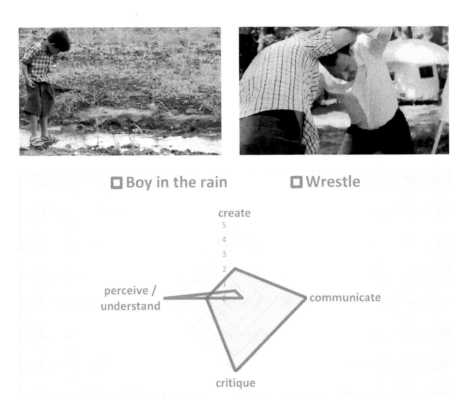

Figure 5.7: Mapping the examples against the core part of the educational model, the skills (visualization by the author).

All these aspects shape a model that can be used as a framework of reference to reflect existing practice and to develop further practice that connects the SDGs and VAE.

Conclusion

If one observes current debates on the topic of ESD in VAE, such as in the webinar series of the International Society for Education through Art (InSEA)[9] conducted in winter 2021/22, it becomes clear that actors' understandings are very different. This is certainly (also) due to the extremely broad understanding of the concept of 'sustainability'. Brundtland's definition, which is still the most convincing one, encompasses everything that is somehow good and important for the future: 'Sustainable development is development that meets the needs of the present without compromising the ability of future generations to meet their own needs' (Brundtland Commission, 1987, p. 5).

This overwhelming and broad claim in an educational subject like 'visual arts' already makes mutual understanding difficult. A critical discussion about the quality of individual measures is also difficult. Not everything that happens under the title 'VAE-ESD' is automatically valid. This makes the necessity of a criterion-led discussion all the more important. As has been shown in this chapter, different methods can help: examining the qualitative profiles of educational settings (see Approach 1), comparing the profiles against normative goals such as the SDGs (Approach 2) or examining the competences that learners can achieve in a project (Approach 3). All these means (and of course more) can help clarify what we are talking about and how.

Notes

1. The *Seoul Agenda* was the major outcome of the *Second UNESCO World Conference in Arts Education* – UNESCO (2010).
2. These dimensions are the sociopolitical dimension (e.g. art education for intercultural dialogue), the economic dimension (e.g. creativity for better employment chances), the ESD dimension (as proposed in this book), and the art-specific (arts for arts' sake) or cultural dimension (e.g. appreciation of cultural heritage).
3. Ben Bolden from Canada, Mousumi De from India, Eckart Liebau from Germany, Lawrence O'Farrell from Canada and Shifra Schonmann from Israel.
4. http://www.backyardnature.net/jinan.htm. Accessed 1 March 2017.
5. This was done contrary to the basic idea of this method, which is to carry out classification with a series of polarities that have no direct relationship to the subject of the assessment but do have a possible associative relationship. While semantic differentials are generally used in data collection strategies like surveys to gather information about attitudes or behaviour, here the polarities were used merely as descriptive aids that facilitated understanding of learning processes.
6. UNESCO. (2014). *UNESCO roadmap for implementing the global action programme on education for sustainable development* (p. 33 (5.a)). Paris: UNESCO.
7. After the start of discussions on the Post 2015 Agenda, many stakeholders tried to promote culture as the fourth dimension in the UN's understanding of sustainable development, unfortunately with no success.
8. Further examples came from Israel (theatre education for peace building), Korea (music education to revitalize a community), Canada (all art forms for inclusion), Australia (visual art education for nature protection), Brazil (heritage education in informal settlements), Egypt (visual art projects for community development), Colombia (dance education for reconciliation), Kenya (music education for entrepreneurship) and Germany (media education for sustainable consumption). For further details, see Wagner et al. (2021).
9. International Society for Education through Art is a non-governmental organization and official partner of UNESCO. InSEA is a non-profit organization whose purpose is to

encourage and advance creative education through art, design and crafts in all countries and promote international understanding (https://www.insea.org/about-us/).

References

Brundtland Commission. (2022). *Our common future*. Brundtland Report. https://www.iisd.org/about-iisd/sustainable-development

Eça, T., & Coutts, G. (2019). *Learning through art: Lessons for the 21st century?* Viseu: InSEA Publications. https://doi.org/10.24981/978-LTA2018

Haanstra, F., & Wagner, E. (2019). A European framework for visual competencies. In R. Hickman, J. Baldacchino, K. Freedman, E. Hall, & N. Meager (Eds.), *The international encyclopedia of art and design education*. New York, NY: John Wiley & Sons. https://doi.org/10.1002/9781118978061.

Hofstätter, P. R. (1971). *Gruppendynamik. Kritik der Massenpsychologie*. Hamburg: Rowohlt.

Latour, B. (2017). *Fight for Gaia*. Berlin: Suhrkamp. http://www.bruno-latour.fr/node/731.html

Liebau, E., & Wagner, E. (2017). *Das Konzept 'Kulturelle Bildung' im globalen Kontext*. In: DgfE (Ed.), *Räume für Bildung – Räume der Bildung*, Veröffentlichung zum 25. DgfE-Kongress.

UNESCO. (2010). *The Seoul Agenda*. https://unesdoc.unesco.org/ark:/48223/pf0000190692

UNITWIN. (2022, 23 January). https://www.unitwin-arts.phil.fau.de/

Wagner, E. (2017). *Research highlight – arts education and education for sustainable development*. German Commission for UNESCO, Scientific Research for Sustainable Development – UNESCO Chairs in Germany (pp. 72–77).

Wagner, E., Nielsen, C., Pachova N., Suominen A., & Veloso L. (2021). Arts, sustainability & education. *ENO yearbook* (Vol. 2). New York, NY: Springer.

Weinert, F. E. (1999). *Concepts of competence. Theoretical and conceptual foundations* Contribution within the OECD project Definition and selection of competencies. DeSeCo. Neuchâtel: Bundesamt für Statistik.

Part 2

Call to Action: Real-World Propositions

Raphael Vella and Victoria Pavlou

Part 1 of the book focuses on the theoretical considerations that need to be contemplated to better prepare teachers in art education. It urges teacher educators to reimagine teacher education in art education as it acknowledges teachers to be one of the most crucial components in bringing change to schools. The new pedagogical possibilities in teacher education – both during initial teacher training and continuous professional development training – include ways of building teachers' competences in applying an art education curriculum infused with education for sustainable development attributes, create new collaborative learning spaces through establishing professional learning communities, connect the training with real-life needs and offer experiences that are transformative enough to challenge stereotypic perceptions and narratives to bring change.

Part 2 contemplates the theoretical considerations of Part 1 and presents examples of projects that promote a new vision of visual arts education (VAE) and the future of museum education. A vision that capitalizes on reflection, collaboration and inclusion as well as on critically interrogating practice in a learning-oriented and growth-promoting way (Stoll & Seashore-Lewis, 2007) results in transformative experiences (Lotz-Sisitka, Wals, Kronlid, & McGarry, 2015). Transformative and emancipatory pedagogies that promote a different way of thinking are essential in bringing change for a sustainable future.

Therefore, Part 2 responds to the challenge of how to utilize 'the complex "pool" of knowledge generated in and through art education research' (Illeris, 2012, p. 77) in sustainable development and to implement useful teaching practices and projects that respond to crucial sustainability issues. The first two chapters focus on the possibilities offered by the formation of professional learning communities in supporting educators through peer mentoring and in promoting inclusivity. The following two chapters focus on competence development that can enable learners (being teachers, or teachers-to-be or children) to become change agents.

Vincent Caruana's chapter focuses on 'Peer mentoring at the intersection of education for sustainable development and visual arts education'. The chapter draws on the findings of two Erasmus+ projects, one on mentoring and peer mentoring and another on the synergies of ESD and VAE for teacher training. It demonstrates how peer mentoring can offer opportunities for personal and professional development of teachers and thus reinforce teachers' engagement and commitment to the teaching of ESD. Affirming that teacher training is one of the most relevant and efficient tools for school innovation and improvement, the chapter moves on to explore the synergies that exist between ESD and

VAE and to suggest a way forward through peer mentoring for further exploiting these synergies.

The importance of fostering peer communities of learning by bringing together diverse teachers is discussed in Chapter 7. In the context of the CARE project, the authors, Soula Mitakidou and Martha Ioannidou, were able to offer an online teacher training programme (TTP) that aimed to link VAE with sustainable development goals and real-life issues. The CARE project's focus on 'real-life' was further problematized by its contextualization in the COVID-19 pandemic, which made many participants ponder what the meaning of 'real-life' could be in a world that was being experienced increasingly as a virtual dimension. VAE was presented as the catalyst for offering attractive, equitable and inclusive learning contexts that explored and nurtured knowledge, abilities and values around real-life issues. The chapter focuses on the concept of inclusion as a sustainability issue, which was brought forward because of the COVID-19 pandemic and the failure in many countries worldwide to offer quality education and reach disadvantaged learners. At the same time, the pandemic opened the discussion on facilitating a new form of growth, focusing on resilience, inclusiveness and well-being. The TTP programme is an example of how to nurture learning communities amongst a very diverse group of teachers to learn through art about compassion and solidarity and also to develop teaching scenarios on the same issues.

Victoria Pavlou and Chrysanthi Kadji-Beltran's chapter 'Envisioning better futures: Integrating sustainability practices into museum education for elementary student teachers' introduces a case study of primary preservice teachers in Cyprus who explored the subject of 'remembrance' in a public art gallery. By infusing ideas from ESD into museum education, this study aligned itself with the new museology, which conceives of museum spaces as spaces of experiences and discussion. While teachers may generally rely on input from museum staff during school visits, this study encouraged them to become change agents by promoting experiential, free-choice and interdisciplinary learning and infusing principles of sustainable development within their plans for educational projects or visits in museums. The case study was significant because it showed that teachers can build new partnerships with museums and their staff.

The final chapter of Part 2, 'Drawing and the global climate emergency: Affective and connective explorations' by Chris Turner and Emese Hall, employs the theory of aesthoecology as a metaphor for the aesthetic and connected nature of the act of drawing. In the act of drawing, an image emerges in a process that is simultaneously playful, unpredictable, dynamic and cognitive. As a part of an issues-based approach to artistic pedagogy, drawing helps practitioners to think differently, which is a significant skill in our contemporary engagement with global issues related to the climate and other ecological concerns. Hence, drawing relies on affective and connective (aesthoecological) dimensions that can be used to explore and communicate emergent phenomena like global warming.

References

Illeris, H. (2012). Nordic contemporary art education and the environment: Constructing an epistemological platform for Art Education for Sustainable Development (AESD). *Nordic Journal of Art and Research, 1*(2), 77–93

Lotz-Sisitka, H., Wals, A. E., Kronlid, D., & McGarry, D. (2015). Transformative, transgressive social learning: Rethinking higher education pedagogy in times of systemic global dysfunction. *Current Opinion in Environmental Sustainability*, 16, 73–80.

Stoll, L., & Seashore-Lewis, K. (2007). *Professional learning communities, divergence, depth and dilemmas*. Buckingham: Open University Press.

Chapter 6

Peer-Mentoring at the Intersection of Education for Sustainable Development and Visual Arts Education

Vincent Caruana

Introduction

The United Nations (UN) 2030 Agenda for Sustainable Development aims, through a collaborative partnership among countries and stakeholders, 'to take the bold and transformative steps which are urgently needed to shift the world onto a sustainable and resilient path' (United Nations [UN], n.d., preamble). This can only be achieved through lifelong learning and education. In fact, the fourth sustainable development goal (SDG), specifically SDG 4.7, aims to 'ensure that by 2030 all learners acquire knowledge and skills needed to promote Sustainable Development (SD), including among others through Education for Sustainable Development (ESD)' (UN, n.d., para. 4.7).

The Erasmus+-funded action research project PEERMENT,[1] which ran between 2017 and 2020, explored the potential of peer-mentoring in enhancing the practice of ESD through sharing knowledge and experience and through providing an opportunity to learn from different perspectives. The need for this project arose from two primary considerations: (1) implementation often lags behind policy in ESD and (2) peer-mentoring is largely untapped in the European formal education systems, even more so regarding ESD.

The aim of this chapter is twofold: to provide a blueprint for organizations that would like to strengthen the practice of ESD through the tool of peer-mentoring and to explore the synergies that exist between ESD and visual arts education (VAE), suggesting a way forward to show how, through peer-mentoring, this synergy could be exploited further.

Implementation lacking behind policy in ESD

Participating partners in PEERMENT understood that despite the clear and growing importance of ESD, as espoused through the various UN Declarations, not least Agenda 2030, most national policies in practice do not reflect this importance. Implementation lags behind policy – in particular, as pertaining to teacher training. In the absence of such support policies, participants realized that they had one thing in common – teachers often leave initial teacher training enthusiastic about implementing ESD, only to feel powerless and have their passion challenged by their inability to apply theory to practice because of resource constraints.

This is an area of concern since research suggests that achieving sustainability is a process requiring both bottom-up and top-down approaches. For example, in his article 'Emerging from Limbo: Environmental Education in Malta', Pace (2009) shows that, while teachers are viewed as significant change agents, this is dependent on the will of people at the top to catalyze such change by providing support and training.

Avenues to rekindle the desire of teachers to be change agents become crucial and urgent. One such avenue worth exploring was mentoring, a model based on a constructivist view of learning, the idea of shared expertise and the model of integrative pedagogy, where teachers are trusted and their professional autonomy respected (Kirsi, 2014). Paradoxically, mentoring and peer-mentoring, while widespread in the world of business and the third sector, are less used in the European formal education systems, though they are increasingly being acknowledged as crucial tools for teachers and school leaders.

Peer-mentoring in European systems of formal education

One definition of mentoring is 'a form of long-term tailored development, with a primary focus on developing capability and potential, which brings benefits both to the individual and to the organization' (University of Sheffield, 2009). Mentoring is considered as a 'just-in-time help, insight into issues, and the sharing of expertise, values, skills, and perspectives' (Educause, n.d., n.p.). In a nutshell, the power of mentoring lies in its catalytic function of provoking change that otherwise would not have taken place or would have taken place at a much slower rate, which is not an option, considering the urgency of the SDGs.

PEERMENT partners were aware of the Finnish model of peer-group mentoring (PGM), which later Tynjälä, Pennanen, Markkanen, and Heikkinen (2021) summarized as based on 'the constructivist theory of learning, the concept of autonomy in (the) teaching profession, peer learning, and narrative identity work' (p. 2). Yet while this model is usually applied to promote the professional development of teachers in primary and secondary education, partners were unaware of the model being explicitly applied to ESD.

Such considerations beg the question: 'What forms of engagement are necessary and effective to rekindle the passion and desire to apply the theory of ESD to practice?'

The need to shed light on this question was first identified by the participating partners in the pre-proposal phase since all partners were well-versed in their country's realities regarding the status and practice of ESD. This was then solidified through initial research that took place during the first phase of the project culminating in the publication 'Mentoring and Peer Mentoring in teachers' training: Good practices in the EU – PEERMENT Partners' Experiences' (Caruana, 2018, n.p.). This publication includes twelve good practices of mentoring and peer-mentoring existing in Europe for initial and in-service teachers' training, setting the scene for identifying aspects that are effective for developing transversal competencies concerning peer-mentoring for ESD and providing the basis for the construction of the new model.

The PEERMENT project

PEERMENT was an innovative and participative intervention to address the need to further ESD, and a methodology to tap the potential of teaching staff. The main innovation was that of turning schools/formal education into learning communities through participating teachers. The innovative contribution of the PEERMENT project was testing and adapting the PGM model for ESD. Partners did so by laying out, testing, improving and disseminating a new model of mentoring and peer-mentoring for ESD that is scalable and can continue to be used and disseminated way beyond the life cycle of the project.

The project created a new space for teachers to exchange their feelings of isolation in their teaching, their preparatory work and even more of ESD, which requires a lot of (personal) research, sorting through valuable information, and is not always easy when faced with 'complex issues' and fake news. Exchanging feelings, views and ideas between peers, even in the same discipline, is rare. Yet, the project gave teachers an opportunity for intradisciplinary exchanges, interdisciplinary exchanges and even inter-generational exchanges (with young and older teachers working together), as well as serving as a break from their teaching and a space for critical reflective thinking. It demonstrated that interdisciplinary approaches were rich and brought both better content on ESD and meaning.

Questionnaires filled in by the teachers participating in the purposefully set up local training groups (the peer-mentoring for ESD groups), as part of the project monitoring and evaluation, indicated the usefulness of the PEERMENT model to be extremely high, way over the originally projected 70 per cent. One other clear indicator of the usefulness and transferability of the model emanated from the feedback received from the multiplier events and website, namely that multiple new organizations were willing to adopt the PEERMENT model for ESD, and that new schools and organizations asked for new training.

One of the basic tenets of the PEERMENT project was to make use of the potential existing inside the schools to guarantee both the personal and professional development of the teaching staff, which is why there was an emphasis on the horizontal aspects of peer-mentoring. This was supported by tailor-made training through inputs from education specialists, thus also acknowledging the vertical aspects of mentoring through outside expertise in ESD where needed. Some participants favoured the use of training in WebQuests, an inquiry-oriented activity based on information from the internet (Dodge, 1997). WebQuests supports critical thinking, diversity, cooperation and creativity while connecting and empowering educators (Taylor, 2001). For other participants, WebQuests would come at a later stage and opted for a detailed analysis of the curriculum so as to re-orient it towards sustainability, as was the case in Malta, where a one-day training for economics and business studies teachers involved a detailed dissection of the diverse syllabi and the brainstorming of ideas on how sustainability can be best infused across the different themes.

Another spillover effect was the endorsement of the learning that took place through incorporating some aspects with other projects, such as the CARE[2] (an acronym for

Connecting Art with REal life issues) Erasmus+ project for the infusion of ESD among art teachers, involving four other institutions. The second part of this chapter will have a look at how CARE is promoting the strengthening of the practice of ESD, including through creating learning communities and peer-mentoring. This focus is particularly important since the intersection of the arts and ESD is still hugely unexplored. Even in the Agenda 2030, science is mentioned eleven times in the document, while there is no mention of the arts, although there is an acknowledgement of the need to appreciate cultural diversity and culture's contribution to sustainable development (UN, n.d., para. 4.7).

The CARE project

The CARE project is about enhancing VAE with ESD elements that promote creative thinking, critical and systemic thinking, reflection, and the development of skills, attitudes and values relevant to today's sustainability challenges. Its focus is on the development and delivery of teacher training and the creation of a culture of collaboration among educators by furthering professional communities of learning. Most of the project was conducted during the difficult times of the COVID-19 pandemic.

Teacher training in ESD and VAE was at the core of CARE, acknowledging that teacher training is one of the most relevant and efficient tools for school innovation and improvement (Vandenberghe, 2002). Due to the pandemic, this training was conducted through an electronic platform and mostly asynchronous in the case of the Maltese partner. Such a platform allowed Maltese students to discuss various themes in the numerous forums opened as part of the training. Furthermore, two Facebook groups were opened, one of which was a private group, which (together with the forums) served as the medium for peer-mentoring, with the possibility also of expert inputs through the tutors. Synchronous online sessions were also held to provide both peer-to-peer and expert feedback on work produced by the teachers. Interviews were also held to further probe and understand the learning process.

Learning communities, what Wengert (1998) calls 'Communities of Practice', have three key features to be considered as such: a domain, a community and a practice. As far as the CARE groups were concerned, these features were:

1. ESD and VAE as the domain, the shared area of interest, which means that the learning communities did not simply learn or meet from time to time, but that there was a commitment to the domain of infusing ESD across VAE.
2. A community that discussed and supported each other in the infusion of sustainable development through the arts curriculum, in particular by learning and discussing six big ideas, namely the *Public, Ecological Literacy, Compassion, Diversity, Conservation and Change,* and *Regeneration*. These big ideas were chosen to provoke teachers to think about ESD in new directions, beyond the regular thematic areas such as climate change

or waste. The Berlin process on ESD considers education to be a 'powerful enabler of positive change of mindsets', that can lead towards 'the well-being of all within planetary boundaries' (UNESCO, 2021, n.p.). The choice of such big ideas centred on this central tenet of changing mindsets, in particular, the need to reconsider the dominant paradigm of development as well as the need to consider new alternative paradigms built on the idea of care and well-being, and discourses initiated through the capability approach of Sen (1984) that encourage us to consider not what we have but what we can do and achieve with what we have.

What created the community was not the mere fact of being teachers but their shared interest in ESD as VAE teachers who engaged in training, activities and discussion. Through the forums and the closed Facebook group, the VAE teachers supported each other in their personal and professional development, as well as engaged in working on the design of the ESD lesson plans and discussing their results. Thanks to engaged interactions – the vertical mentorship through the expert tutors and the peer-to-peer methodology – teachers built relationships that made it possible for them to learn from each other, creating *de facto* learning communities.

3. The development of the competencies created and used lesson plans that infuse ESD across the VAE curriculum. It is not enough to have a shared interest – this needs to be complemented by the active participation of teachers. CARE saw the design and elaboration of a shared repertoire of lesson plans that were subsequently implemented in the classroom and subsequently evaluated, with the learning that took place fed back into the group, as well as the participating partners. This dynamic of provoking creative thought in new directions through the big ideas, on the one hand, and, on the other hand, individualized support through the training sessions and one-on-one mentoring, created a new space for in-depth reflections, leading to innovative lesson plans and hence transformation in the VAE curriculum.

A peer-mentoring blueprint for organizations

VAE is often at risk of being squeezed out of the curriculum and thus it is crucial to acknowledge its value in teaching children about sustainability challenges. As the experience of the PEERMENT project indicated, when change towards infusing ESD across the school is initiated through the school leadership, there is potential for including teachers from all subject matters. Working with the visual arts is a particularly good window opportunity to introduce the young child to understanding, seeing and feeling the world, and at a later stage to connect art with real-life issues and learn, investigate and act creatively upon them. The learning communities or communities of practice by both PEERMENT and CARE are ultimately a means to provide training, promote innovation, develop social competencies, and facilitate and spread knowledge within a group (Wenger, 1998). What follows are some more practical considerations, based on the outcome of PEERMENT and the works in progress of CARE, that can provide a blueprint for other organizations that see the benefit of such projects, and want to embark on similar processes, in particular, the strengthening of ESD through peer-mentoring in the context of VAE.

As part of the PEERMENT project, a checklist for the PEERMENT ESD model for teachers' community of practice was created, focusing on three main pillars: ESD, peer-mentoring groups and the development of new methodologies (Šibalić, 2020). This checklist can be adapted to all subject matter and is here adapted for the needs of VAE. Concerning the first pillar, VAE teachers who adopt this path can consider the following questions:

- What is the extent of commitment among VAE teachers regarding learning about ESD and including it in the curriculum planning? Are there any strong shared areas of interest?
- What opportunities exist within the VAE curriculum to infuse ESD successfully across the curriculum?
- What comparative advantage does VAE have in infusing ESD successfully across the curriculum and in developing a whole-school approach to ESD?
- What is the comparative advantage of VAE in promoting a positive change of mindsets as intended by the Berlin process and a subjective evaluation of one's well-being?

Here, it is pertinent to point out that not all VAE teachers will be conversant with the main tenets and pedagogies related to ESD, and so any training ought to be tailor-made to the particular cohort. In particular, there might be a tendency to go towards soft green issues such as one-off projects recycling material without considering the bigger issues related to the need to challenge lifestyles, change behaviours, consider social justice, take concrete actions and create a sustainability mindset.

Concerning the second pillar, the following questions are relevant:

- What opportunities exist in engaging in joint training on VAE, activities and discussion? What opportunities exist to share knowledge and information and support each other in their personal and social development?
- How can one go about working together on the design of lesson plans, based on the best ESD and VAE methodologies? How can one work together in identifying and sourcing more eco-friendly material to work with?
- How can one strengthen existing peer relationships and build new relationships, including new intergenerational relationships?
- What opportunities exist for regular interactions – whether face-to-face, or online, both synchronous and asynchronous?

Concerning the third pillar regarding the development of new methodologies, the following questions are applicable:

- What artworks, both local and international, are helpful in the development of inquiry-based learning, in particular as dealing with the SDGs and sustainable development?
- How can one filter reliable news from fake news, regarding online sources related to sustainable development or greenwashing?
- How can one build a shared repertoire of didactic and educational tools, inspiring works of art, lesson plans and WebQuests related to VAE and ESD? What big ideas enhance good lesson plans? What are the roles of values clarification, care and compassion in such an endeavour?

Particularly in the case of VAE and ESD, the question of fake news is often linked to greenwashing, with various claims of going green that make it in the news ultimately proving to be more of an alienation or marketing than a solution. One thus needs to carefully consider the whole life cycle of resources. For example, material that could have easily gone to the recycling facilities might have been used in the name of 're-using' in the classroom, only to be changed into a new format that makes recycling impossible, thus creating a new problem of what to do with the new installation. It is here that VAE educators can work with ESD experts to try to come out as much as possible with solutions that are compatible with preserving the environment and eradicating poverty, as well as where possible restoring and beautifying the environment.

In the case of both PEERMENT and CARE, the projects themselves served as the first entry points of the processes. However, these entry points are not project-specific, and the learning that took place during such projects can serve as an inspiration to catalyze other VAE and ESD practitioners to start similar processes. Valid entry points experienced during the PEERMENT project, some of which were also used for the CARE project, include starting with a small group of already motivated teachers, starting with a continuous professional development training at the school or with teachers through a coordinating body such as the subject coordinator or education officer, working on creating local training groups of teachers (the name was adopted by PEERMENT for the peer-mentoring circles) that are committed to engaging with each other regularly and working with the administration of the school to get the support of the school leadership and engage in a whole school approach (Šibalić, 2020).

Topics to discuss during such sessions of the local training groups are best identified by the teachers themselves. However, good starting points could be:

1. What do you understand by the transformative power of ESD through VAE? What type of support do you need to unleash this full power? How can we support each other? Who can we enlist to provide us with further expertise? Which artworks inspire you in your ESD work?

2. What VAE lesson or story can you share that you think successfully communicated a sustainable way of thinking to your students? Which artworks inspired you? What problems did you encounter? What will you do differently another time?

As we have seen, the practice of a learning community can take place online. In the case of both projects, most of the training and expert mentoring was conducted online, while participants also used social media to mentor each other. While the COVID-19 played a role, there is scope for considering online environments beyond the pandemic. In the case of the PEERMENT project, for example, an online environment was used to overcome geographical limitations, where more than one school (often with considerable distances between them) was involved in such training and learning communities or where a specific subject teacher would be the only one in a particular school, and thus local training groups and learning communities will need to be organized by necessity among different schools rather than within the same school. Participating partners in PEERMENT also opted for using the Electronic Platform for Adult Learning in Europe (EPALE), which allows for communities of practice to be set up, thus also allowing for a wider outreach across different organizations and countries.

The blueprint outlined here offers a clear way to embark on the journey of integrating ESD across VAE, on the understanding that context is important and that revisions and changes will be done, to better reflect the specific situations and to integrate the new learning that will surely take place on the way.

Accelerating SDG 4.7

We have seen that implementation of policy often lags behind official commitments, such as those concerning the SDGs, in particular SDG 4.7. In the absence of much-needed top-down approaches to complement and catalyze the role of teachers as change makers, PEERMENT and CARE have both demonstrated that bottom-up initiatives, where teachers and universities act as 'champions' of the cause and move within global and national policy directions, can be effective.

Through the PEERMENT and CARE projects, we have shown how the Finnish model of PGM, or aspects of it, could be adapted to ESD and further adapted for specific subjects, in this case, the infusion of ESD with VAE. Both projects foresaw the development of competencies linked to delivering ESD as a transversal topic and the role of the teacher in transformative education. The peer-mentoring spaces provided were designed to strengthen competencies linked to personal and social development. They were also designed to deal with difficulties arising from implementing ESD across the curriculum, which, as the PEERMENT initial work indicated, often carries a low status in schools and is not always supported in practice by educational leaders. The main focus was on what takes place in the classroom, often through the use of WebQuests in the case of PEERMENT and lesson plans across six big ideas in the case of CARE – a 'territory' where the teacher often has a lot of influence and potential for taking initiatives.

The PEERMENT project considered the following aspects, amongst others, as essential in developing teachers' knowledge and skills in peer-mentoring systems for ESD: fluidity in the roles of mentor and mentee, the centrality of networking, the role of 'accompaniment', added value in international cooperation, the centrality of children empowerment, the necessity for continuous monitoring and evaluation, the necessity for knowledge and experience sharing, the distinction between information and formation, and environmental sustainability as the basis of social sustainability (Šibalić, 2020). It is still too early to confirm this concerning the CARE project, however, most of the aforementioned aspects seem to be in common.

However, more research is needed to gauge the development through such projects of what Silverman (2012) called key sustainability competencies, namely systems-thinking, anticipatory, normative, strategic and interpersonal competencies. The research, so far, suggests that the PEERMENT model allows participants to reinforce their engagement and commitment to the teaching of ESD and their self-consciousness in their potential as ESD educators. Interviews conducted amongst CARE participating teachers indicate the same. Of particular mention is that participants remarked that they only understood the concept of a learning community by experiencing it through CARE training, that they learned new things and got inspired from each other, and that the CARE course was much more helpful and engaging than they expected it would be when they enrolled.

Learning communities and peer-mentoring processes can be important vehicles in strengthening the educational processes collectively in creating a different world to the status quo we have inherited. While such collaborative or cooperative practices are still rare, when implemented, such practices offer teachers the opportunity to break out of isolation and engage in a cross-fertilization of ideas (Solidarité Laïque, 2020). PEERMENT and CARE, though perhaps unintentionally, also highlight the crucial political roles of universities in taking the initiative to follow up on the missing gaps in the SDGs.

It remains to be seen if such learning communities stay, regroup, or serve as a springboard for new initiatives after the project interventions are ended. However, given the success of the PEERMENT experience and the enthusiasm and good quality products created through the ongoing CARE project, it is clear that the practice of ESD through various subjects, not least VAE, is not wishful thinking nor something hard to attain. The value of such projects often lies in their ability to create a new sense of possibility and to rekindle the passion in teachers to show that another world is possible and another education is possible.

Notes

1. See https://peerment.eu/ for details.
2. See http://care.frederick.ac.cy/ for more details.

References

Caruana, V. (2018). *Mentoring and peer mentoring in teachers' training: Good practices in the EU – PEERMENT partners' experiences.* https://peerment.eu/wp-content/uploads/2020/04/MENTORING-AND-PEER-MENTORING-IN-TEACHERS-TRAINING_-GOOD-PRACTICES-IN-THE-EU-PEERMENT-Partners%e2%80%99-Experiences-.pdf

Dodge, B. (1997). *Some thoughts about WebQuests.* https://webquest.org/sdsu/about_webquests.html

Educause. (n.d.). *Mentoring styles.* http://www.educause.edu/careers/special-topicprograms/mentoring/about-mentoring/mentoring-styles

Filho, W., Manolas, E., & Pace, P. (2009). Education for sustainable development: Current discourses and practices and their relevance to technology education. *International Journal of Technology and Design Education, 19,* 149–165. https://doi.org/10.1007/s10798-008-9079-z

Kirsi, T. (2014). Peer-group mentoring for teacher development. *Journal of Education for Teaching, 40*(3), 322–323. https://doi.org/10.1080/02607476.2014.886918

Pace, P. (2009). Emerging from Limbo: Environmental education in Malta. In *Environmental education in context* (pp. 71–82). Austria: Brill. https://doi.org/10.1163/9789087909635_009

Sen, A. K. (1984). Wellbeing, agency and freedom: The Dewey Lectures 1984. *Journal of Philosophy, 82*(4), 169–221.

Šibalić, I. (2020). *Teachers' guidelines: Peer-mentoring system for ESD.* https://peerment.eu/news/teachers-guidelines-peer-mentoring-system-for-esd/

Silverman, H. (2012). *Key competencies in sustainability.* https://www.solvingforpattern.org/2012/08/14/kcompetencies-in-sustainability/

Solidarité Laïque. (2020a). *How does peer-mentoring contribute to education for sustainable development in schools?* https://peerment.eu/wp-content/uploads/2020/12/solidarite_laique_etude_et_analyse_eng_vf_0.pdf

Taylor, H. G. (2001). *The WebQuest model for inquiry-based learning using the resources of the world wide web.* Copenhagen: WCCE.

Tynjälä, P., Pennanen, M., Markkanen, I., & Heikkinen, H. L. T. (2021). Finnish model of peer-group mentoring: Review of research. *Annals of the New York Academy of Sciences, 1483*(1), 208–223. https://doi.org/10.1111/nyas.14296

United Nations. (n.d.). *Transforming our world: The 2030 agenda for sustainable development.* https://sdgs.un.org/2030agenda

University of Sheffield. (2009). *Mentoring – CIPD factsheet.* https://www.shef.ac.uk/polopoly_fs/1.110468!/file/cipd_mentoring_factsheet.pdf

UNESCO. (2021). *Berlin declaration on education for sustainable development.* https://en.unesco.org/sites/default/files/esdfor2030-berlin-declaration-en.pdf

Vandenberghe, R. (2002). Teachers' professional development as the core of school improvement. *International Journal of Educational Research, 37,* 653–659. https://doi.org/10.1016/S0883-0355(03)00063-6

Wenger, E. (1998). *Communities of practice: Learning, meaning, and identity.* Cambridge: Cambridge University Press.

Chapter 7

Visual Arts for Inclusion in Diverse School Contexts: A Kaleidoscope of Learning

Soula Mitakidou and Martha Ioannidou

Just as the rhetoric on inclusion started to weigh towards the idea that inclusion is a 'good thing' (Levitas, 2003) and the concept of inclusion extended to include all children with increased educational needs, the pandemic of COVID-19 broke out. Unrelated as they may seem, the two subjects are strongly interconnected. According to United Nations estimates, the pandemic will cause 100 million more people worldwide to move below the poverty line and urges governments, organizations and people to seek sustainable solutions to avoid irreparable post-COVID 19 disasters (United Nations, 2020).

If we turn to educational outcomes, according to UNICEF (2020a, n.p.) data, 'more than 1 billion children are at risk of falling behind due to school closures aimed at containing the spread of COVID-19'. Approximately 40 per cent of low and lower-middle-income countries have failed to support disadvantaged learners during often extended school lockdowns (UNESCO, n.d.). At least one-third of schoolchildren worldwide cannot benefit from remote learning programmes, mainly due to a lack of the necessary household resources or the inadequacy of policies that could meet their needs. Preschool education is suffering the hardest blow, as 40 per cent of countries failed to provide preschoolers with remote learning opportunities (UNESCO, 2020; UNICEF, 2020b). The world is not a fair place and obviously, the COVID-19 crisis has further exacerbated pre-existing inequalities (digital and traditional), undermining the already precarious vision of inclusion for all.

It is perhaps not a surprise that the COVID-19 health crisis has intensified the sustainability discussion, as people have painfully experienced the severe disruption of every pillar of the sustainability equation, social, economic, political and environmental. However, despite its severe consequences, the pandemic has at the same time resulted in positive impacts, primarily due to reduced human activity (Bashir, Ma, & Shahzad, 2020; Corlett et al., 2020; Garrido-Cumbrera et al., 2021; Mahato, Pal, & Ghosh, 2020). One of these positive outcomes, relative to our discussion here, is a decisive shift in public consciousness for sustainability issues. Based on their research findings, Rousseau and Deschacht (2020, p. 1157) claim that 'public support for programs aiming at more resilient and sustainable living environments may have increased' but they also warn us that 'while we find evidence of changes in public awareness, these changes may be short-lived, and people may revert to previous patterns once the crisis is past'. Their suggestion is to act quickly 'to initiate a transformation to a new form of growth, focusing on resilience, well-being and sustainability' (Rousseau & Deschacht, 2020, p. 1157). Teachers can capitalize on the lessons the global health crisis has taught us and try to frame their teaching in the sustainability paradigm better, thus working towards a successful transition to a sustainable post-COVID-19 world (Leal Filho et al., 2021).

Education for sustainable development (ESD) can facilitate in learners the development 'of the knowledge, skills, attitudes and values required to become active participants, individually and collectively, in decision-making processes, both at local and global levels that will improve the quality of life of present and future generations' (Vella, 2022, p. 10). Fortunately, the sustainability discourse had already disclaimed the urgency traditionally granted to ecological degradation and adopted three more equally important, interconnected pillars for sustainable development: the economic, social and cultural. This crucial expansion embraces all aspects of the human-inflicted catastrophes on the world and promises the reconstruction of the broken human–nature–society ties, provided that the addition of sustainability to the development equation is reflective of a shift away from the narrow concerns of mainstream economics and modernization theories that emphasize economic growth to the disregard of other concerns such as the relationship between ecology, inter- and intra-generational equity, and social justice (Nurse, 2006, p. 35).

In this sense, a viable sustainability model should avoid 'the narrow confines of modernization theories of development scripted in the tenets of Western technological civilization that is often promoted as the "universal" and the "obvious"' (Nurse, 2006, p. 35); instead, the objectives of sustainable development should be strictly pursued within the framework of social, ecological, economic and cultural equity and viability.

The intensified sustainability discourse is positive, but it is far from sufficient. '[I]t is not enough to present beautiful aims and theories; it is the actual pedagogical means and acts that matter' (Knif & Kairavuori, 2020, p. 76). In this vein, educators are invited 'to move beyond knowledge into action […] both at an individual level and at an organisational level, in this case the school' (Vella, 2022, p. 4). It seems that ESD can teach us ways to understand and act to solve the social, economic, cultural and environmental problems we have created.

The same is true of visual arts education (VAE). The Seoul Agenda, formulated during UNESCO's Second World Conference on Arts Education, firmly proclaims the central role that arts education plays

> in the constructive transformation of educational systems that are struggling to meet the needs of learners in a rapidly changing world characterized by remarkable advances in technology on the one hand and intractable social and cultural injustices on the other.
> (UNESCO, 2010, p. 2)

Learning through the arts can make the school more attractive by increasing the children's interest and motivation for learning. VAE can create flexible, purposeful and meaningful learning spaces and promote unique ways of viewing the world and achieving learning. It has the potential to challenge inequities and invite diversity, build ecological literacy, inspire alternative views of the world and suggest a paradigm shift that allows us to envision more viable and promising futures (Ioannidou & Mitakidou, 2018). The use of visual arts in the classroom can liberate art from its often-stereotypical character of simple entertainment, transforming it into a potential and potent educational tool that maximizes the prospects of all learners. VAE holds promising possibilities provided its use:

- calls for active student engagement with the artwork,
- encourages equitable collaboration and group work,
- invites children to discover their own and their classmates' talents and thus reassess their abilities,
- enables freedom, multiple means of expression, promoting learning and creative expression for all,
- pursues critical, cognitive as well as creative goals,
- ensures equitable access to quality education for every child regardless of his/her difference from the mainstream norm in terms of ability, language, culture, identity and origin.

Thus delivered, VAE becomes a powerful teaching tool that fosters 'critical, reflective, and creative thinking in the context of society, coupled with expression. The expression might be an attempt to change society or to simply explore its complexities' (Goldberg, 2001, p. 33). VAE can support inclusion and equality for all, as advocated by the fourth[2] sustainable development goal (SDG); and as Sonetti, Barioglio, and Campobenedetto (2020) claim, SDG4 can be considered as the means of achieving all other SDGs.

VAE contributes towards inclusion in education by creating a multimodal, diverse, hospitable learning space that positions all children at the same starting point, eliminating arbitrary dichotomies that evoke different expectations and, inevitably, different performances. VAE speaks 'to the whole group and thus exceeds but at the same time addresses personal pursuits. In this framework, different languages and cultures are embedded in the learning process in a natural, instrumental way' (Mitakidou & Tressou, 2017, p. 1159). Differences become a springboard for learning and children are encouraged to use their skills and funds of knowledge (including their home language and culture) to make sense of new learning. Visual arts convert the class into a learning community usually diminishing conflict among children, especially in mixed multicultural classes (Goldberg, 2001).

VAE can contribute to restoring the disrupted human–nature and human–society bonds by educating students to understand the fragility of man's position in the world and inspire them to act for its protection. The attractiveness of VAE increases when teachers manage to weave the visual arts across the curriculum, i.e., creatively interconnect it with the school subjects they teach. This approach enhances the appeal of VAE to sceptical educators, offering an example of holistic learning that counters the dominant practice of fragmented and segregated school subjects.

The potential of visual arts to build attractive, equitable and inclusive learning contexts has been documented through research studies (Bamford, 2006; Bamford & Wimmer, 2012; Hunter, 2005; Ioannidou, 2014; LaJevic, 2013). To verify the validity of this claim, especially in the face of a universal crisis, we rely on the example of a case study recently completed. It was carried out in the framework of the CARE Teacher Training Programme (TTP).

A case study paradigm

The context

The overarching aim of the European project *CARE: Visual arts education in new times: Connecting Art with REal life issues* (2019–22)[3] is to empower teachers to build on the interconnection between the aims of VAE and ESD and pursue them through the arts and broader cultural products. The Greek TTP, a core of the CARE project, lasted from January 2021 to June 2021 and was conducted by the Aristotle University research team. Entitled 'Visual Arts and Sustainability in Education', it attempted to prepare Greek elementary school teachers to plan and implement a teaching scenario in their learning settings.

It followed the framework suggested by the text written as a guide for TTTPs (Vella, 2022), enriched by relevant artworks and often by workshops presented by the proposed Greek artists themselves. Except for sessions and workshops, a rich array of educational materials (e.g. videos, presentations, online training sessions and lots of art/art projects related to CARE objectives) was made available to participants through the interactive platform CARE-full, created by the Aristotle University of Thessaloniki (AUTH) training team. The participation requirements included the teachers' active involvement in the training courses, the maintenance of a reflective visual journal (individual work), the design of a teaching scenario based on VAE and ESD principles (group work) and its implementation at school (group work).

Data were collected, processed and interpreted during the training and implementation phase. The research tools deployed included observation of the participants' active involvement in the sessions (recorded and analyzed); the teachers' frequent comments about the sessions (personal communications with trainers throughout the training programme); extracts from their reflective visual journals; teachers' interim group interviews; the final evaluation questionnaires and reports of their scenario's implementation. Children's reactions to the implementation were collected by teachers through children's group interviews and were included in their final reports. Children's responses were both verbal and visual. Digital data were transcribed, and all data were processed using a mixed-method research scheme (frequency as well as content analysis), thus adding validity and credibility to findings (Johnson & Onwuegbuzie, 2004). Also, triangulation facilitated data validation and comparison.

Inclusion enhanced

Inclusive, quality and fair education has been both the means as well as one of the main targets of the CARE project. The selected data indicated an increased level of inclusion in teacher–teacher collaborations. To verify this, in addition to the aggregate data of the main study, a supplementary group interview was conducted among eighteen of the participating teachers (divided into two groups). All our discussants – to the point of data saturation – acknowledged that the programme contributed to enhanced collegial partnerships among them and that their inclusive participatory behaviours were immediately filtered down and reflected on their associations with children and the children's relationships among them, contributing to class cohesion and inclusive participation in face-to-face sessions.

The case study presented here focuses on the collaboration patterns of a very diverse group of teachers both regarding their teaching experience and backgrounds and their implementation settings. Equally diverse were the participating students in these settings. Despite their diversity, the teachers felt empowered and inspired by their mutual commitment to the principles of VAE and ESD and ventured to bridge their differences by creating and applying a flexible and all-encompassing teaching scenario.

The case study group comprised six generalist teachers: Two fresh graduates, still not appointed to a school, and four experienced (ranging from 19 to 30 years of experience) public school teachers. The group met many times online, often with their mentor and on their own, for brainstorming, trying to figure out ways to plan a scenario that would involve them all and be versatile enough to be implemented in very dissimilar settings. One of the settings was a social centre for creative art activities in Portugal, where one of the two younger teachers was spending the school year as a volunteer teacher. Another setting was a Greek language school in Poland, where one of the mature teachers was seconded. The third setting was an experimental public school attached to the university of a town in northwest Greece, where another experienced teacher was seconded. Of the rest, the two experienced teachers worked in rural public schools and the second younger teacher was not employed in an educational setting.

Decisions were taken through inclusive and democratic processes, aiming at satisfactory levels of consensus, despite overt differences. Younger teachers were surprised to realize that their voice was equally valued: 'We felt 100% included. The experienced teachers asked and respected our opinion, they said that we were the ideas, we brought the newest scientific developments in the field, and they often adopted our suggestions'. The experienced teachers were also happy to 'be exposed to fresh ideas' and felt 'vaccinated with new ideas that rejuvenated their practice'. This mutual respect contributed to enhanced and eager participation: 'The planning period of our scenario was an exciting, pleasant process; it had a certain charm, we talked for hours on ZOOM or VIBER, all ideas were heard and processed as equal'.

The implementation was conducted by the teachers appointed to the corresponding settings, with the rest of the teachers playing the role of critical friends to their colleagues through regular communication. For example, one member of the critical friends' team travelled to Warsaw and collaborated ad hoc for a few days. Teachers' shared responsibility for planning, implementing and assessing their scenarios was a source of strength and motivation and greatly enhanced their classroom performance, a fact highlighted in their interviews and evaluation. For example, one teacher noted 'I have benefitted and learnt a lot by working with people who use different approaches to teaching; I trusted them and took the risk of trying what works for them and adapting it to my style'.

Their scenario was based on the themes of compassion and solidarity. They aimed at cognitive goals (e.g. acquaint children with artists whose work reflects social, political, environmental and cultural concerns, introduce them to their methods, materials and techniques, their artistic vocabulary and symbolic language), emotional goals (e.g. facilitate children to acknowledge and express their emotions, understand the emotions of others, comprehend the impact of feelings on decision making and personal relationships) and social goals (e.g. communicate their ideas and concerns, develop empathy and solidarity for others, and assume social responsibility and action). Children were familiarized with artistic techniques, such as paper ageing and papier-mâché, to create their artworks. The activities designed involved children in observing, appreciating, interpreting, discussing and reflecting on the artists' and their own creations.

All the subgroups sought to accomplish the same objectives while making appropriate differentiations to adapt their lesson plans to the learning environments in which they were teaching. For instance, in Portugal, students came after school from different areas to study for the next day and be creatively involved for the rest of the time. Students' numbers fluctuated each day. That was a challenge that obliged the repetition of several activities in cycles to expose all students to the main activities and ideas each time, depriving some of the students of a deeper and more comprehensive understanding of the activity goals. Nevertheless, the level of participation of the children was very high (see Figures 7.1–7.4). The teacher cherished their enthusiasm for the programme and the collegial atmosphere created each time. Her own partnership with three of her colleagues at the Social Centre (not related to the programme), initially necessary due to her limited Portuguese language proficiency, developed into a dynamic collaboration. This 'unique experience' inspired her and worked as a model for the children. The children felt closer to her, trying to act as intermediaries for her language understanding. 'This exchange of languages, experiences and feelings gave me the sense that I participated with all of my senses' (interview quote). The teacher pointed out several highlights of the patterns of participation developed:

> To begin with, *I felt included* (*her emphasis*), which, I could see, was true for the children as well. Time after time, the children learnt more, talked more, understood more, and were rewarded. Yes, the atmosphere was inclusive, touchingly solidary.

And the teacher concluded:

> I cannot begin to describe how lucky and happy I feel to have met and collaborated with such a group of wonderful people. We 'planted' together the 'seed' of compassion and solidarity and hoped to see it grow to be a tree and then a whole forest, a proof that the location or the language do not really matter; what is essential is the desire to co-create.

Visual Arts for Inclusion in Diverse School Contexts

Figure 7.1: Communal artistic work by the subgroup in Portugal.

In Poland, the student population was steady, but they represented a wide array of ages, from 6 to 18 years, which posed a different challenge: differentiating the designed activities and making them attractive and appealing to the whole group. In any case, the broad age range did not affect the cohesion of the class; on the contrary, the mixed age/ability group worked harmoniously with gains for everyone: older students learnt the value of offering and collegiality, playing the role of mentors for the younger; the younger students were happy for the attention and the ensuing language growth. In a way, students were enacting the theme of the project they were involved in, i.e., compassion and solidarity.

As the teachers of the Polish project reported, they managed to achieve successfully the targets set by their professional group; the students were excited to be involved in the visual arts project and gained a deeper understanding of the value of collaboration; 'they realized that they needed each other's help to complete activities. They managed to voice their emotions. They recognized that they shared common feelings with many of their classmates, despite their differences' (interview quote). An added benefit was that the children's families were captured by their enthusiasm, and as a result, they showed keen interest in the project and its goals.

At the end of the school year, the children's artwork was displayed at a special function at the Greek Embassy in Warsaw. It was well attended by the children and their parents

Art, Sustainability and Learning Communities

Figure 7.2: Paper-ageing and torso by the subgroup in Ioannina, Greece.

Figure 7.3: Invitation and a sample image of the exhibition in Poland.

and honoured by the Ambassador and the Consul. It remained in exhibition till September 2021.

The title of the exhibition *I am because we are* triggered the visitors' curiosity, so children were engaged in conversations with visitors trying to explain, as their teachers reported, that 'compassion and solidarity make our world a better, more sustainable and fairer place to live in'. Parents confessed to the teachers that they were impressed at how children learned to listen and how they started to listen to their children more in return. They also observed reduced outbursts of anger and jealousy at home, which positively changed children's relationships with family members.

Figure 7.4: Children of the subgroup in Poland preparing their artworks for the exhibition.

In Greece, the students involved in the scenario implementation were very diverse in origin, with many in-group tensions, seriously disrupting the lesson's harmony, an 'explosive mix', according to their teacher. There was no class cohesion, and collaborations were rare and exclusive. As stressed in the teachers' interview, 'the programme worked miracles for that class. Even though most of the meetings [five out of seven] were online, the children showed keen and unwavering interest. In fact, they welcomed the challenge of working on completing artworks online'. Despite the confines of online classes, the teacher highlights eager participation: 'There was not even one child that did not participate, and we were amazed to see that all children were meaningfully involved'. The teacher shared a 'success story' of a reserved, secluded student girl 'who had never participated in anything before but was highly motivated and contributed to all these artistic activities enthusiastically'.

It is true that the necessity of online sessions failed to foster and reveal collaboration patterns among children in this class. The teachers regretted that the children missed the chance to collaborate to complete engaging activities in realistic settings and experience the development of inclusive, collaborative forms in this highly fragmented class. Even so, 'the students shared a common point of interest, i.e., the artwork they were viewing, discussing or creating that worked like the glue that attracted their attention' (interview quote). Among the discernible benefits that the children gained were 'their enhanced ability to observe closely and appreciate their classmates' contributions, value and take pride in their contributions, and accept and respect difference to a significant degree, which is a step towards the inclusive direction, I think' (interview quote).

Discussion

Teachers in this case study saw the potential of sharing common interests and values, a shared vision, and treasured their participation in the newly launched professional learning community; this boosted their self-esteem and gave them the confidence to engage in professional conversations and try out new ideas in their classes and careers. 'Even a small-scale project such as ours demands collaborations built firmly on principles and values, on a common vision and common goals that instigate and inspire people even at their everyday local level' (teacher report). Teachers acknowledged that the TTP liberated them to a greater or lesser degree from their fear of art, a result of their basic education that did not prepare them to use the arts in their practice, and this lack of knowledge was a source of anxiety and inhibition.

The equitable collaboration developed among participants in this study was an outcome they welcomed, but they did not expect: 'We were all honestly surprised at this spark, we were not aware we had it in us, the usual school culture did not foster alliances of this kind.' To the question of what might have triggered this welcome change, teachers unanimously agreed it was art. Visual arts were the perfect means of permeating and sustaining their ventures, liberating senses, impressions and ideas, bonding groups, and facilitating growth. Most teachers acknowledged that the collegial atmosphere and the sense of community they were sharing touched the children's interrelations as well.

Having relished the fruits of their collaboration, these teachers spontaneously opted to create inclusive learning communities for their students. Even in online classes that limit interactions, teachers noticed that children learnt how to take turns in talking and showed respect for and interest in their classmates' work and ideas. In the face-to-face sessions, teachers reported concrete gains in terms of the children's inclusive participation. They were thrilled to see students with poor performance or learning difficulties be meaningfully involved in every activity. Through their inclusion in group work, children increased their sociability, teamwork spirit and respect for the product of their work and the work of others. They realized that protecting public and common assets were their own obligation and opted to take initiatives and risks, thus increasing their responsibility and reliability.

Equitable inclusion and respectful partnerships were the main traits of this case study that would be interesting to duplicate in various settings and groups. Perhaps future research could investigate how these professionals, who were not previously related, managed to find common pacing in planning and implementing an intervention in their dissimilar settings when long-time colleagues in the same setting do not often rely on collaborations in their efforts to scaffold their students' learning more creatively and effectively. Furthermore, to find out if other conditions except visual arts can account for the paradigm shift in this case.

This brief intervention contained fractions of what Sleeter and Cornbleth (2011) call 'socially aware teaching', which 'is based on the idea that education is a resource for the public good, particularly in a democratic society' (p. 7). Socially aware teaching aims at building a community of learners that share common values: 'Educating young people for democratic participation in a diverse society entails fostering habits that enable them to hear and engage with diverse perspectives, including those that are routinely marginalized, and to practice working for justice' (Sleeter & Cornbleth, 2011, p. 7).

Ladson-Billings (2009) maintains that community building is 'a lifelong practice that extends beyond the classroom' (p. 78). Participating teachers worked consciously and eagerly to build safe and intellectually challenging learning communities. They invited their students to explore critically current social, environmental, political and economic issues, thus opting to contribute to the making of active citizens, who could secure a sustainable future for themselves and the world.

Concluding remarks

This case study, conducted at a time of a profound crisis that affected all sectors of private and public life, has both suffered and benefited from it. Almost all participants regretted functioning without the immediacy of face-to-face contact that deprived them of the joy of collegial live partnerships. The positive outcome of the pandemic confines was that it allowed teachers from various areas of the country/the world to participate.

In conclusion, VAE empowered and inspired this group of teachers, so diverse among themselves, to work creatively and systematically to fulfil a course requirement; in the process, by identifying and building on their abilities and imagination, they grew as professionals. Teachers felt they gained professional expertise through co-planning and teaching, mentor guidance, joint reflection, observation of colleagues and common efforts for professional growth. In addition, they recognized the need to create exciting learning communities that inspire all their members to imagine a sustainable, equitable future and work harmoniously together to accomplish their vision.

Notes

1. CARE, *Visual arts education in new times: Connecting Art with REal Life Issues* is an EU-funded, Erasmus + project (2019–22).
2. 'Ensure inclusive and equitable quality education and promote lifelong learning opportunities for all'.
3. Run by Frederick University in Cyprus, lead partner, University of Malta in Malta, Exeter University in the United Kingdom, and Aristotle University of Thessaloniki (AUTH) in Thessaloniki, Greece. http://care.frederick.ac.cy/

References

Bamford, A. (2006). *The wow factor: Global research compendium on the impact of arts in education*. Germany: Waxmann Verlag.

Bamford, A., & Wimmer, M. (2012). Audience building and the future Creative Europe Programme. *EENC Short Report*. https://www.interarts.net/publications/report-audience-building-and-the-future-creative-europe-programme/

Bashir, M.F., Ma, B., & Shahzad, L. (2020). A brief review of socio-economic and environmental impact of Covid-19. *Air Quality, Atmosphere, and Health, 13*, 1403–1409. https://doi.org/10.1007/s11869-020-00894-8

Corlett, R. T., Primack, R. B., Devictor, V., Maas, B., Goswami, V. R., Bates, A. E., ... Roth, R. (2020). Impacts of the coronavirus pandemic on biodiversity conservation. *Biological Conservation, 246*, 108571. https://doi.org/10.1016/j.biocon.2020.108571

Garrido-Cumbrera, M., Foley, R., Braçe, O., Correa-Fernández, J., López-Lara, E., Guzman, V., ... Hewlett, D. (2021). Perceptions of change in the natural environment produced by the first wave of the COVID-19 pandemic across three European countries. Results from the GreenCOVID study. *Urban Forestry & Urban Greening, 64*, 127260. https://doi.org/10.1016/j.ufug.2021.127260

Goldberg, M. (2001). *Arts and learning: An integrated approach to teaching and learning in multicultural and multilingual settings* (2nd ed.). New York, NY: Addison Wesley Longman.

Hunter, M. A. (2005). *Education and the arts: Research overview*. Sydney: Commonwealth of Australia.

Ioannidou, M. (2014). 'Web-ism': A new art movement for e-generation children. *Eurasian Journal of Social Sciences, 2*(2), 15–21. https://doi.org/10.15604/ejjss.2014.02.02.002

Ioannidou, M., & Mitakidou, S. (2018). Taking tableaux vivants a step further: Using multicultural and cross-readings of living pictures and literature texts in class. In *IAI Academic Conference Proceedings Education and Social Sciences*, Université de la Sorbonne Nouvelle, Paris (pp. 6–14). https://ia-institute.com/iai-academic-conference-proceedings-paris-2018/

Johnson, R. B., & Onwuegbuzie, A. J. (2004). Mixed methods research: A research paradigm whose time has come. *Educational Researcher, 33*, 14–26. https://doi.org/10.3102/0013189X033007014

Knif, L., & Kairavuori, S. (2020). Student teachers building a sustainable future through constructing equality in visual arts education. *Discourse and Communication for Sustainable Education, 11*(1), 74–90. https://doi.org/10.2478/dcse-2020-0008

Ladson-Billings, G. (2009). *The dream-keepers*. New York, NY: John Wiley & Sons, Inc.

LaJevic, L. (2013). Arts integration: What is really happening in the elementary classroom? *Journal for Learning Through the Arts, 9*(1), 1–30.

Leal Filho, W., Price, E., Wall, T., Shiel, C., Azeiteiro, U., Mifsud, M., ... LeVasser, T. J. (2021). COVID-19: The impact of a global crisis on sustainable development teaching. *Environment, Development and Sustainability, 23*, 11257–11278. https://doi.org/10.1007/s10668-020-01107-z

Levitas, R. (2003). The idea of social inclusion. In *2003 Social Inclusion Research Conference*. Kanata, ON: Canadian Council on Social Development. http://www.ccsd.ca/events/inclusion/papers

Mahato, S., Pal, S., & Ghosh, K. G. (2020). Effect of lockdown amid COVID-19 pandemic on air quality of the megacity Delhi, India. *Science of the Total Environment, 730*, 139086. https://doi.org/10.1016/j.scitotenv.2020.139086

Mitakidou, S., & Tressou, E. (2017). The arts as a vehicle to school literacy. In *EDULEARN17 Proceedings of 9th International Conference on Education and New Learning Technologies*, Barcelona (pp. 1157–1161). https://library.iated.org/view/MITAKIDOU2017ART. IATED

Nurse, K. (2006). Culture as the fourth pillar of sustainable development. *Small States: Economic Review and Basic Statistics, 11*, 28–40. https://doi.org/10.14217/smalst-2007-en

Rousseau, S., & Deschacht, N. (2020). Public awareness of nature and the environment during the COVID-19 crisis. *Environmental and Resource Economics, 76*, 1149–1159.

Sleeter, C. E., & Cornbleth, C. (Eds.). (2011). *Teaching with vision: Culturally responsive teaching in standards-based classrooms*. New York, NY: Teachers College Press.

Sonetti, G., Barioglio, C., & Campobenedetto, D. (2020). Education for sustainability in practice: A review of current strategies within Italian universities. *Sustainability, 12*, 5246. https://doi.org/10.3390/su12135246

Vella, R. (Ed.). (2022). *Integrating principles of education for sustainable development into visual art education in teacher education programmes*. Cyprus: Frederick University.

UNESCO. (2010). *The Seoul Agenda: Goals for the development of arts education*. https://unesdoc.unesco.org/ark:/48223/pf0000190692

UNESCO. (2020). *Press release*. https://www.unesco.org/en/articles/unesco-report-inclusion-education-shows-40-poorest-countries-did-not-provide-specific-support

UNESCO. (n.d.). *Press release*. https://en.unesco.org/gem-report/sites/default/files/2020_Press_Release_EN.pdf

UNICEF. (2020a). *Educate a child*. https://www.unicef.org/partnerships/educate-a-child

UNICEF. (2020b). *COVID-19 – Are children able to continue learning during school closures? A global analysis of the potential reach of remote learning policies using data from 100 countries*. New York, NY: United Nations Children's Fund. https://data.unicef.org/resources/remote-learning-reachability-factsheet

United Nations. (2020). *In face of pandemic, 100 million people worldwide on brink of extreme poverty*. https://www.un.org/press/en/2020/gaef3534.doc.htm

Chapter 8

Envisioning Better Futures: Integrating Sustainability Practices Into Museum Education for Elementary Student Teachers

Victoria Pavlou and Chrysanthi Kadji-Beltran

The international community is now committed to sustainable development (SD) as a vision that incorporates responses to the most pressing modern environmental, economic and social issues that humanity is facing. United Nations 2030 Agenda for Sustainable Development and its seventeen sustainable development goals (SDGs) are certainly the most ambitious and widely accepted political texts to guide efforts towards this vision. Quality education (target 4.7) and education for sustainable development (ESD) in particular, is the vehicle that will lead the SDGs' roadmap and promote the Agenda 2030 as a whole (UN General Assembly, 2019).

To address SD issues, we need competent and committed educators, 'multipliers', who can act as change agents for SD in the different educational sectors. In teacher education programmes, we need to see ESD as an important and full component of teacher professionalism and integrate it into different disciplines (Dahl, 2019; Timm & Barth, 2021) so that teachers will infuse ESD into their curricula and school practice and not simply have it as an additional component (González, 2021). This chapter provides an example of how ESD can enrich museum education in the context of teacher education. We focus on developing elementary preservice teachers' ESD competences by responding to artworks and by engaging them in curriculum design and instruction activities in museum/gallery settings that will enable them to transfer these competences to their future learners.

Museum education

The educational role of cultural institutions and learning outside school is an established and well-known reality. Museums, as active preservers and interpreters of culture, are exciting places for visitors; they tell us stories about the objects they hold and the research they undertake in a diversity of ways (Hein, 1998). The new museology in the 2000s highlights further that museums are more than simple spaces for learning and more than places of preserving memory; they are spaces of experiences, critical thinking, discussion and coming together where the aim is to connect the past with the present. The new museology also values representation, access and providing opportunities to create, preserve and distribute human values for the benefit of society (Nikonanou, Bounia, Filippoupoliti, Chourmouziadis, & Giannoutsou, 2015). Museums offer unique learning environments, which have the potential to shape identities, encourage active participation and educate for future citizenship. Visitors – through access to objects – receive information and knowledge that relates to them, their culture and that of others, in ways that encourage new connections and provide meaningful learning (Falk & Dierking, 2000).

School trips are critical in influencing lifelong visiting habits, and educational authorities in many countries often encourage or even require schools to visit museums, ensuring thus a number of visits. Evidence on the benefits of these visits on children is nevertheless limited, while research shows that teachers are often unprepared to make the most of such visits and are not confident in their ability to use museum collections to teach critically and creatively, despite acknowledging their educational potential (Robins & Woodland, 2005; Talboys, 2012). Teachers appear to have little training relating to the processes involved in planning and preparing school visits in museums and tend to rely completely on the museum staff (Behrendt & Franklin, 2014). However, not all museums have educational departments or museum educators to support teachers (Zbuchea, 2013). While museum educators should be the experts in implementing the new museology, their position/profession is not well established in the organizational structures of museums (Kristinsdóttir, 2017). Thus, the main responsibility for organizing meaningful school trips to the museum lies with teachers (Robins & Woodland, 2005).

Sustainability practices in museum education

Museums have the potential to embrace SD since their mission is about collecting, conserving, researching and exhibiting the tangible and intangible heritage of humanity and its environment for the purposes of education, from generation to generation, linking the past, the present and the future and thus forming the core of cultural sustainability (Brown & Mairesse, 2018). Cultural sustainability, in the context of museums, can be identified in seven specific parameters: heritage preservation, cultural skills and knowledge, memory/identity, new audiences/inclusion, cultural diversity/intercultural dialogue, creativity and innovation, and artistic vitality (Stylianou-Lambert et al., 2014). Despite the obvious connections between museums, culture and sustainability, not much research has examined how museum education might fit into cultural sustainability and, in particular, how teachers – as a significant group of stakeholders that visit museums with their classes – might contribute to different aspects of cultural sustainability by organizing school trips to museums. It is important to consider what museums and their exhibitions can bring to ESD (Ott, 2014) and in particular what is the role of higher educational institutions in preparing and supporting preservice teachers to understand the potential of using museums and their resources in ESD. In the context of this chapter and the case study presented next we aimed to explore:

> What kind of competences (knowledge, skills and dispositions) do preservice teachers need to have in museum education in order to embrace sustainability practices?

Can preservice teachers explore the museum parameters of memory/identity, creativity, innovation and artistic vitality to develop curriculum units for their future learners by integrating sustainability issues/practices?

Background

The study took place within the context of the compulsory 'museum education' course that is offered during the four-year Bachelor's degree in elementary education at Frederick University in Cyprus. The museum education course aims to increase preservice teachers' confidence in their ability to use museums and their collections as educational resources. It is an interdisciplinary course that embraces knowledge, skills and attitudes gained in many different subject matter areas. It offers opportunities for students to engage with a variety of cultural institutions and having first-hand experiences with interpreting exhibits and visiting museums/galleries is an integrated part of the delivery of the course. It takes into consideration stereotypes or misconceptions that preservice teachers might have about the role of museums and of visitors due to their past experiences and in particular participant passivity (Kristinsdóttir, 2017).

The purpose of the course is:

- to enable students to understand the important role of cultural institutions and out-of-school activities in the well-rounded education of children.
- to provide them with the basic principles for planning and organizing meaningful school visits to cultural institutions by adopting learning theories related to active, experiential, free-choice and interdisciplinary learning.
- to infuse SD issues within their planning of educational interventions in museums.

The first two goals were always part of the course, since its introduction, more than ten years ago while the third goal is a new one aiming to align with current calls for building teachers' capacities in preparing children for the varied and interrelated environmental, social and economic challenges they will meet as they confront the changing world (Bell, 2016). The museum education course curriculum was reviewed to meet this goal with the collaboration among the two authors; a specialist in art and museum education and a specialist in ESD. The curriculum alignment included reflection on learning outcomes and introduction of ESD concepts within them, addition of transversal competences (which were ESD competences proposed by the RSP model for teacher education; Vare et al., 2019), enrichment of content to include SDGs within the big ideas addressed, and use of common pedagogical approaches between ESD and museum education.

The case study described next focuses on the visit to the Limassol Municipality Gallery, a gallery that presents challenges for the students as it adopts a traditional way of presenting its collections, with emphasis on object preservation rather than on visitors' connections with the collections (Stylianou-Lambert et al., 2014). The Gallery has no educational department and no specialized personnel for museum education. It hosts the National Revolution Tribute collection, a series of artworks about Greek-Cypriots' struggle for independence during 1955–59.[1] The Gallery was purposefully chosen because of the uniqueness of its collections, its potential to bring to life Greek-Cypriot history through artworks, to deal with issues of history/memory and offer meaningful connections between the present and the past. As a topic, it is connected to SD as it concerns peace and justice, goals that are prerequisites for the achievement of all the rest. Engaging with and interpreting artworks related to these issues can be beneficial in simultaneously developing systemic thinking, empathy, critical and creative competences. Apart from honouring the sacrifice of people for a better future (freedom), it has the potential to promote future thinking by inviting visitors to contemplate how they envision their own future today.

The case study

Ten senior students, seven women and three men, aged 21–37 years were enrolled in the course during the academic year 2020–21. Six of them were Cypriots (Greek-Cypriots) and four of them were Greeks. This was the only physical visit that took place because of the COVID-19 pandemic. Next, the activities that took place before, during and after the visit are described. These present the pedagogical approaches that were adopted to promote learning in museums, connecting the past with the present and the future while supporting the development of systemic, empathy, future, critical and creative competences.

The visit to the Limassol Municipal Art Gallery

1. Pre-visit activities

Prior to the visit, the students (preservice teachers) were introduced to basic concepts of museum education and learning in museums through presentations, readings and examples of activities for children within art gallery settings. To this end, the students were invited to recall past knowledge and experiences from their art education courses. They were also invited to respond to artworks that deal with the SDGs and to talk about the activist role of art in society, such as the sculpture *Follow the leaders* by Isaac Cordal[2] showing politicians discussing global warming and street art in Melilla, Spain by BLU,[3] showing the European Union (EU) flag as a barbed wire that prevents people to enter EU. Using the artworks as a springboard, the students were also challenged to recall past knowledge and experiences from their ESD courses. Further, through a presentation about sustainability competences the students were asked to explore ESD competences that could be addressed through viewing artworks. The process of connecting the viewing of an artwork and its concept with a big idea, one SDG and ESD competences proved to be a challenge for the students. Their explanation of their work was short, and they needed several prompts to elaborate. It appeared that they had compartmentalized their knowledge by course (e.g. knowledge gained during the sustainable education course and knowledge gained during the art education course), and it was difficult for them to bring that knowledge together (Spectre, 2019). Therefore, they were invited to develop concept maps to explore ideas connecting the artworks and the SDGs. This resulted in an enhanced ability to elaborate on their responses to the artworks and also search for other artworks that might connect with SDGs.

2. Activities during the visit

The purpose of the visit was to challenge students' attitudes towards museum visits and also build knowledge and understanding of the potential of museum learning to contribute to children's empowerment by improving dialogue and understanding, empathy, criticality and creativity. Further, the chosen artworks could easily connect with big ideas and SDGs. The visit included experiential and active engagement with selected artworks, first from the different collections of the gallery and secondly from the National Revolution Tribute collection.

In part A, students were invited to respond to selected artworks by playing games, immersing themselves in the artworks, enacting figures of the artworks, listening to music and making imaginary trips, dressing up and making sketches. All students engaged actively in all activities; they gave in-depth descriptions of the artworks, offered their own interpretations, laughed at the enactment of dialogues, dressed up and took magical trips. Critical and creative thinking along with the ability to collaborate and show empathy towards the figures in the artworks was also evident in their responses. During the post-course interview (a couple of months after the end of the semester), students reflected on their feelings regarding the first part:

- The activities were so enjoyable that I could remember them while reading about our final exams (*she laughs*)!! And I caught myself laughing while remembering my classmates enacting the dialogue of a woman in the fields and a superintendent. It was then that I truly understand what you meant when you were talking about making children active learners in a museum, and let them play in the museum.
- I enjoyed the activities regarding the life under water! The materials that we used to immerse into the painting, the sounds and the music enabled us to make an imaginary dive into the bottom of the sea.

- So, different experiences from what I had before in a museum!!! When I was a child, my teachers never did anything like these. We (*children*) simply saw exhibits and they (*teachers*) talked to us.

In part B, upon entering the hall of the National Revolution Tribute collection, students started commenting on the mood of the artworks, which was much more serious than those viewed before. In the beginning, there was puzzlement about the purpose of the collection. However, soon they found enough clues in the artworks to understand that the collection was a tribute to the Greek-Cypriot liberation struggle. They all engaged deeply with the first artwork that was chosen, answered prompts, wondered and posed questions, and offered their own interpretations. Identifying symbols in the artwork and attributing personal meaning appeared easier than before. It was also easy to identify the big idea, that of freedom and human rights. However, they found it hard to make any connections with sustainable living or sustainable societies as the misconception of the mono-dimensional environmental interpretation of sustainability apparently dominated their understanding. Further, students were divided into three groups, given the opportunity to choose an artwork as a group, have a private encounter with the artwork and then work collaboratively to reach a shared understanding and interpretation. Students had vivid discussions about the artworks, took notes and made sketches (Figure 8.1).

Figure 8.1: Example of an artwork that deals with SDG 16: EU borders as a circle with barbed wire that replaces the stars of the EU flag (mural by Italian street artist BLU in Melilla, Spain).

They were also invited to share their interpretations with the other groups. The students appeared to have a beautified (embellished) image of the liberation struggle. However, the artworks in front of them were communicating emotions of pain, sadness, death, unfulfilled dreams and abrupt loss of life. During the post-course interview, students noted:

- Every year when I was at school, we talked about the fight for independence against British rule. But I had never felt so emotional before. I felt awe at the gallery. It was the first time I truly understood their contribution and their sacrifice for the ideal of freedom.
- I didn't know much about the Cypriots' struggle for freedom. And what we did at the gallery is something that is imprinted in me. The artworks were so powerful that I would never forget whatever we saw, discussed and did in the gallery.
- Listening to some contextual information about the struggle after seeing the artwork, I shivered … I really felt their sacrifice.

3. Post-visit activities

After the visit, the students were asked to reflect on the visit, discuss particular artworks and connect the artworks with big ideas and subsequently with SDGs. The students reported enjoyment and surprise because they could 'play' with the artworks. They also talked about the concept of the artworks and managed to connect these with big ideas. For example, they connected an artwork that depicted women working in the fields in the 1950s with women's place in society in Cyprus in the past and the present and thus with SDG5 'Gender equality'. Also, an artwork depicting the bottom of the sea was connected with the pollution of water and thus with SDG17 'Life under water'. Finally, the artworks from the National Tribute Collection were connected with the big idea of freedom, with imagining a better future and with SDG16 'Peace, justice and strong institutions'. To support connections with SDG16, students retrieved information from past courses on ESD and were asked to draw concept maps connecting the ideas of independence (the result of the Greek-Cypriots' struggle), identity (Greek-Cypriot identity) and sustainability. The concept maps provided evidence that the students started to better understand potential connections, leading to systemic thinking (Figure 8.2).

Finally, the students were given the task of developing an educational programme for children that would include a visit to the National Tribute Collection of the Gallery. The programme's title was 'I envision a better future', an important underlying aspect of all SDGs, of the key principles of ESD (think holistically, envision change, achieve transformation) and the ESD competences (Vare et al., 2019). A template was given (see Table 8.1) to the students to develop their assignment, which was an adaptation of the template format proposed by Pavlou and Kadji-Beltran (2021) on how to develop resources that enrich art education activities with sustainability pedagogies.

Figure 8.2: Students making sketches in the gallery setting.

Envisioning Better Futures

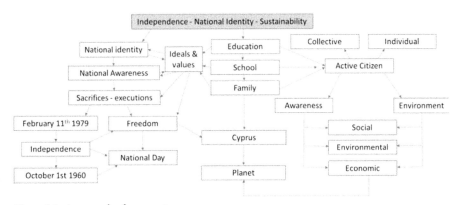

Figure 8.3: An example of a concept map.

Table 8.1: Template for developing the assignment.

Educational programme	I envision a better future
School-subjects	Art, … (*add*)
Class	
Duration	
Big idea	Explain the concept of developing this unit. WHY? Explain the big ideas/key concepts you want to work on with children. WHAT? Indicate briefly what the unit will include HOW? Mention your methodology at school and the gallery
Transversal aims	Connect the big idea with the purpose of education in general. What kind of future citizens do we want to have?
Specific aims	Include aims that are specifically connected with the subjects you will integrate for developing this unit of lessons.
Evaluation	How will you know that your goals were achieved?
Before the visit	Lesson plan 1: School subject, Aims, time, resources, class organization, activities
During the visit	Lesson plan 2: Aims, time, resources, class organization, activities
After the visit	Lesson plan 3: School subject, Aims, time, resources, class organization, activities

Assessment

In this section, we explore preservice teachers' ability to use the museum parameters of memory/identity, creativity, innovation and artistic vitality to develop curriculum units

Table 8.2: Scoring rubric for assessing the assignment.

1 – Insufficient	The issue is incomplete, or there is no description, or the information is unclear. A little familiarity with how children learn. Little integration of the planning with sustainability issues.
2 – Improvement needed	The issue is addressed, but it is poorly written, or it is not convincing. There is somewhat familiarity with how children learn. There is some thinking about sustainability issues.
3 – Effective	The issue is clearly addressed, and there is consistency, but some detail is lacking. There is a good grasp of how children learn. There is good integration of sustainability issues.
4 – Highly effective	The issue is clear, appropriately addressed, well-structured and well-thought. There is a very good grasp of how children learn. There is an effective integration of sustainability issues.

connected to sustainability issues. A rubric was used to assess the assignment. Each issue received a score in the one to four range.

One assignment received a total score below 50 per cent, which was considered unacceptable since several pieces of information were missing and several issues were incomplete or unclear. The student was fascinated by the historical facts of the National Tribute Collection and focused on national identity issues but from a very traditional, teacher-centred point of view. The student's views were not 'translated' into child-centred, concrete, valid lesson plans that endorsed sustainability issues. Three assignments received a score between 51 and 70 per cent, and they needed improvement. These assignments included inconsistencies. There were some acceptable objectives, some familiarity with standards and assessment and some integration of sustainability issues, but at the same time, some key points of the units were not convicting or were poorly written. Four assignments received a score between 70 and 86 per cent and were considered effective. They were clear and consistent. Some detail was lacking, and at times, it was difficult for a third party to follow the development of the unit, but otherwise, they were well-structured. Two assignments received a score over 86 per cent and were considered exemplary. They were clear, appropriate, well-structured, consistent, well-thought and rich in resources. There was a logical flow of activities, enough details for a third party to understand the development of the unit, and they included appropriate, interesting and engaging activities for the age group of children that the unit was planned for.

While only two assignments were considered to be 'highly effective' and four were 'effective', further qualitative analysis of the assignments in terms of the most cited aims and methodological approaches revealed interesting findings for most students (eight out of ten). In relation to the aims, students focused both on knowledge and competences, especially on the competence of empathy that related to emotions and values; of criticality that related to the critical interpretation of artworks; and of future thinking that related to the concept of active citizens. Further, they embraced interdisciplinarity and developed programmes that integrated the visit to the Gallery with art, history, language and health education lessons. Regarding methodological approaches that provide space and time for learners to share their voice and insights, students used pedagogies that endorsed the new museology, and in particular, participatory pedagogies, active and experiential learning, as well as free-choice learning (in the gallery setting) and they valued the learners' own interpretations. Activities included analysis of (including discussions around) videos, photographs, artworks, songs and poems as well as enactment/making 'alive' artworks, creative writing, creating artworks and drawing concept maps. The latter also functioned as evaluation activities, since the students noted that they would like to employ creative methodologies for their evaluation activities as these were more appropriate for evaluating competences.

Finally, four students enriched their planning with a more global view. One student included a discussion on indigenous people's rights after viewing a part of a Disney movie in the pre-visit lesson plan. Another student included a discussion activity on today's 'struggles' of people in other countries connected to what children learn through media in the post-visit lesson plan. Two other students included discussions about how the pandemic has influenced our lives today, focusing on human rights and obligations, individual rights and the common good, in their post-visit lesson plan. To conclude, the fact that students' planning included (a) aims related to both knowledge and transversal competences, (b) methodologies that embrace interdisciplinary and participatory, active and experiential pedagogies, and (c) discussion on issues from both local and global points of view provided evidence of preservice teacher professionalism (Dahl, 2019).

Discussion

This chapter contemplates the competences (knowledge, skills and dispositions) that preservice teachers need to have in museum education to embrace sustainability practices and develop meaningful curriculum units for their future students. The activities and assignments presented highlight opportunities and challenges for two important aspects of teacher training: the development of preservice teachers' own competences and the development of their professionalism in designing appropriate museum educational programmes. Regarding systemic thinking, students were able to identify the level of complexity and look for interconnections between the concepts of 'Independence – Identity – Sustainable living' by developing concept maps. They also used different forms of thinking and logic to aid analysis, such as scientific methods and artistic interpretation. However, there was no evidence in their planning regarding their ability to develop their future learners' systemic thinking. Regarding empathy, there was evidence for their own development as well as for the development of their future learners' empathy. Preservice teachers embraced activities that were affective and focused on values, such as interpretation of artworks and role-play, and they listened actively and authentically to others and built on each other's views. They used their imagination to put themselves in the position of others. Consequently, they were able to plan learning activities that encouraged learners to listen to their own emotions and those of others, to apply strategies for dealing with emotions of pain and sadness as well as hope and happiness. A similar finding was noted regarding the futures thinking competence. Preservice teachers were able to creatively imagine several different future scenarios related to sustainable living and plan similar activities in the unit they developed. However, in both cases, they avoided using the term 'sustainable living' and preferred the term 'social issues' or 'social challenges'. The competence of criticality was mainly identified in the critical viewing and interpretation of artworks and partly in the identification of other relevant sources for developing their assignments. Lastly, regarding the creativity competence, preservice teachers demonstrated creative interpretations of artworks and recognized the opportunities for creatively building an educational programme around the given task. They used creative and innovative teaching techniques, positioning the teaching processes in the real world and facilitating a process of generating new ideas and inviting the learners to create artworks, write poems or letters and enact roles.

In light of these findings as well as the evidence provided regarding preservice teacher professionalism in the previous section, it is worth contemplating the role that teachers can have in influencing museums' approaches, given that some museums – including the ones in this study – do not have museum specialists. This largely depends on how schools and museums may establish partnerships without museum education specialists, which is an unmapped territory that future research might address. Exploring the connections between formal education curricula and museums' thematic areas and mission could also highlight areas where educational programmes in the museums can be developed in support of formal education and with the employment of ESD competences.

An inquiry that emerges from the reflections above poses the question: What were the most important factors that significantly impacted the changes observed? Why do we consider that museums, their exhibitions and the educational programmes in museums can have an important contribution to achieving SDGs and connecting school life with real-life needs (Ott, 2014)? Art collections about historical events have the potential to move beyond the facts into the way people in the past experienced the events (focus on emotions and values) and thus be valuable SD educational resources. Preservice teachers had an optimal experience in the gallery setting which was interesting enough to have a deep concentration/engagement, and mobilized their senses (visual, kinesthetic, audio), their cognitive side (reason, historical knowledge) and their emotional side (empathy, feelings). In other words, they experienced *flow* in what they were doing (Csikszentmihalyi, 2015), which influenced their curriculum planning. Preservice teachers 'played' with the exhibits, enjoyed the process and were immersed in the activities; they experienced challenging active learning through participatory practices that embodied ESD methodologies, free-choice learning, etc.

Flow theory can point the way if our goal is to improve the quality of life and education. We need teacher training that invites learners/future teachers to immerse into activities, intensively concentrate, and as a result, experience intrinsic motivation, which propels critical thinking and creativity (Csikszentmihalyi, 2015). Training to teach for a sustainable society should be a component in teacher education programmes (Dahl, 2019) and this case study exemplified how this aspect of teacher professionalism can become a part of teacher education, especially in disciplines such as museum education. The museum education course adopted a dual focus; on the one hand, it focused on content, pedagogy and teaching approaches in museum education – a technical-rational model for teacher professionality – and, on the other hand, it focused on values and ethics through the SD context – a creative-interpretive model for teacher professionality (Dahl, 2019; Martin, Summers, & Sjerps-Jones, 2007). This combined focus led to reconsidering pedagogy and identifying aspects of creative teaching-learning situations conducive to preservice teacher engagement. Consequently, preservice teachers worked in planning curriculum units that could increase learner engagement, maximize learning opportunities and restore creativity (Csikszentmihalyi, 2015). The full potential of the course was not really explored as the study coincided with the COVID-19 pandemic and no further physical visits to museums/galleries than the one described in the chapter were made.

Future challenges

So why did a group of students that had already attended an ESD course find it difficult at the beginning to integrate ESD into museum education?

Museum education, per se, is a non-formal type of education, drawing from innovative contexts and educational approaches. This fact on its own is challenging for an inexperienced preservice teacher. The compartmentalization of teacher education curricula and formal education overall places an additional burden as it operates as a role model for preservice teachers and hinders the development of a holistic and transdisciplinary way of approaching a topic. Thus, preservice teachers face challenges in putting theory into practice and although aware of the connections and the benefits, these cannot be fully reflected in their lessons. The implications for teacher education are huge if we consider that higher education needs to uproot the traditional limiting practice that supports unsustainability and revolutionize education through new educational paradigms. We need to practise what we preach, and we need more courses that exceed the frontiers of their disciplines and enable a broader, critical, systemic eye-opening way of thinking. Education is challenging, and preparing preservice teachers to respond to future demands in a creative way is important. Otherwise, they would feel that the situation is too complex and will not be able to know what to do about it.

Notes

1. Cyprus' history of occupation by different rulers is quite rich since the ancient times. In 1878, Cyprus was placed under the British Empire ruling. The future of the island became a matter of disagreement between the two prominent ethnic communities, Greek Cypriots, who made up 77 per cent of the population in 1960, and Turkish Cypriots, who made up 18 per cent of the population. From the nineteenth century onwards, the Greek Cypriot population pursued *enosis*, union with Greece. Following the Greek Cypriots' national struggle for freedom during 1955–59, Cyprus was granted independence in 1960.
2. https://streetartutopia.com/2021/09/28/politicians-discussing-climate-change/
3. https://streetartnews.net/2012/04/blu-new-mural-in-melila-spain.html

References

Behrendt, M., & Franklin T. (2014). A review of research on school field trips and their value in education. *International Journal of Environmental and Science Education, 9*(3), 235–245.

Bell, D. (2016). Twenty-first century education: Transformative education for sustainability and responsible citizenship. *Journal of Teacher Education for Sustainability, 18*(1), 48–56.

Brown, K., & Mairesse, F. (2018). The definition of the museum through its social role. *Curator: The Museum Journal, 61*(4), 525–539.

Csikszentmihalyi, M. (2015). *The systems model of creativity: The collected works of Mihaly Csikszentmihalyi*. New York, NY: Springer.

Dahl, T. (2019). Prepared to teach for sustainable development? Student teachers' beliefs in their ability to teach for sustainable development. *Sustainability, 11*(7), 1993.

Falk, J., & Dierking, L. (2000). *Learning from museums*. Lanham, MD: Altamira Press

González, E. P. (2021). Toward education for sustainable development: Lessons from Asia and the Americas. In R. Iyengar, & C.T. Kwauk (Eds.), *Curriculum and learning for climate action* (pp. 291–308). Leiden: Brill.

Hein, G. (1998). *Learning in the museum*. New York, NY: Routledge.

Kristinsdóttir, A. (2017). Toward sustainable museum education practices: Confronting challenges and uncertainties. *Museum Management and Curatorship, 32*(5), 424–439.

Martin, K., Summers, D., & Sjerps-Jones, H. (2007). Sustainability and teacher education. *Journal of Further and Higher Education, 31*(4), 351–362.

Nikonanou, N., Bounia, A., Filippoupoliti, A., Chourmouziadis, A., & Giannoutsou, N. (2015). *Museum learning and experience in the 21st century [in Greek]*. Athens: Association of Greek Academic Libraries.

Ott, A. (2014). *Museums, learning centers and education for sustainable development: Practices and possibilities in the Oslo area* [Master's Thesis]. University of Oslo.

Pavlou, V., & Kadji-Beltran, C. (2021). Enhancing arts education with education for sustainable development competences: A proposed framework for visual arts education educators. In

E. Wagner, C. S. Nielsen, L. Veloso, T. Suominen, & N. Pachova (Eds.), *Arts. Sustainability. Education. ENO yearbook* (Vol. 2, pp. 217–235). Berlin: Springer Verlag.

Robins, C., & Woodland, V. (2005). *Creative connections: Teaching and learning in museums and galleries*. London: Art Design and Museology Department, IOE, University of London.

Spectre, L. (2019). Compartmentalized knowledge. *Philosophical Studies, 176*(10), 2785–2805.

Stylianou-Lambert, T., Boukas, N., & Christodoulou-Yerali, M. (2014). Museums and cultural sustainability: Stakeholders, forces, and cultural policies. *International Journal of Cultural Policy, 20*(5), 566–587.

Talboys, G. (2012). *Using museums as an educational resource: An introductory handbook for students and teachers*. Farnham: Ashgate Publishing Ltd.

Timm, J. M., & Barth, M. (2021). Making education for sustainable development happen in elementary schools: The role of teachers. *Environmental Education Research, 27*(1), 50–66.

UN General Assembly. (2019). Political declaration of the high-level political forum on sustainable development convened under the auspices of the General Assembly. Resolution adopted by the General Assembly on 15 October 2019. A/RES/74/4. https://undocs.org/en/A/RES/74/4

Vare, P., Arro, G., De Hamer, A., Del Gobbo, G., De Vries, G., Farioli, F., ... & Zachariou, A. (2019). Devising a competence-based training program for educators of sustainable development: Lessons learned. *Sustainability, 11*(7), 1890.

Zbuchea, A. (2013). Human resources management in education department of museums: A worldwide survey. *Management & marketing. Challenges for the Knowledge Society, 8*, 479–510.

Chapter 9

Drawing and the Global Climate Emergency: Affective and Connective Explorations

Chris Turner and Emese Hall

Introduction

In this chapter, we propose that by embracing a pedagogy founded on the theory of aesthoecology (Turner, 2019), drawing activity brings together the aesthetic (*affective*) and the ecological (*connected*) in a powerful way through which to examine the potentiality of an unknown and *emerging future*. Drawing, in all its forms, is a journey of discovery. Fundamental to the act of drawing is line making (Ingold, 2016) and through drawing as a form of intellectual play (Wood & Hall, 2011), we suggest that the ideas, observations and questions of emergence are exemplified. Not knowing is to be valued.

A condensed explanation of aesthoecology in this introduction cannot do justice to its nuances, but it is notable that the words in italics in the previous paragraph are essential components. One of our key arguments is this: as an onto-epistemology, aesthoecology encompasses beliefs about ways of being with ways of knowing and it has profound educational implications. To expand briefly upon our ontological interests, which must come first, 'in considering aesthetics and ecology, we are always brought back to a philosophy of life itself' (Turner, 2019, p. 57). Following this, in terms of epistemology, we hold that 'education is the process of bringing learning into consciousness and, in order to do so, a connectivity is required' (Turner, 2019, p. 75). Art connects us in our common humanity, and we will provide some illustration of how an aesthoecologically informed approach to art in schools, here with a particular focus on drawing, offers immense scope for young people's connectivity and learning.

We are framing our proposal within the context of issues-based art education (IBAE), in which topics of study are external to art as a discipline – learning through the subject is foregrounded. IBAE offers a useful and meaningful approach to contemporary art education where teachers are looking to enhance students' knowledge and understanding of what it means to be a global citizen in the twenty-first century. Reiterating the significance of our theoretical stance, 'Aesthoecology adds value to an understanding of our global scale of existence and the impact, individually and collectively, we have on the future' (Turner, 2019, p. 163). We focus on the global climate emergency in this chapter, as it is an issue with which all readers are likely to be familiar and one that is especially 'visible' and pertinent. Young people's concern about the global climate emergency must be harnessed in a positive and careful manner.

Crucially, at this time of global crisis concerning the future of our planet (Laininen, 2019), we stress an urgent need to question the purpose of education, to ensure that young people are equipped with the necessary knowledge, understanding, skills – and sensitivities – to make a positive difference as change agents (Jimenez & Moorhead, 2001). Although we are far from alone in making this assertion, our chapter offers a fresh perspective and brings together the following fields of interest: IBAE, the global climate emergency; aesthoecology; and drawing activity. As we have only recently started to explore these ideas through reading, reflection and dialogue, we must clarify that the discussion here is more tentative than certain. The chapter is organized to address the four topics in the order listed above, but we wish to highlight that there is no intended hierarchy, and considerable overlaps to exist.

IBAE

It is notable that debates in contemporary art education increasingly tend to focus on topics that are broader than the subject. This shift away from an academic interest in art-specific knowledge and skills seems to reflect a 'global' educational perspective and a desire to underline art's versatility and universal relevance. Although this agenda might be welcomed, there is a counter-perspective, because too frequently art educators find themselves having to justify the relevance of their subject to address misconceptions about its educational role and value (Payne & Hall, 2018). IBAE is likely to be engaging for students, but adds complication for the teacher in terms of scope because choosing topics of study can be time-consuming, with so many possibilities vying for attention (Smith, 2011). Issues explored within IBAE can be local, national, international or global; we suggest that no one of these categories is more important than another, from an educational perspective, but different in scale and affording its own opportunities and challenges (Hall, 2019). We contend that a transdisciplinary approach to curriculum design and pedagogy is one way to integrate and co-create knowledge of the global crisis (Mauser et al., 2013).

One opportunity in IBAE is to emphasize how art can be used as a learning vehicle to connect to other curriculum areas (Turner & Hall, 2021). This could lead to increased visibility for art, especially within other subject departments in secondary schools, and invite teachers to consider transdisciplinary and interdisciplinary approaches. A challenge is to ensure that, in emphasizing the potential of extrinsic learning through art, intrinsic learning within art is not compromised. For instance, technical skills in the subject can enhance expressive communication, and this, in particular, is an area in which we argue that drawing can have a powerful role as it is such a versatile activity.

The global climate emergency

It is widely accepted in the scientific community that we face the biggest and most widespread crisis that the human species has ever encountered. The evidence for this has become more apparent as the past decade has seen a warming of the planet that is equal to, or even greater than, that predicted by the modelling of scientists throughout the latter part of the twentieth century. Global warming has had widespread environmental impacts that have, in too many cases, resulted in devastating outcomes affecting both human and non-human life. This is evidenced by organizations such as the World Future Fund and the World Economic Forum.

The global climate emergency is a complex issue to investigate because one cannot use the normal products of reductionism to arrive at smaller and smaller aspects of the problem to be studied in detail. It is the whole or it is nothing (Schmidt, 2014). Scientific method looks at individual components of a system, whereas climate change is compounded by multiple entities that, although driven by increases in carbon dioxide, have a myriad of complex impacts (environmental as well as socio-economic) that are difficult, if not impossible, to disentangle and, therefore, to predict accurately. The effects are variously emergent over time.

The effects of global warming are evidenced by a rapid decline in biodiversity and major climatic events that lead to rises in sea levels, melting of the polar ice caps, devastating fires, life-threatening droughts and catastrophic floods. Scientists suggest that it is crucial to take action in the next decade to keep rises in temperature to manageable levels (Schmidt, 2014). Concerningly, most commitments set at the *21st United Nations Climate Change Conference of the Parties (COP21)*, which took place in Paris in 2015, have not been met and, therefore, limiting global warming to 1.5 degrees has not succeeded. It is vital that commitments made at COP26, taking place in Glasgow, Scotland, at the time of writing, are met, in order to achieve the reductions in global warming that are required by 2030. Politicians, informed by scientists and campaigners, need to take big and effective decisions that will determine the fate of the planet, one way or another, for future generations. The concerns that heads of state need to address are not just complicated issues; they demand a complexity of understanding and decision-making that few other political issues have ever required.

Experts are continually sharing their growing awareness of the many factors that have led to the current climate emergency but just turning back the clock to pre-industrial times is, first, not possible and, second, not desirable. It is universally accepted that there is a pressing need to adapt to the current situation, which means, amongst other changes, the expansion of new green industries to ensure responsible production, significant change in many people's daily ways of living to ensure responsible consumption, and, all-in-all, a different way of looking to the future. Many young people across the globe, such as the climate activist Greta Thunberg, are fully aware of the importance of making changes now rather than later and are actively trying to make a positive difference. They urgently call on older and more powerful members of society to enact the changes that are required to enable the younger generation to survive and prosper in a potentially more hostile global environment and climate that is not of their making.

Not only does the older generation need to make those changes for the sake of children and young people but, crucially, the education system has to adapt quickly to provide young people with the skills, understanding and ways of thinking necessary to support the hope, optimism, tenacity and creativity to deal with a rapidly changing and unpredictable world: one that, more than ever, is steeped in complexity. We refer to this as an ethical pedagogy of ecological action.

An ethical pedagogy of ecological action

Educationalists in the twenty-first century should seek ways to make schools radically different and significantly more adaptable to the prevailing changes on the planet and within the societies that inhabit it. This requires deep consideration of the ethicality of both curriculum and pedagogy.

Students sampled in higher education, for example, seem to have a consensus on desired educational outcomes that transcend disciplines. These outcomes focus on the ethical and the affective, and include creativity, criticality, sensitivity, imagination, curiosity, tolerance, clarity of expression, intellectual flexibility and a passion for learning for its own sake (Gregory & Gregory, 2013). Each of these characteristics can be engaged in a transdisciplinary way to address the current climate crisis.

This requires a shift, not just by redesigning our current curriculum (the equivalent of moving the deckchairs on the Titanic) or adding topics labelled 'climate change' or 'nature study', but a fundamental realignment in the values and theories that underpin the fundamental purposes of schools, their curricula and their pedagogies. Thus, a wide-ranging, in-depth debate that builds upon the existing consensus of the inclusion of global issues in education and the importance of a critical approach is required (Pashby, Sund, & Corcoran, 2019).

We do not pretend to have all the answers, but we do believe that educationalists should be enthusiastically engaged in this debate. Even giving thought to these issues is a step in the right direction, as reflection is a type of action. It is at times like this, when massive and fundamental problems such as pandemics and the global climate crisis beset humanity, that the most creative solutions emerge, which, in more quiescent times, would not be considered at all. Crises, small or large, act as catalysts for change. Below we consider three different examples of an educational solution to the climate crisis.

Example one of an educational solution

Many people will have different views on if, how and why we should make changes to our schools. White (2020), for example, proposes that in England – our own geographical context – there should be a National Curriculum Commission (NCC) with a key focus on educational aims. White (2020) argues that considering aims over content as a starting point is essential:

> An urgent NCC aim for the 2020s would be equipping students to deal with the climate emergency. Here we might expect it to point schools in the direction of a mix of disciplinary and interdisciplinary work, using internet facilities where appropriate; to urge them to look kindly on student action in favour of climate change, including the use of the web

and social media in school time and in out-of-school activity in place of some lessons; to favour more discussion of the issues, collaborative planning of courses of action and personalised learning by building time for these, including internet explorations, into the school day.

(p. 872)

White's (2020) recommendation promotes the active role of young people in tasks and projects aimed at enhancing their knowledge and understanding of the global climate emergency, which is positive. However, it also seems to reflect the perspective that there are answers 'out there' to be discovered as opposed to the answers *emerging* from a creative, discursive and critical pedagogy.

Example two of an educational solution

The British Educational Research Association (BERA) calls on sustainability to become a key feature of the curriculum. In their recent publication, *A Manifesto for Education for Environmental Sustainability* (BERA, 2021), they stress some key characteristics that relate closely to the ideas of an ethical pedagogy of ecological action. They stress the importance of collaboration, coherence and involvement. This cannot be the domain of one teacher, one subject area or even one school. The school must draw on its community and its environment playing a part in influencing and being influenced by those beyond the school walls. This holistic approach, both within and beyond, must be reinforced by practical action in all that is said and done. In this way, sustainability is embedded as a central tenet in educational life – an ethical pedagogy of ecological action. This is reinforced in the BERA manifesto through references to love, respect, compassion, connection, honesty and social justice – affective characteristics that should run deep in our educational systems and now are brought to stark attention due to the climate crisis we face.

Example three of an educational solution – Aesthoecology

In order to explore the educational implications of the global climate crisis, we draw on the theory of aesthoecology (Turner, 2019), which we have explained and applied in different educational contexts in previous publications and conference presentations – namely in higher education (Turner & Hall, 2021) and in early years education (Hall & Turner, 2021). Our argument here is that aesthoecology offers an approach to thinking about life and its meaning that sits perfectly with the belief system that we suggest are required to inform ethically responsible approaches to the global climate emergency in schools, for a wide age-range of learners. In the next section, aesthoecology is further explained.

Aesthoecology

Aesthoecology is an onto-epistemology (a way of being and a way of knowing), which we assert highlights some of the most fundamental issues to be considered in any education proposed for the future. Aesthoecology represents a symbiotic relationship between aesthetics and ecology, in which aesthetics is defined as the affective domain and ecology as the connected domain.

The aesthetic aspect refers to our sensorium (Duncum, 2012) – the ways in which we *affectively* sense our environment, our appreciation of it, the experiences that arise from it and the actions and reactions that result. Affect is concerned with potentiality and the changes that are elicited through the making and breaking of a myriad of inter- and intra-connections.

These connections represent our ecology, linking our somatic responses to that which lies beyond our bodies, and are essential in our understanding of our environment. This happens frequently as an autonomic response. Testing our environment, and experiencing it, is an essential part of our learning, first through our senses and then cognitively. The theory of aesthoecology contends that this represents the way in which education brings learning into consciousness (Turner, 2019) and explains why the arts are so important. Consciously using the body, through art, dance and movement, for example, embodies our learning experiences and makes sense of them.

We use drawing as an example of this embodied way of learning. Affectivity and connectivity represent the comparative relationships we see between drawing as a meaning-making activity and an understanding of the complexities involved in coming to terms with the global climate crisis. We contend that an important thing to understand is that we cannot always predict the result of actions, but drawing activity potentially allows students to understand and express the nature of how events arise spontaneously. This is an example of emergence. This association between drawing and the climate crisis might seem somewhat obscure, but we suggest that it has useful potential as one way of engaging students in activities from which outcomes evolve and emerge as opposed to activities in which there is a presumption of a definitive solution. The idea of emergence through embodied action is implicit within our theory of aesthoecology and helps students embrace notions of complex phenomena to which there is no simple answer. In this way, students can engage in futures thinking and develop confidence in embracing radical and transformative creativity.

It is in that spirit of proactive action that this chapter, in a small but potentially significant way, engages in the futures-thinking debate by looking at drawing as a way to creatively involve students in the methods of understanding and coming to terms with the complexities inherent in phenomena such as the climate crisis and the emergence of patterns of change of the type that human-induced global warming present.

The global climate emergency as a hyperobject

Characteristics that relate aesthetics to the world of education need to be explored through an understanding of their overall ecological significance and through notions of inter-connectivity and the identification and importance of space and place. An ecological hierarchy that relates to both space and time, through both aesthetics and ecology, might be seen as a series of different levels, perhaps very loosely equating to a meta-state, a meso-state, and a micro-state (Turner, 2019). The meta-state would reasonably seem to represent an understanding of our global situation and issues facing the planet. The meso-state represents the multitudinous connections and nodes that play a definable part in the process of lifelong education – all those spaces, places and contexts within which education is enacted. The micro-state is related to the individual – the level at which learning becomes education through the emergence and construction of an educational landscape that operates through the meso regions and out to the meta regions and back. The individual can only exist in relation to these areas and by transcending the boundaries. It is by accepting these series of transitions that the ideas of superficial and constructed boundaries are negated.

The meta-state is similar to that which Morton (2013) describes as hyperobjects and Lovelock (2000) describes as Gaia. Each of these are all-encompassing phenomena, which connect us to something far greater and yet which impinge on us as humans in every way, much of the time not realized, which represents an understanding of our global situation and issues facing the planet (Turner, 2019; Turner & Hall, 2021). Hyperobjects are entities of such vast and complex dimensions that they challenge all traditional understandings of simply an assemblage of things or objects, in which individual interactions can be studied in order to understand the whole.

Global warming is a very good example of a hyperobject in which the connectivity between things produces effects that are largely unpredictable apart from in the most general of terms. The outcomes are emergent and, from an educational perspective, present to us a world that is unfamiliar. The objects from which this emergent world is composed are referred to by Morton (2013, pp. 216–217) as 'strange strangers' and by Bennett (2010) as actants, in that they are strange to each other and, therefore, irreducible in understanding nature or place. This is radically different from any sense of conventional environmental relationality, which 'characterizes ecological spaces as (tacitly) homogenous knowable planes or ecosystems' (Saari & Mullen, 2018, p. 6). In educational terms, this suggests an epistemology in which is situated 'the idea that knowledge does not bring us closer to what is already present but, rather, moves us into a new reality which is incalculable from what came before' (Osberg & Biesta, 2007, p. 46).

Osberg and Biesta's (2007) perspective shown in the above quotation has profound implications for how we define and promote knowledge within school curricula, pedagogy and learning. How can this new reality be predicted? The simple answer is that it cannot. We would like the uncertain nature of knowledge to be welcomed by educators as an invitation to promote creative teaching and teaching for creativity (Craft, 2000) in which questions are valued as highly as answers. However, we recognize that this is an unconventional philosophy that some may find difficult to understand or even accept as an alternative to the status quo.

Aesthoecology embraces the affective domain of education. We relate this to the aesthetic but, contrary to more conventional views, consider it to be much more than just art. It has to do with the liminal, which represents awareness, sensitivity and active anticipation of the next event. Liminality is an important concept that can be considered as an in-between space, determined by being both 'a point in time and state of being' (Barradell & Kennedy-Jones, 2015, pp. 541–542). This entails recognition of the next state of emergence, which situates the aesthetic, the affective dimension, as an in-between relationship in which anticipation, action and emergence coalesce in a continuously organic process. This might be applied to a global meta-state, such as changing weather conditions. Alternatively, the micro-state, which related to the individual, might be the action of an artist in developing thought processes on paper.

Affecting and being affected may be considered to be two aspects of the same event that alternate dynamically between object and subject. The interaction between the two governs the transition from one liminal state to the next. This transition is a quality of experience that leaves a trace or memory that sets up 'a reactivation of the past in passage towards a changed future' (Massumi, 2015, p. 49). This embodied process, as evident in drawing, is captured by a form of aesthoecological cognition in which action upon action develops a co-ordinated and yet emergent way of thinking that embraces complexity and might be referred to as aesthoecologically informed drawing.

Re-thinking the activity of drawing

Drawing is not only a fundamental artistic skill but also a tool for thinking and a tool for learning (Adams, 2017). The vast learning potential of drawing as an activity should not be underestimated, but in formal education settings, all too often 'drawing' is misunderstood and undervalued. Even if teachers know that drawings can be created from observation, imagination or memory, they may be unaware of the pedagogical implications of this knowledge. Further to this, and notably linked to the philosophy of aesthoecology, children's communicative purposes for drawing can be both cognitive and affective (Hall, 2010; Hope, 2008). We see great potential to exploit drawing as an activity within IBAE.

Drawing is a ubiquitous activity that pre-dates writing as a form of communication (Ingold, 2016). It can offer students the means to understand the complexity and the ways in which a dynamic process can develop the thinking process. Drawing represents a continual process of testing the world and connecting with it through the senses of both vision and touch. The activity of drawing is a significant way of sensing, playing and relating to and with the environment. But it is not just a sensory process. Through feedback mechanisms, it becomes a cognitive process as well, which progressively develops the skills of hand-eye co-ordination. This ability to think through the hands is beneficial for thinking differently and assimilating knowledge in a haptic, experiential way, which we feel fits well within IBAE.

Drawing always exemplifies emergence: what is observed or imagined by the drawer does not simply translate from eyes or brain to paper. Similarly, in futures thinking, one must explore possibilities to prepare for an imagined but inevitable future, the details of which are largely unknown. We propose that tackling the current global climate emergency requires a similar creative process to that of aesthoecologically informed drawing activity, which relies upon ideas of emergence and the production of the unexpected. For example, in climate science, it is known that tipping points are important (Lenton, 2021) and 'challenging to predict because of their non-linearity: change appears to be happening smoothly and then suddenly it becomes abrupt and/or irreversible' (Lenton, 2021, p. 325). This is a moment when a small change triggers a large, often irreversible, response. This relates to aesthoecology in that we maintain that nothing is stable, and our proposed links between the act of drawing and the anticipation of environmental disaster bring about largely unpredictable and self-organizing learning experiences, which may be positively incorporated into an ethical pedagogy of ecological action as described previously. The ethical aspects come from affective responses of engaging with the emergent.

Although all forms of drawing involve communication (Adams, 2017; Hall, 2010), it is recognized that that there is some sort of modifying feedback process between the drawer, a broader culture and the work (Kantrowiitz, Brew, & Fara, 2011). To expand upon this, Wilkinson (2016) asserts that:

> there is something about the eye–brain–hand coordination that seems to stimulate ideas, just as it serves to communicate them. It can also be said that although rendering conveys a design in a superbly accurate way, a freehand sketch can often express the emotions and thinking behind the concept, which can be more successful.
>
> (p. 4)

Wilkinson (2016) suggests that drawing activity is a complex, diverse and adaptive emergence. Crucially, due to its emergent nature, drawing may be a process that unintentionally transforms ideas.

Wasserman (2013) refers to the work of Clark (2008, p. xxv), a cognitive scientist, who suggests that working on paper is 'actually thinking on paper' and that activities like drawing 'quite literally extend […] the machinery of the mind out into the world' (2008, p. xxvi) and should, therefore, be considered as a part of the mind. Clark (2008) regards sketching as 'an integral process of artistic cognition itself' (p. 77). Conceiving of the mind as extending beyond the brain is called the extended mind view of cognition. This involves the affective nature of thinking and perceiving, such that the senses produce not only tangible thought but also evoke emotion and a sensitivity that binds subject to object, draws on previous experiences and extends to the hopes and fears of an anticipation of future. This gives access to multiple layers of mind and world. This opposes, or at least extends, the theory of 'drawing as expression', argues Wasserman (2013, p. 2).

Wasserman explores why encoding the outcome of thought processes in a sketch or drawing should play an important part in stimulating visual invention and therefore the understanding of previously obscure phenomena. This, combined with observations on the 'nature and emergence of imaginative mental imagery' suggests that drawing exploits and extends the activity of the 'opportunistic brain' (Wasserman, 2013, p. 9). The 'opportunistic brain' does not operate in set predictable ways but will be involved in emergent behaviours in which continuous imaginative interpretation of marks on paper represents hybrid thoughts that rely on affectivity (feelings, emotions and sensitivity) alongside the connectivity between past and future. This is very important in educational contexts because it capitalizes on those happenings that spontaneously arise and presents spaces for new thinking. Thus, aesthoecologically informed (relying on affectivity and connectivity) drawing arising from the personal micro-state can help students to come to terms with, and understand better, the complexities of emergent phenomena (the meta-state) such as the global warming crisis that young people will need to discuss as a part of any new educational system (pedagogy, curriculum). Emergent phenomena often rely on taking advantage of chance events that are largely unpredictable. These are conditions that IBAE can usefully exploit.

Creativity, artistic originality and naturally occurring phenomena share an underlying pattern of emergent behaviours that work at a variety of levels of inter- and intra-action. The theory of aesthoecology relates these emergent events to affective anticipation – processes of rhythmic melding of aesthetics and ecology 'that seem to connect affective responses and anticipation in an almost instantaneous way' (Turner, 2019, p. 140). This emphasizes the idea that not knowing is an important element of education, reinforcing the vitality of constantly seeking answers and grasping opportunities to do so as they arise. IBAE should be driven by students' questions, and drawing as an activity facilitates this complex thinking.

This ability to react in the present, and carry something radically new into the future, suggests that the processes involved in affective anticipation are much more complex than just an extrapolation of what has happened in the past determining some sort of preconceived future. Radical newness can only be perceived when it comes into being and is enacted such that 'anticipation disappears the moment uncertainty is overcome' (Osberg, 2018, p. 15). This moment of transition is reliant on 'an affective way of being – a liminal state of openness and receptivity to change' (Turner, 2019, p. 143) or, as MacCormack and Gardner suggest (2018, p. 11), 'affects are not concrete entities but rather self-constituting interfaces that generate both interiority and exteriority through affective encounters'. This relates to the way in which subject and object interact such that material entities produce particular reactions. That interface between the two – the touch of a stone wall, the sound of a bell or the comfort of a chair – are examples of affective encounters with materiality that alter the way you perceive them in the future.

That is why both in the act of drawing at the micro level and in meta-phenomena such as global warming, the trends are apparent, but particular outcomes are unpredictable. Micro-states and meta-states are separable by magnitudes of space and time, but moving between the two and making connections allow a broader spectrum of thinking and understanding.

This is the richness of learning, the divergent thinking, that IBAE hopes to achieve for all students. We argue that making drawing relevant and based on life issues connects the imagination with the real in a way that can be very powerful.

Conclusion

We recognize that our discussion here can only offer a relatively superficial insight into some very important matters that demand further attention. We are being bold in our assertions in the expectation that novel ways of making connections between actions and phenomena will help students to understand very complex issues.

These four main topics (IBAE; the global climate emergency; aesthoecology; the activity of drawing) can be considered from a multitude of other angles. However, in bringing together these topics, which may otherwise not have been seen to be connected, we may have created our own hyperobject by eliciting new and emergent thinking. We hope, at the least, that it will stimulate further discussion. As we have suggested in previous writing (Turner & Hall, 2021), introducing readers to the principles of aesthoecology is an invitation to reflect upon its meaning and significance, particularly in relation to a transdisciplinary approach to the school curriculum and pedagogy.

References

Adams, E. (2017). Thinking drawing. *International Journal of Art and Design Education, 31*(2), 166–179. https://doi.org/10.1111/jade.12153

Addison, N. (2011). Moments of intensity: Affect and the making and teaching of art. *International Journal of Art and Design Education, 30*(3), 363–378. https://doi.org/10.1111/j.1476-8070.2011.01729.x

Barradell, S., & Kennedy-Jones, M. (2015). Threshold concepts, student learning and curriculum: Making connections between theory and practice. *Innovations in Education and Teaching International, 52*(5), 536–545. https://doi.org/10.1080/14703297.2013.866592

Bennett, J. (2010). *Vibrant matter: A political ecology of things*. Durham, NC: Duke University Press.

BERA. (2021). *A Manifesto for Education for Environmental Sustainability*. London: British Educational Research Association.

Chang, E., Lim, M., & Kim, M. (2012). Three approaches to teaching art methods courses: Child art, visual culture, and issues-based art education. *Art Education, 65*(3), 17–24. https://doi.org/10.1080/00043125.2012.11519172

Clark, A. (2008). *Supersizing the mind: Embodiment, action, and cognitive extension*. Oxford: Oxford University Press.

Craft, A. (2000). *Creativity across the curriculum*. London: Routledge.

Duncum, P. (2012). An eye does not make an I: Expanding the sensorium. *Studies in Art Education, 53*(3), 182–193.

Gregory, M., & Gregory, M.V. (2013). Ethical pedagogy. In M.V. Gregory (Ed.), *Teaching excellence in higher education* (pp. 73–94). London: Palgrave MacMillan.

Hall, E. (2010). *The communicative potential of young children's drawings* (Doctoral thesis). University of Exeter, UK. Open Research Exeter. https://ore.exeter.ac.uk/repository/handle/10036/105041?show=full

Hall, E. (2019). *The opportunities and challenges of issues-based art education [IBAE] in English schools* [Conference presentation]. In InSEA Seminar, Malta.

Hall, E., & Turner, C. (2021). Aesthoecology and its implications for art and design education: Examining the foundations. *International Journal of Art and Design Education,* 40(4), 761–772. https://doi.org/10.1111/jade.12387

Hope, G. (2008). *Thinking and learning through drawing in primary classrooms.* London: Sage.

Ingold, T. (2016). *Lines.* London: Routledge.

Jimenez, J., & Moorhead, L. (2001). 'Don't say it's going to be okay': How international educators embrace transformative education to support their students navigating our global climate emergency. *Education Sciences,* 11, 593. https://doi.org/10.3390/educsci11100593

Kantrowitz, A., Brew, A. & Fara, M. (2011). Thinking through drawing: Practice into knowledge. In *Proceedings of an Interdisciplinary Symposium on Drawing, Cognition and Education* (pp. 123–125). New York, NY: Teachers College, Columbia University.

Laininen, E. (2019). Transforming our worldview towards a sustainable future. In J. Cook (Ed.), *Sustainability, human well-being, and the future of education.* Cham: Palgrave Macmillan. https:/doi.org/10.1007/978-3-319-78580-6_5

Lenton, T. M. (2021). Tipping points in the climate system. *Royal Meteorological Society, Weather,* 76(10), 325–326.

Lovelock, J. (2000). *Gaia: A new look at life on earth.* Oxford: Oxford University Press.

MacCormack, P., & Gardner, C. (Eds.). (2018). *Ecosophical aesthetics: Arts, ethics and ecology with Guattari.* London: Bloomsbury Academic.

Massumi, B. (2015). *The politics of affect.* Cambridge: Polity Press.

Mauser, W., Klepper, G., Rice, M., Schmalzbauer, B., Hackmann, H., Leemans, R., & Moore, H. (2013). Transdisciplinarity global change research: The co-creation of knowledge for sustainability. *Current Opinion in Environmental Sustainability,* 5(3/4), 420–431.

Morton, T. (2013). *Hyperobjects.* Minneapolis, MN: University of Minnesota Press.

Osberg, D. (2018). Education and the future. In R. Poli (Ed.), *Handbook of anticipation.* New York, NY: Springer. https://doi.org/10.1007/978-3-319-31737-3_88-1

Osberg, D., & Biesta, G. (2007). Beyond re/presentation: A case for updating the epistemology of schooling. *Interchange,* 38(1), 15–29. https://doi10.1007/s10780-007-9015-2

Osberg, D., & Biesta, G. (2018). *Beyond the educational machine: Prolegomena for an aesthetic theory of education* [Conference presentation]. In European Conference on Educational Research (ECER), Bozen/Bolzano, Italy.

Pashby, K., Sund, L., & Corcoran, S. L. (2019). *Teaching for sustainable development through ethical global issues pedagogy: Participatory research with teachers.* Manchester: Manchester Metropolitan University, Faculty of Education.

Payne, R., & Hall, E. (2018). The NSEAD survey report 2015–16: Political reflections from two art and design educators. *International Journal of Art and Design Education, 37*(2), 167–176. https://doi.org/10.1111/jade.12142

Saari, A., & Mullen, J. (2018). Dark places: Environmental education research in a world of hyperobjects. *Environmental Education Research, 26*(9–10), 1466–1478. https://doi.org?10.1080/13504622.2018.1522618

Schmidt, G. (2014). *The emergent patterns of climate change. TedX, YouTube*, 1 May 2014. https://www.ted.com/talks/gavin_schmidt_the_emergent_patterns_of_climate_change

Smith, D. L. (2011). Material culture and issues-based art education. *The International Journal of Arts Education, 9*(2), 92–100. https://ed.arte.gov.tw/uploadfile/periodical/3056_9-2-p.92-100.pdf

Turner, C. (2019). *Education as aesthoecology* (Doctoral thesis). University of Exeter, UK. Open Research Exeter. https://ore.exeter.ac.uk/repository/handle/10871/40105

Turner, C., & Hall, E. (2021). Transformation through aesthoecology: Affectivity, connectivity, and the role of art in promoting transdisciplinarity. In *Innovative Practice in Higher Education. GLAD-HE Special Edition*. Staffordshire: University of Staffordshire. http://journals.staffs.ac.uk/index.php/ipihe/article/view/219?fbclid=IwAR0Qt8ASHc9wEClYiGp6RzAfMFk84Dq9PtvDWs-N4ewnb47DFClP_tB6Enw

Wasserman, M. L. (2013). *Drawing as thinking: An enquiry into the art of drawing as embodied extension of the mind* (MA dissertation). KwaZulu-Natal: University of KwaZulu-Natal.

White, J. (2020). The climate emergency and the transformed school. *Journal of Philosophy of Education, 54*(4), 867–873. https://doi.org/10.1111/1467-9752.12461

Wilkinson, W. (2016). Thinking through drawing. *The Architectural Review*, 4 November, 2016. https://www.architecturalreview.com/essays/thinking-through-drawing

Wood, E., & Hall, E. (2011). Drawings as spaces for intellectual play. *International Journal of Early Years Education, 19*(3–4), 267–281. https://doi.org/10.1080/09669760.2011.642253

Part 3

Sustaining Diverse Epistemological Frameworks
Through the Arts

Raphael Vella and Victoria Pavlou

The widespread use of practice-based methods in artistic and qualitative research supports the idea that knowledge can be transmitted in different ways. Language is not sufficiently representative of everything that can be known. The arts can mould new epistemological parameters that subsist outside the propositional structures of language. Non-verbal practices interrogate the world, ask difficult questions, communicate unfamiliar interpretations and generate new knowledge. Cross-disciplinary connections between artistic and scientific inquiry can be developed to conduct social research (Leavy, 2009). As creative practices enter the research domain, they unsettle more conventional qualitative and quantitative paradigms and redefine what it means to know.

Similarly, radically alternative epistemological debates and research around art education, sustainability and learning communities need to take into account diverse epistemological perspectives that collectively present decolonial shifts in power and global practices in the arts and pedagogies. It is becoming increasingly evident that learning about and from different ways of knowing can inform sustainable thinking and gradual yet necessary processes of recovery in the world. Boaventura de Sousa Santos has written about the tendency in western thought to silence, exclude and hence 'waste' the rich diversity of epistemologies that emerge from the Global South (Santos, 2016). Our understanding of the world and our interactions with it, relations between humans and nonhumans and creative paradigms stand to gain from a broader and deeper engagement with different worldviews. The development of novel strategies at the macro and micro levels for dealing with sustainability issues relies on modelling alternative conceptualizations of 'relevant' knowledge and creative methodologies for expressing and communicating this knowledge.

Part 3 recognizes the need to explore locally informed research about sustainability, communities and art by bringing together contributions from different parts of the world. The contributions were selected from a much larger number of abstracts sent to the editors following an international open call and eventually developed into full articles and visual essays by their authors. The authors represent different backgrounds – artists, environmentalists, art educators, curators, among others – and they collectively weave a rich tapestry of stories referring to different places around the world: Chile, the United States, Finland, Cyprus, Malta, Cambodia, Spain, Japan, Canada, Turkey and Ghana. The essays are presented here in an order that proceeds from artistic, poetic or curatorial positions to community-based actions, finally ending with more explicitly educational projects.

Bob Jickling's 'Lyric convergences: Bringing together art, philosophy, and places we can love' is inspired by lyric philosophy and presents a creative essay that merges photographic images into text. Through the emotive force of art, the chapter argues for a stronger bond with the places we love, avoiding approaches to education that have become too analytical and rationalistic. Influenced by the thought of philosopher Jan Zwicky, this aesthetic approach to art and philosophy allows us to appreciate forms of knowledge, including ideas that are difficult to articulate in words that educational systems may ignore.

Costas Mantzalos' chapter 'The TWO|FOUR|TWO art group: Can contemporary art practice act as a vehicle for sustainable development?' describes a handful of artworks produced by the TWO|FOUR|TWO art group in Cyprus, which relate to various UN sustainable goals. Employing experimental methods and materials like signs, installation and socially engaged practice, the two members of the group engage with topics like inequalities, poverty and hunger, teasing viewers with works that often revolve around linguistic play.

'Now we Know' by Margerita Pulè and Maren Richter brings a fresh perspective on the notion of 'knowing' and 'belonging'. The chapter reflects on the artistic experimental platform Debatable Land(s) that took place in Malta and explores the notions of land-use, (de)territorial thinking and generative concepts of belonging. It demonstrates how artists can work together to build communities of learning around essential issues of caring, passing on responsibility, memory and belonging, thus composing sustainable senses of collectiveness.

'Cross-cultural dialogue: Searching traces and the Mahalla Festival' presents the development of a festival in response to the refugee crisis of 2014. The authors, Sabine Küper-Büsch and Thomas Büsch, demonstrate how art practices can contribute to community communication around migration and serve to raise awareness of international conflicts and social justice through workshops that offer opportunities for collaborative filmmaking. The festival's success as a space of diversity and inclusion in the arts, culture and sustainability led to a repetition of the repeated workshops, thus highlighting innovative ways to build synergies and structures to facilitate collaborative and co-creative art projects for the benefit of communities and their members.

In the chapter 'Participatory art with trees: A pedagogical approach', Maria Huhmarniemi discusses the value and potential of contemporary art in informal education that facilitates healing and creates an opportunity for including other-than-human into a sense of community. It presents contemporary innovative artistic practices that have the potential to strengthen local communities and sustainability initiatives in Finland that can inspire artistic practices worldwide.

'"Ngen" ancient spirits of the woods: Art-based environmental education in Chiloé Archipelago' by Francisco Schwember, Felipe Palma, Antonia Condeza-Marmentini and Guillermo Marini studies a project carried out with persons of different ages from a rural community in southern Chile. By partnering with an informal educational initiative in the region, the researchers developed an interdisciplinary methodology that used alternative, including ancient, ways of knowing revolving particularly around the figure of the Ngen – a spirit or force in traditional culture in the area.

Introduction

In 'Trash to Treasure: Sustaining and preserving the Krobo bead culture through community learning', Felix Amofa Gyebi describes a practice-led research project leading to the production of a collaborative smartphone documentary. The film documents the recycling of glass bottles into beads by the Krobo people in Ghana, while the chapter assesses how the filmmaking process gave the participants a voice and facilitated community learning.

'Changing climate, changing communities' by Stephanie Danker, Shafkat Khan and Katie Feilen describes an example of a place-based community art exhibition that brought together learning communities, including local school districts, universities, lifelong learners, artists, and environmental organizations, to discuss difficult topics related to environmental problems such as climate change. This case study recognizes the power of art to engage the public, encourage diversity of voices and raise awareness. It also highlights the critical role of art education in driving community conversations and learning about important environmental issues.

'Reclaiming the street: The expanded garden' by Eva Marín Peinado is inspired by what one might think as the seemingly simple action of an elderly woman who places plants on her street in a town on the outskirts of Barcelona. The author/artist discusses the effects of this action in creating a community of caring and connected people, and explores the activist role of contemporary art in engaging the public in a way that encourages them to see common spaces, specifically spaces in the periphery and in their neighbourhoods.

Susan (Susie) Lachal's 'Diffractive methodology as a posthuman approach to engaging with human equity through socially engaged artistic practice' discusses a socially engaged artistic project which connected participants from Australia and Cambodia. Sited in the Kampong Thom education community in Cambodia, the research sets the tone for a posthuman analysis in the chapter, which seeks to underline the interdependent, or entangled, nature of the social practice and the relations that were nurtured in it.

In 'Inviting teacher candidates in art education to become global agents for sustainability', Kazuyo Nakamura and Anita Sinner present perspectives from Concordia University in Canada and Hiroshima University in Japan that explore ways of promoting engagement with issues of sustainable development amongst teacher candidates in each country. By referencing the UN's 2030 Agenda for Sustainable Development and nurturing an understanding of the interdependency of global issues, the study shows how collaborative work on shared goals can be developed even when participants are based in different contexts.

In the chapter 'Social sculpture perspective: Re-sculpting or de-sculpting citizenship by shaping art as an element for social change', Ana María Marqués Ibáñez explores the application of the concept of social sculpture to the educational field. The chapter presents designs for educational projects and classroom activities developed by students of early childhood and elementary education degrees and offers guidance for implementing social sculpture activities inspired by the work of Beuys and contemporary collaborative art.

References

Leavy, P. (2009). *Method meets art: Arts-based research practice.* New York, NY: The Guilford Press.

Santos, B. d. S. (2016). Epistemologies of the south and the future. *European South: A Transdisciplinary Journal of Postcolonial Humanities*, 1, 17–29.

Chapter 10

Lyric Convergences: Bringing Together Art, Philosophy and Places We Can Love

Bob Jickling

We are living on an increasingly threadbare planet. We cannot continue to do the same things – perpetuate the same relationships – and hope to have a viable future. In responding as educators and researchers, we must search for alternative pedagogies and experiment with new research methodologies. We must be different.

In this chapter, I embrace art, art education and creative pedagogies as meaningful alternatives. I experiment with a tantalizing convergence of philosophy and art in ways that are pedagogical and research-oriented. And I riff off the work of philosopher Jan Zwicky. For her, philosophy is too narrowly categorized when thought of as only logico-linguistic analysis. I believe that the same can be said about mainstream education. When conceived of as primarily logico-linguistic, both remain too narrowly categorized and do not attempt to understand experiences that affect us as whole beings with bodies and emotions. Zwicky aims for a more expansive vision through her lyric philosophy, enacted through lyric arguments (1992, 2003, 2015). For her, it ceases to be useful to distinguish between art and philosophy when experiencing lyric arguments. They are artful. Thus, it seems that lyric arguments can add breadth to both pedagogies and educational research (Zwicky, 2015).

In this chapter, my interpretations of lyric arguments are comprised of written text and photographic art. They were crafted by me and two young participants during a canoeing journey where we sought interesting ways to represent our experiences and ideas.[1] The photographs were created using a homemade pinhole camera with neither a lens nor a viewfinder. Making photographs thus demanded sensual presence during creation (Jickling, 2015; Morse, Jickling, & Morse, 2018). Importantly, the aesthetics of this process are also reminiscent of Suzi Gablik's connective aesthetics (1992).[2]

The written expression of this work is derived from interviews that asked these young participants to consider the photographic images and their experiences while making them and, also, from my own reflections on lyric philosophy in practice. The core aim of this experimental journey was to loosen control over our experiences and to see what aspects of the landscapes would call us to make photographs. It was to see and feel what learning might arise from being in these places when the leash, tethered to controlling instincts, was loosened. This could be called self-willed learning – or learning that is always a little wild (Jickling, Blenkinsop, Timmerman, & Sitka-Sage, 2018).

In my interpretation of lyric philosophy, I have arranged elements of experiences as side-by-side comparisons. In representational terms, this consists of a series of 'left-hand pages' comprised of the texts, and a series of 'right-hand pages' comprised of the pinhole photographs. Such an arrangement is reminiscent of Zwicky's own arrangement of lyric philosophy (1992, 2003). If successful, the creative tensions between these paired pages will constitute a lyric argument that will invite the connoisseur – the reader of text and the viewer of images – to perceive resonances with their own experiences of being in the world beyond what linguistic expression and artistic representation can singularly provide (Lee, 2010). Thus, readers are invited to realize some shared experience that is not simply contained by logic and language.

This work is also an act of resistance. It aims to resist globalized educational trends weighted in favour of tightly controlled analytical, rationalistic and abstract versions of a living world. I fear that without such bold moves to seek and represent existential experiences in multiple ways, education will be hamstrung in attempting to create radical breaks that resist the status quo. Sadly, we will also fail to connect with places we can love.

Viewing the work

The following pages are designed to be viewed as pairs – text on the left and photographs on the right. Together, these pairings invite connoisseurs to explore resonances in the world and to move their understanding to positions in spaces beyond what linguistic expression and artistic representation provide. Lyric arguments arise on their own terms. If successful, outcomes will be expressive, emotive and individual (Eisner, 1985) – and a little wild. Thus, I resist describing the work further. However, some parting thoughts follow in a brief afterword. Enjoy!

Frame 1: The Wernecke Mountains

Stephanie is 15. And, determined to make a pinhole picture of camp.[3]

That Wernecke gap really caught me. I loved the mountains, and that small area where we camped, just at the end of it. Those two mountains with the water represent life and the place. The tent in front represents us passing through, and living there and being there.

In a place, attention is in response to particularities: This pair of mountains, this gap, this waterfall, this camp, this tent.

Jan Zwicky says we are pierced: *The **this** strikes into us like a shaft of light.*

A bolt of **thisness**.

A wild education in these Wernecke mountains.

***

When you're in the place, whether you like it or you absolutely hate it, you have a feeling for that place, says Stephanie, *and when you take the pinhole picture, after all the steps, it captures the feeling because you have the bond, after having spent so much time with it.*

***

What did you learn, Stephanie?

Going out and actually doing it and getting the feel of everything that's around you, and what it means to you, and how it affects you, and everything.

Frame 2: The unlanguaged world

Andrew's 13. Together we walk ahead, up this valley of limestone cliffs and lemonade poppies.[4]

Well, Andrew, what do you think?

I don't have a word to describe it.

What do you mean?

It's like the flowers, the birds, the animals, the scenery – everything.

His wild understanding of this place just announced itself. A gestalt, a coherent whole, an ecology of connections, intelligible in an unlanguaged world.

***

Cool winds shiver the poppies, and the idea of framed objectivity.

Legs shiver, too, pierced by the chill and the stillness of a 30-second exposure. A pinhole gestalt is always more than a moment in time.

Frame 3: What cannot be said

Andrew, what do you feel when you see the picture we made at the end of that valley?[5]

Wow!

What else? No answer.

He grasps this place in an exclamation of recognition, *the vibrant spoor of what cannot be said.*

***

The cliff will no longer announce cliffness when reduced to a pile of boulders. And more questions will turn Andrew's wonder to rubble.

With their own loss of this youthful perspective, educators can be awestruck by the joy exhibited by students on field trips, free from the constraints of systematized learning.

It is sometimes enough to just point and wander.

Frame 4: Three canoes

For Stephanie, the three canoes are: *being with the river, paddling, learning about different parts of the river, the pinhole, canoeing, camping, how you have to respect the environment, different things…*[6]

Oh yes, Andrew adds, *what I remember about that photo was being tired, and skipping rocks, and having twizzlers.*

That's enough questions!

***

Dennis Lee asks, *How should we test a gestalt when it is simply* **shown**? *Not by hacking its bounty back into logical form and subjugating it to analytic verification; everything of substance is likely to be leached out in the process.*

Self-willed learning is unaccountable in the language of learning outcomes and measurable achievements.

It just announces itself.

And, that's its joy.

Afterword

If I have been successful in constructing the preceding lyric arguments, you will likely already know. You will have felt a moment of recognition. You might have smiled, laughed or shed a tear. Something in these pairings of text and images will have resonated; it will have rekindled past experiences. It may have challenged you to look further into your past or given shape to future resolutions. Some outcomes might be pedagogical. The validity of the outcomes – the lyric arguments – is found in this resonance of lived experience. And, there is verisimilitude in resonance.

If the above is true for you as a reader, then you will have felt an aesthetic convergence of art and philosophy. That is enough; you can stop reading now. However, I think it may be worthwhile to speak a little more to those who are called to these experiments – as teachers and researchers.

First, consider Rosi Braidotti's (2019) claim that the quotidian exhaustion felt by so many academics – and surely practitioners, too – is not a pathological state that needs to be cured; rather, it is a transformative threshold that calls for less fatigue and more conceptual creativity. Experiences with COVID-19 have undoubtedly amplified these claims. Colleagues and I have attempted to rise to that call and respond to the creative moment.[7] If Braidotti is correct, we may have opportunities to take hold of this window of opportunity. However, meaningful change is never easy, and I offer a few thoughts for consideration.

On rationality

Zwicky's lyric philosophy embraces understandings that arise suddenly and affect us as sensuous beings. Think about Stephanie's experience with the Wernecke Gap or Andrew's response to the valley of limestone cliffs and lemonade poppies. Their experiences suddenly announce themselves, not as a collection of logically linked parts; rather, they arrive in a moment as whole understandings. Zwicky calls these whole understandings gestalts and considers them neither rational nor irrational; they are, she suggests, *arational*, in that they elude adequate capture in words (Zwicky, 2019).

Here, one question arises: should we create another category to describe these additional understandings, or should we rethink our conceptions of rationality? The Norwegian philosopher Arne Naess, for example, once suggested that any form of rationality that did not have room for feelings is a petty rationality (2002).

On perils of analysis

Zwicky raises the disturbing possibility that, in her terms, *arational* understanding might crumble and decay under analysis. That is, asking seemingly harmless questions, like 'What do you think?' can be problematic. Perhaps we can trace this in Andrew's responses. In Frame 2, he takes a stab at explaining what he thinks. In Frame 3, he answers with the single word 'Wow'. By Frame 4, Andrew is refreshingly honest about his daily needs. But I wonder if, by now, I have just asked him too many questions. In other words, this gestalt-knowing is not amenable to being further reduced to components. Could it be said that the same is sometimes true of art critics? Such analysis can undermine learning and suck the joy from wonder. Care is required.

On control

I have pondered the durability of the status quo as framed in a variety of ways – modernist, globalized, westernized, eurocentric, neo-liberal, colonial, Cartesian, anthropocentric – and the educational structures that support it (Jickling et al., 2018). Its resilience seems to rest on an uncanny human drive for control – over each other, other beings, socially acceptable behaviour, economic dogma, conceptions of truth and even what constitutes rationality. And why, 'are we so deeply susceptible to the charms of epistemological security?' (Zwicky, 2019, p. 95). It is a loosening of this control that is intriguing and leads me to wonder about other forms of knowing beyond those prioritized by mainstream educational systems.

Zwicky reminds us that our inclination towards logical 'rules of thought' may be in tension with an underlying proclivity to accept unexamined gestalt – the capacity of children to wonder at cliffs and flowers, waterfalls and rivers. She adds,

> There is no series of steps we can implement to precipitate gestalts in all audiences. Real thinking does not always occur in words; it can decay under analysis; its processes are not always reportable. This means that real thinking is in some sense wild: it cannot be corralled or regulated. But it is also the only access humans have to the experience of insight, to moral and mathematical beauty, to ontological vision.
> (Zwicky, 2019, p. 95)

It is risky business for educators to stray so far from expected norms. Yet, in Zwicky's words, 'where the danger lies, there too lies meaningful life' (2019, p. 95). So, we are challenged to ask what is lost: when thinking is limited to only thinking in words when we rely on a narrowly conceived notion of rational logic when we prefer to teach students to see a world that is reduced to its constituent parts? Can we be diligent in fulfilling our educational responsibilities if we do not embrace learning that increases our capacity for thinking with and in the world? Is it reasonable to arbitrarily deprive learners of access to meaningful forms of knowing? I think not. We are vulnerable, but the reward is the precious insight that goes well beyond rationality and knowledge as they are currently conceived.

Acknowledgements

A version of the lyric arguments presented here was first published in *Cultural Studies of Science Education* (Jickling, 2015). The final publication is available at Springer via https://doi.org/10.1007/s11422-014-9587-y

Notes

1. This line of research weaves in and out of a *Wild Pedagogies* project concerned with re-wilding education and disrupting the status quo (Jickling et al., 2018).
2. Gablik embraces a shift in emphasis from artistic ideals of freedom and individuality to ones of relatedness and connection, and concrete expressions of being in the world. Thus, her 'connective aesthetics' attempts to build social and environmental connections. This is mentioned in passing but warrants further attention elsewhere.
3. The pinhole pictures were made collaboratively by Bob Jickling and Stephanie and Andrew Potter. Stephanie and Andrew also answered my questions. Throughout the frames, quotations are italicized and identified in these Notes. The conversational quotations in this frame are by Stephanie Potter. *The **this** strikes into us …* Zwicky (2002, p. 53, left).
4. All quotations are by Andrew Potter.
5. *… the vibrant spoor …* Lee (2010, p. 22).
6. *How should we test a gestalt …* Lee (2010, p. 37).
7. See Jickling (2015), Morse, Jickling, and Morse (2018), and Jickling and Morse (2022).

References

Braidotti, R. (2019). *Posthuman knowledge*. Cambridge: Polity Press.
Eisner, E. (1985). *The educational imagination* (2nd ed.). London: Macmillan.
Gablik, S. (1992). Connective aesthetics. *American Art*, 6(2), 2–7.
Jickling, B. (2015) Self-willed learning: Experiments in wild pedagogy. *Cultural Studies of Science Education*, 10, 149–161.
Jickling, B., Blenkinsop, S., Timmerman, N., & Sitka-Sage, M. (2018). *Wild pedagogies: Touchstones for re-negotiating education and the environment in the anthropocene*. London: Palgrave-MacMillan.
Jickling, B., & Morse, M (2022). Experiments with lyric philosophy and the wilding of educational research. *Canadian Journal of Environmental Education*, 25, 13–36.
Lee, D. (2010). The music of thinking: The structural logic of 'Lyric Philosophy'. In M. Dickinson & C. Goulet (Eds.), *Lyric ecology: An appreciation of the work of Jan Zwicky* (pp. 19–39). Toronto: Cormorant Books.
Morse, M., Jickling, B., & Morse, P. (2018). Views from a pinhole: Experiments in wild pedagogy on the Franklin river. *Journal of Outdoor and Environmental Education*, 21(3), 255–275.

Næss, A. (2002). *Life's philosophy: Reason and feeling in a deeper world*. Athens, GA: University of Georgia Press.

Zwicky, J. (1992). *Lyric philosophy*. Toronto: University of Toronto Press.

Zwicky, J. (2003). *Wisdom and metaphor*. Kentville: Gaspereau Press.

Zwicky, J. (2015). What is lyric philosophy? In J. Zwicky (Ed.), *Alkibiades' love: Essays in philosophy* (pp. 3–18). Montreal: McGill-Queen's University Press.

Zwicky, J. (2019). *The experience of meaning*. Montreal: McGill-Queen's University Press.

Chapter 11

The TWO|FOUR|TWO Art Group: Can Contemporary Art Practice Act as a Vehicle for Sustainable Development?

Costas Mantzalos

The TWO|FOUR|TWO art group

Throughout the twentieth century, the boundaries of artistic genres were fluid and constantly changing. In the contemporary art scene, it is not rare to find works that require a whole new 'reading' to be interpreted. This new reading, which involves an interdisciplinary practice, can accommodate a hybrid of disciplines such as design, architecture, fashion or even literature. In the practice of the group, it becomes obvious that the art product has in many ways been replaced by a process that engaged audiences with real-life issues in response to sustainability and the UN sustainable development goals (SDGs).

The TWO|FOUR|TWO art group embarked on a voyage of collaboration under the umbrella term of the 'group'. Deriving from different backgrounds – a visual artist and an architect – both explore their common experience to produce a visual base on which they can communicate between themselves and with viewers. Their work does not pretend to be a traditionally accepted art form; instead, it seeks a place in its own right. The creative displacement and their stance in a diverse creative mindset – that of architecture and art – led them to work as a collective!

The TWO|FOUR|TWO art group was formed on 21 August 1996 in Nicosia, Cyprus, by Costas Mantzalos and Constantinos Kounnis. It is an art group that lives and believes in art as an evolutionary institution, which changes and mutates with time; however, like democracy, it remains a supreme power vested in the people and characterized by the recognition of the equality of opinions and voices.

The oeuvre of the TWO|FOUR|TWO art group has progressed towards appropriation and action in recent years. In many cases, their work since 2012 involved a process where the art object became a series of interactive events, allowing audience participation and interaction. Despite this development, and although the visual vocabulary of the work has shifted towards a different direction, the TWO|FOUR|TWO art group religiously follows the self-exploration and an autobiographical journey towards the investigation of interpersonal relationships as these are governed by personal identity and social behaviour. The messages that come out of the work are stable and consistent and try to illustrate human relationships which, consciously or not, have determined the cultural, social, geographical, professional and personal behaviour of both members of the group as well as the general social sphere.

The art group uses appropriation, reuse and anagrammatism to transfer concepts about consumerism, greed and megalomania that can be directed towards a further sociopolitical investigation and analysis of identity and ownership. At one level, the appropriating action of the TWO|FOUR|TWO art group is an act of recycling; at a different level, it extends to issues that deal with the UN SDGs and specifically those goals that concern 'decent work and economic growth', 'reduced inequalities', 'zero hunger', 'zero poverty' and 'good health and well-being'. The UN SDGs were set up in 2015 by the United Nations General Assembly and are intended to be achieved by 2030.

The latest work by the TWO|FOUR|TWO art group addresses contemporary social matters, such as personal or social identity politics, economic disasters, corruption and the vanity of excessive consumerism, via an artistic methodology characterized by humour and unconventional thinking. Within this context, the latest works of the art group fall within the scope of the UN SDGs. In an effort to criticize as well as create public awareness about these issues, the group's works revolve around concepts of political, social and financial corruption, which opened the doors to inequalities, poverty, migration and exploitation.

Social Ride

In the 'Social Ride' project (see Figure 11.1), which ran from July to December 2012, the art object is a series of interactive events, allowing audience participation. The concept of the TWO|FOUR|TWO art group was inspired first by the proposed site determined by the curator of the exhibition. The 'Old Powerhouse' restaurant became the arena of the group's artistic production. The final concept revolved around three main axes. The first axis was mainly determined by the actual space's character and the operational behaviour, a restaurant open to the community and in constant use as a space that provides food and drinks. The second axis was formulated by the constant search for artistic production where action and process, as well as community engagement and activism, replace the traditional and conventional art object. The third axis was determined by the sociopolitical situation, particularly the financial crisis that started internationally in 2008 and hit Cyprus in 2012.

Through these three axes, the TWO|FOUR|TWO art group proposed the creation of the 'Social Ride'. Costas Mantzalos and Constantinos Kounnis of the TWO|FOUR|TWO art group, together with the exhibition curator, Yiannis Toumazis, and a diverse network of individuals who came from the artistic and design industry (artists, designers, architects, cultural officers and producers), converted the restaurant into a place which welcomed and accommodated 24 persons who came from various sensitive levels of society, such as financial immigrants, prisoners, people with addictions, etc. Once a month, groups of these people were welcomed. Their selection was pre-decided and implemented after consultation with Ms Andrea Athanasiou from the Social Work Department of Frederick University and through official bodies and various social services and welfare programmes. The kick-off involved a guided tour of the Nicosia Municipal Art Centre and concluded with a dinner in the specially converted space. Dinner was designed and prepared by the TWO|FOUR|TWO art group and the associates who worked on the 'Social Ride' project. Every month the dinner

Figure 11.1: 'Social Ride', Installation View, Nimac, Nicosia, 2012.

preparation and the whole process differed accordingly. The entire activity was supported by the management and staff of the restaurant 'The Old Powerhouse'.

'ΛΑΙΚ ΟΡΦΑΝΣ'

The TWO|FOUR|TWO art group has been producing images that abstract and summarize human relationships that consciously or unconsciously shape their social universe. The ability to transform objects and people into meaningful spiritual and mental sources of information is a seductive act. In a playfully perverse mode, the two members of the group dictated control over their world and started to identify the irony underlying our everyday lives. The TWO|FOUR|TWO art group has been able to poke fun at the complex nature of human interaction through a series of images of the self (Das Party, 2006; Publish Me, 2005), a museum-like set up of portraits (Threesomes, 2008), a sculptural ideal new world (Espace Blanc, 2011) and a charitable performance-like interactive action (Social Ride, 2012).

Within the framework of the aforementioned concept, the TWO|FOUR|TWO art group proposed an installation entitled 'ΛΑΙΚ ΟΡΦΑΝΣ' (LIKE ORPHANS). Keeping in mind various semiological meanings, the group invented words sourced from existing unused signs and various other three-dimensional letter light signs. This new installation included two autonomous works that used the word twister, which illustrates daily routines in

Figure 11.2: 'ΛΑΙΚ ΟΡΦΑΝΣ', Installation View, Argo Gallery, Nicosia, 2015.

Cyprus. The life-size light sign 'ΛΑΙΚ' (LIKE) replicated a prototype outdoor sign of the second largest bank in Cyprus, which now is part of the economy's past. The large-scale work 'ΟΡΦΑΝΣ' (ORPHANS) – which used to be part of a basic signage from a chain of supermarkets in Cyprus that went bankrupt – contains illuminated letters in an order that changes its meaning to the phrase 'Like Orfans' – a 'Greeklish' word corresponding to the word orphans. 'Greeklish' is a portmanteau of the words Greek and English, also known as Grenglish, *Latinoellinika/Λατινοελληνικά* ('Latin-Greek') or ASCII Greek, and is the Greek language written with the Latin alphabet. This develops a new understanding that as 'orphans' – through the concepts of consumerism, greed and megalomania – we bluntly 'like' and accept the new de facto situation of our daily lives.

Through this installation, the TWO|FOUR|TWO art group suggests a new mode of inquiry while remaining loyal to its visual vocabulary. As a result of the financial crisis, the latest development in Cypriot society offers new questions. Is the financial crisis the 'New Cyprus Problem'?[1] Are the words 'occupied land' and 'refugees' going to be replaced by the words 'divestments' and 'unemployment'?

'Postcards from Cyprus'

The work of the TWO|FOUR|TWO art group kicked off as a very personal need to explore the notion of togetherness, the self and the other. The work evolved and has developed into an investigation of the notion of the private and the public, the personal and the common, the domestic and the international.

Figure 11.3: 'Postcards from Cyprus', Installation View, S:2F2, Nicosia, 2017.

'Postcards from Cyprus' is an ongoing activity that began in 2015 and initially derived from the critical stance that the TWO|FOUR|TWO art group took towards the current sociopolitical situation of Cyprus since the financial crisis of 2013 and the aftermath caused by the collapse of the banking system.

The TWO|FOUR|TWO art group uses appropriation in its oeuvre. It has used and reinvented new concepts from numerous industrial signs that came down from bankrupt businesses due to the financial crisis. Additionally, the group's members recontextualized the work by twisting the meaning of these signs to re-create new names/words that promote a critical view of the current situation in Cyprus. These twisters and combinations of text and images illustrate daily routines in Cyprus. These routines refer to the changing social character of the community: from a well-off society to a society that is now on the verge of poverty. The latest work uses touristic images from Cyprus in juxtaposition with the text 'care for u', which 'twists' the Carrefour sign, one of the latest casualties of Cyprus' and Greece's crippling recession.

The new juxtaposition of word and image teases the viewer and confirms that Cyprus cares for you. It is a paradox and a huge antithesis of semiological meanings, which can extend to various other interpretations. The TWO|FOUR|TWO art group asks different questions with their 'Postcards from Cyprus'. Their visual vocabulary involves interdisciplinary practices that employ industrialized objects and installations and questions the notion of a country as 'patria', a home, a refuge or a holiday destination.

Welcome/not welcome

The TWO|FOUR|TWO art group's investigative exploration of immigration and the subject of refugees are communicated via the imagery of its landscape photographs, which focus on the sea and the shoreline, as in Figure 11.4. The viewer's mind drifts towards the current international lingua franca used to communicate these images, for example, 'flow of refugees', 'uprooting' and the haunting 'human cargo'. A double-faced sign reading καλώς/ κακώς ήλθατε ('welcome/not welcome') reminds us that the journey leads to a precarious future. The deliberate addition of a letter results in many contrasting meanings. It reads as 'welcome' and then changes to 'not welcome' or even reads as 'good or bad you may still be welcome'.

The actual sign was sourced once again from the 'Orphanides' chain of supermarkets when this chain collapsed financially in 2013. Although at first the sign only served as a word twister combining the meanings of good and bad when it was initially presented in a gallery space in Nicosia in 2015, the actual translation of the work took a different meaning in the following years. This meaning was mainly affected by the dislocation of the work from the gallery space and its relocation to various other spots by the shoreline. In spoken language, culture plays an important role in the understanding and cognition of an idea. Similarly, in visual language, it is space that plays an important role and determines the awareness as well as the interpretation of its messages. It has to be said that although visual language is becoming more and more an accepted form of communication in current times, it has not yet been formalized like spoken language.

Figure 11.4: 'WELCOME/NOT WELCOME', A2 Printed Giveaway, Petah Tikva Museum of Art, Tel Aviv, 2017.

Conclusion

Taking the above-mentioned works of the TWO|FOUR|TWO art group into consideration, it becomes evident that contemporary art practice in the twenty-first century has taken a completely new approach towards social and political issues. Like the TWO|FOUR|TWO art group, many contemporary artists work around themes and concepts that revolve around all the seventeen UN SDGs, integrating ecological, humanitarian and sociological dimensions. The role of contemporary art has become much more educational, and it is not only focused on profiling the contemporary culture but is also committed to making a change and an impact towards the sustainable development of the sociopolitical sphere.

Note

1. The Cyprus problem is an ongoing dispute between Greek Cypriots in the south and Turkish Cypriots in the north, which started with the establishment of the Republic of Cyprus after independence from the British Empire in 1960 and which intensified as of the 1974 Turkish military invasion and occupation of the northern third of Cyprus (Wikipedia, n.d.).

References

Certoma, C., Clewer, N., & Elsey D. (2012). *The politics of space and place*. London: Cambridge Scholars.

Deleuze, G., & Guattari, F. (1987). *A thousand plateaus: Capitalism and schizophrenia*. Minneapolis, MN: University of Minnesota.

Eleftheriadou, A. (2005). Publish Me! [Exhibition Catalogue]. Nicosia/Cyprus. The TWOFOURTWO Art Group.

Evans, J., & Hall, S. (2013). *Visual culture: The reader*. London: SAGE Publications in Association with the Open University.

McLuhan, M. (1964). *Understanding media; the extensions of man*. New York, NY: MIT Press.

Wikipedia. (n.d.). *Cyprus problem*. https://en.wikipedia.org/wiki/Cyprus_problem

Wittgenstein, L. (1922). *Tractatus logico: Philosophicus*. London: Keagan Paul.

Wolfe, T. (1976, August 23). The 'Me' decade and the third great awakening. *New York Magazine*, pp. 27–48.

Chapter 12

'Now We Know': On Coming Together as an Artistic Practice

Margerita Pulè and Maren Richter

During the final presentation weekend of the project Debatable Land(s) (DL),[1] performance artist Charlene Galea (2021) told a story about her childhood in Malta's countryside helping her father in his fields and the conflict she felt when, as a young adult, she left for a more cosmopolitan life (see Figure 12.1). Her description of the repetitive nature of harvesting by hand revealed her father's love for the land he tends. Galea conveyed the practical, spiritual and aesthetic value of the small plot, ending her performance with the declaration, 'Now that you know about this land, this story, you are responsible to look after it'. Galea's act of passing on responsibility by sharing the story turned 'knowing' into a collective process of caring and the act of handing over responsibility into a social practice, which begins at the moment of becoming unable to 'not know'. In retrospect, this act could be taken as the working philosophy of the entire DL process; with the transference of individual knowledge comes collective responsibility and the creation of a sustainable learning community.

The performance was one of many interventions created for the DL final weekend, which took place as an artistic experimental platform through which we – a temporary collective of four art practitioners – collectively explored notions of land-use, (de)territorial thinking and generative concepts of belonging. Taking place in an empty house in the coastal town of Kalkara (Malta) in October 2021, the weekend constituted the concluding phase of a series of steps each with different methodologies, including a presentation of research findings alongside artists' responses at Kunsthalle Exnergasse (KEXVienna) in 2020, and a sequence of 'performative debates' with collaborators throughout 2021. In this context, what we call 'performative' refers both to an artistic form and to a criticality towards existing regimes of knowledge. Gender theorist Judith Butler (2006), in particular, conceptualizes performing as a way of (co-)becoming within the rendering and crafting of knowledge in which knowledge is never given, but is always a process that 'proves to be performative'.

This chapter focuses on the interplay between knowledge and community, on what 'knowing' – produced by practices arising from coming together – implies; and its potential community-building capacity by means of methodological experimentation on the advocacy of knowledge. During the project's process, our aim was not to collaborate with one specific or homogeneous community. Instead, we took Malta as an artistic case study to examine how an alternative sense of collectiveness can be composed through a set of spatial relations using dialogue as an aesthetic discipline and a principle for exhibition-making, to critically explore how territories as products of intersecting interests can create new artistic fields for 'knowing'. We considered emotional and responsive aspects of knowledge transfer

Figure 12.1: Charlene Galea performing Ħawwel żerriegħa ('Sow a Seed') during Debatable Land(s), October 2021. @ Photo Elisa von Brockdorff.

and understood belonging as emergent co-becoming that may allow for new geographies, simultaneously caring and careful, and which – as Galea exemplified in her performance – may adopt a different mode of responsibility.

The term 'Debatable Lands' (DL), which we borrowed for our project, originally referred to a piece of land on the border between Scotland and England where sovereignty was in question. For centuries, this land and its borders were intangible, until a map of the territory was drawn, and it became a 'knowable place' to which a borderline was added. Following Frances Stonor Saunders's observation, borderlines, manifesting the knowable place, can be equally seen as places of risk, symbols of a step into the unknown, or a 'nothing place' that is simultaneously a place on a map, a line, or a void (2020). This ambivalence around conceptualizing borders partly fuelled our investigation into whether becoming knowable through a bureaucratic process manifests another definition of 'knowable' than a piece of farmland being made knowable by a shared experience. Who can truly claim to 'know' a piece of land, and who are the carers in those different scenarios?

However, lines on a map drawn as a result of claims of belonging are not themselves free of the ambiguities that may escape the rigorous theorization of other key concepts of space. This is how DL sought to reflect on the texture of how they are felt, practised and transmitted and what different concepts of belonging, owning and knowing they may generate. Throughout the project's various stages, we aimed to bring forward definitions of shared, open or safe space, immaterial or new imaginary categories beyond the dichotomy of the private and public realm, and, in doing so, to consider the roles of memory and history in these nomenclatures of ownership or otherwise, for designing a participatory, interdisciplinary project that envisions territory beyond the concept of occupation or physicality.

In Malta, space is delineated by a highly contested field of spatial vectors. The island nation is not only one of the smallest European countries but also one of the most densely populated in the world. The notion of place is strongly linked to the politics of space, departing from a long colonial history and rhetoric of survival, filled with blind spots and ambivalences in reception and discourse. Under the intense lens of the microstate, as we argue, events and conflicts become magnified for identifying materialities and regimes of spatial concepts. Nevertheless, the conducted research was not exclusive to the archipelago, and our viewpoint shifted back and forth from the minutiae to the global spectacle. Similarly, we took facts, current global events and behaviours – like border controls, coercive behaviours or populist rhetoric, to name a few – as symbolic tokens of the ideologies they represent.

This initial research served as a portfolio of information, propositions and questions inspired by accumulated materials from academia, mainstream media, literature, propaganda and visual culture, which was then arranged into nine exploratory essayistic chapters with the intention to deconstruct classical chronological narratives or 'logical' chains of arguments.[2] The nine sections lent structure to the project's methodologies, around which a temporary community of artists, researchers and experts in their fields was built.

While DL's first public manifestation, the exhibition at KEXVienna, which presented its chapters with collaged materials and artefacts alongside the artistic responses of twelve artists, acknowledged – as Hilary Mantel (2017) stated – that information does not equate with knowledge and historical record is just that – a record – not the event itself, for the second part of the project, dialogue was utilized as an aesthetic and artistic discipline in itself. Using our nine-chapter structure, a series of what we called 'performative debates' brought 30 (non)experts and (non)artists from diverse fields together to discuss areas revolving around histories, identities and territories, including speculations around sovereignty, land-use, metaphorical or factual marine territories, cottage industries, cosmic views, otherness and more-than-human matters as well as the possibilities of 'caring and curing' in a prophesied dystopia.

At the same time, we took a deeper look at comparative methodologies such as wet ontology, which suggests conceptualizing the land from the sea's perspective to destabilize the static and linear framings that typify human geographical understanding of place, territory and time (Peters & Steinberg, 2015); or Archipelagic Thinking, a spatial counter-model to continental paradigms and perspectives for structuring ways of thinking about the world and our place in it differently. This research made up the underlying principles of our essayistic method – as a free-style process of disrupting old assemblages, of experimentation, of exploration, of inquiry, of provocation (Stephens & Martínez-San Miguel, 2020) – towards the initial step of inviting artists and thinkers from different fields and disciplines, scholars,

Figure 12.2: Debatable Land(s) exhibition view showing the information gathered during the online Performative Debates. @ Photo Elisa von Brockdorff.

activists and what we call everyday-experts to respond to the project's chapters in group online-sessions by means of horizontal debating.

The debates were ultimately conducted online due to COVID-19 restrictions; in the absence of the planned physicality and performative rituality of the debates, we endeavoured to encourage dialogue through some adjustments to a 'dry' online meeting atmosphere with the use of sensorial aids such as a sprig of rosemary, or a particular blend of tea, which were posted to participants in time for their debate. During other sessions, a short breathing exercise was proposed, while during one memorable meeting, participants were asked to go to the nearest window and gaze up at the sky for a few minutes before the session began. We used several methods like online mind-mapping and synonymic exercises to structure the documentation of the debates. This gathering of material eventually culminated in a spatial walk-through installation and a central sound installation at the final presentation days in the dilapidated house in Kalkara, along with artistic and performative interventions which used the collected materials and documentations as inspiration. The interventions ranged from movement, poetry and video, to sound-based, text-based, image-based and speech-based contributions, which for three days circulated through the entire building, trying to incorporate its unknown but vividly present stories.

'Now We Know'

The temporary 'community house' not only provided a physical space but, more importantly, offered an open and safe space for experimentation, in which all participants felt encouraged to articulate concerns and showcase alternative ways of physically experiencing spatial coordinates. The contributions laid claims, challenged us to take action, lamented binaries, cast spells on capitalist thinking and staged or deconstructed protests. For both the performers and the visitors, this temporary space, with its immediacy and physicality, became the site of a collective act of sharing stories and points of view in an intimate setting.

This returns us to questions about what it means 'to know' collectively in the moment of a shared experience, and how this 'knowing' can transfer responsibility, leading ultimately to the act of care. Is 'knowing', in the way we understood it within our project, in conflict with the radical pedagogy's claim to unlearn? Can 'to know' diverge from the blurred field of reproduced patterns of relationalities of knowledge, as theories of unlearning are concerned with?[3] And how does knowing affect the 'responsibility' gained through a collective act? What about tacit knowledge, as opposed to formal, codified or explicit knowledge – skills that cannot be captured through words alone that are difficult to express or extract, and which Michael Polanyi (1966) calls 'we know more than we can tell' (p. 4)?[4]

The environmentalist Thom van Dooren (2015) suggests replacing 'knowing' with 'knowing more' within the necessity that care involves an ongoing critical engagement with the terms of its own production and practice. For van Dooren, 'knowing more' articulates

Figure 12.3: Fatima Amn performing *UN/EARTH* (2021) within the Debatable Land(s) exhibition. @Photo Elisa von Brockdorff.

Figure 12.4: Mohamed Ali (Dali) Aguerbi & Chakib Zidi performing *Dress Code* (2021) within the Debatable Land(s) exhibition, with Rachelle Deguara's *Tor ta' Min?* ('Whose Fault?') (2021) visible in the background. @ Photo Elisa von Brockdorff.

an ongoing, deep and, at the same time, self-critical, conceptual knowledge, a vital practice of critique of what feminist theorist Donna Haraway (1988) referred to as the 'God Trick' of academic, good judgment (p. 581). For Haraway, caring means becoming subject to the unsettling obligation of curiosity, which requires knowing more at the end of the day than at the beginning.

Throughout the DL process, 'knowing more' was an essential critical force to community-building, knowledge-making and care-taking that resulted from response and responsibility. The process explored how we might learn to be affected in new ways; how practices of compassionate immersion might create new avenues for narratives which – as became evident during those closing days – can interfere with tidy images, coherent truths or stories with clear edges. Here, the obligation to 'know more' could emerge as a demand for deep contextual and critical knowledge about the object of our care, a knowledge that simultaneously demands collective responsibility by negotiating what counts as care and why. How else might care-through-knowing be imagined and practised?

In conclusion, the year-long DL process brought to the fore that the practice of coming together and sharing stories as a central artistic element has the capacity to load the conventions of spatial thinking with multiple meanings. This did not result in the accumulation of more knowledge per se but instead enabled the construction of alternative readings through the act of collectively 'knowing more', favouring neither one or another exclusive methodology or pedagogy. This organic experimental understanding allowed

Figure 12.5: Niels Plotard performing *Last Sweep* (2021) within Debatable Land(s), October 2021. @ Photo Elisa von Brockdorff.

space for empathy and imagination, forming a learning community and thus a social practice towards a connecting space of knowledge, which can be utilized as an investigative process into the constituting conditions and contexts of its making.

Notes

1. Debatable Land(s) took place between August 2020 and November 2021, produced by Maren Richter and Klaus Schafler (*Fleeting Territories*), Margerita Pulè (*Unfinished Art Space*) and Greta Muscat Azzopardi and engaged with more than 50 collaborators from various (non)academic, and (non)artistic fields and disciplines.
2. The chapters were islandness; one divides into two, two doesn't merge into one; Zeroland, of horizons and trails in the sky; the shadow lines; strange fruit; ragments and traces; hunters and collectors; the next revolution will not be funded (or televised); terrain vague.
3. There are several critical studies on 'unlearning' as new forms of education but not limited to education. In particular, in postcolonial debates, unlearning serves to rethink the structures of power relations by forgetting old patterns of thinking.
4. In *The Tacit Dimension*, Michael Polanyi declares, '*I shall reconsider human knowledge by starting from the fact that we can know more than we can tell*' (1966, p. 4; original emphasis). *The Tacit Dimension* argues that tacit knowledge – tradition, inherited practices, implied values and prejudgments – is a crucial part of scientific knowledge.

References

Butler, J. (2006). *Gender trouble*. London: Routledge.

Butler, J. (2011). *Bodies in alliance and the politics of the treet*. Lecture held in Venice, 7 September 2011, in the framework of the series *The State of Things*, organized by the Office for Contemporary Art Norway (OCA). http://eipcp.net/transversal/1011/butler/en/#_ftnref2

Galea, C. (2021). *Ħawwel żerriegħa* ('Sow a Seed'). Performance, 23 October 2021. Debatable Land(s), Kalkara, Malta.

Haraway, D. (1988). Situated knowledges: The science question in feminism and the privilege of partial perspective. *Feminist Studies, 14*(3), 575–599.

Mantel, H. (2017, June 3). Why I became a historical novelist. *The Guardian*. https://www.theguardian.com/books/2017/jun/03/hilary-mantel-why-i-became-a-historical-novelist

Polanyi, M. (1966). *The tacit dimension*. New York, NY: Doubleday & Co.

Seery, A., & Dunne, É. (Eds.). (2016). *The pedagogics of unlearning*. Santa Barbara, CA: Punktum Books.

Steinberg, P., & Peters, K. (2015). Wet ontologies, fluid spaces: Giving depth to volume through oceanic thinking. *Society and Space, 33*(2), 247–264. https://doi.org/10.1068/d14148p

Stephens, M., & Martínez-San Miguel Y. (2020). *Contemporary archipelagic thinking towards new comparative methodologies and disciplinary formations*. Lanham, MD: Rowman & Littlefield International.

Stonor Saunders, F. (2020, July). The suitcase. *London Review of Books, 42*(15), 16–17

van Dooren, T. (2014). *Flight ways: Life and loss at the edge of extinction*. New York, NY: Columbia University Press.

van Dooren, T. (2015). The last snail: Loss, hope, and care for the future. In A. Springer & E. Turpin (Eds.), *Land & Animal & Nonanimal* in association with K. Einfeld & D. K. Wolf, Publishing and Haus der Kulturen der Welt.

Chapter 13

Cross-Cultural Dialogue: Searching Traces and the Mahalla Festival

Sabine Küper-Büsch and Thomas Büsch

The Istanbul-based association Diyalog Derneği developed the Mahalla Festival in response to the refugee crisis of 2014 when attacks by the Islamic State in Syria and Iraq caused internal and international mass migration. One of its basic actions was the 'Searching Traces' programme, which offered filmmaking-based workshops to facilitate cross-cultural collaboration and dialogue.

Sustainable development strategies

A group of researchers recently looked at global migration movements and asked whether a paradox exists between migration and sustainability (Granovel et al., 2021). They concluded that migration could contribute to sustainability by increasing well-being and reducing inequality and called for policies to embrace migration to achieve these goals by triggering synergistic benefits.

In the past eight years, the Mahalla Festival developed and implemented strategies for creating these synergies. It is a travelling event of contemporary art, film and literature, with several ancillary events running alongside it. It aims to promote cultural and artistic discourse in urban space that corresponds to global political, social and environmental challenges, believing that the 'migrant issues' are an opportunity for communities to engage in discussions about global conflicts and to process them locally. The festival's title, Mahalla, is a metaphor for a space of diversity and inclusion in the fields of arts and culture. It refers to the word 'mahalla' (root: Arabic), used in many languages and countries to mean 'neighbourhood'. The general vision is to question a dystopian reality of excluding 'the other' in the form of the migrant, the poor, the opposite sex, the environment and all entities considered as unknown and to raise awareness in communities about inclusion and topics connected to sustainable development. For newcomers, such as those living in Turkey, Syrians or African migrants residing in Malta, artistic platforms can serve as an invaluable vehicle for self-representation. Facilitating cross-cultural collaboration and dialogue between different groups via the tools of film and artistic expression was the motivation to start Searching Traces.

The Searching Traces programme

The experience with the first group of participants in a workshop about short film production shaped the following programmes and the outline of the festival. Two million Syrians fled to

Figure 13.1: *Film Workshop*, 2014.

Turkey from the ongoing civil war in their home country in 2014. Most migrants attending the first film workshops responded to the association's open call over social media. Twenty participants attended intensive daily sessions of four hours during two weeks in November 2014 and May 2015. The majority were Syrians with urban backgrounds from across different regions of Syria. There were an equal number of male and female participants between the ages of 22–35 years old.

As a basic result, we observed that the participants were not looking for psychological support but were highly motivated to share their complex experiences from Syria. They were searching for adequate artistic tools of expression, practical guidance for settling in Istanbul and a platform to share their own narratives. In the following section, we share several moments from these workshops as snapshots of how cross-cultural dialogue can be fostered through the arts.

Encountering victimization

Most participants in the Searching Traces workshop were inexperienced in filmmaking. The single-shot-film technique was chosen as a basic tool. It teaches the participants to focus on one topic and complex handling of camera devices with the management of video- and sound-tools. Syrian Filmmaker Ziad Homsi and German Filmmakers Thomas Büsch and Sabine Küper-Büsch conducted the first video workshop in the winter of 2014. The participants were mainly Syrians and two Turkish, one Bosnian and two Germans. Homsi screened parts of some video footage from Syria. Some footage included sequences of violence between the Syrian military and the Free Syrian Army. The non-Syrians reacted by discussing the possibility that the Syrians might get re-traumatized. An immediate discussion arose. The Syrians mainly expressed an aversion to being victimized. They disliked generalizing TV-documentary formats showing traumatized kids from refugee camps or Syrians begging in the streets of Istanbul. They argued that the images commonly depicted by the mass media produced stereotypes of refugees, leading to their stigmatization.

Sublime experiences

The next step was the development of film ideas. The formats for the films were not limited to any style. Documentary, fiction and experimental formats were equally welcomed. During the brainstorming sessions, the forced migrants were the first to come up with ideas because they had immediate experiences to process and the desire to share them. Two Palestinian-Syrians, Bassam and Mahmoud,[1] shared their idea of working on a film using a suitcase as a metaphorical object. For them, the suitcase represents an object in one's personal history that travels everywhere with the person. In 2001, Mahmoud was forced to leave high school in Baghdad due to the US bombardment of Iraq, and he then moved to Damascus with his family. The Tigris River appeared in front of his eyes whenever he was looking at the waters of the Golden Horn. Both shared an apartment in Fener on the banks of the Golden Horn. The movie starts with Bassam as the main character picking photos from a wall inside his

Figure 13.2: *Beyond the Station,* 2014.

Spartan room. He climbs into a big suitcase and closes it. In the next scene, Bassam carries the big suitcase on his back through the streets. He constantly struggles with the load; finally, he reaches the shore of the Golden Horn, pushes it into a pit and runs away. The end is open. Does he free himself from the object, or does he run away from his tormented self?

Creating safe spaces

During the shooting, the leading actor was coached by the participants of the workshop and the instructors. Migrants and locals inhabit Fener equally. The Syrians in the workshop often felt bullied in public spaces. During the filming activity, they were acting in a protected frame. Many people were asking about the purpose of the filming, delighted about the educational purpose and impressed by the seriousness of the performance. The first screening of the film during the workshop startled everyone. Bassam and Mahmoud had added the sound of an early performance of artist Yoko Ono on Japanese haiku from the 1960s. The shrill tones successfully developed the performance around themes related to memories, loss and pain. Even though this was Bassam's first experience in acting and Mahmoud's pioneering experience with the camera, the video was amazingly strong both visually and in terms of content. They chose *Beyond the Station* as a title to express that there are a few normal ways of mobility available for refugees.

Building a sense of belonging

In this particular example, collaborative filmmaking served as a vehicle to mediate between the past and the present. Memories from the old home were intertwined with the new surroundings, creating reflections about past journeys, new memories and experiences of belonging. The interaction during the production process inspired an important, new spirit for community life. The Syrians communicated with their new environment for the first time as equals and respected filmmakers. The different films produced in the first Searching Traces workshop dealt with complex realities related to different cases. Screenings in prominent spaces such as the Salt Museum and the Pera Museum provided a platform for Syrians and locals to communicate based on a sublimated content of a real crisis. The audience learned about a globally relevant conflict and its relevance in places outside of their own context.

Encountering borders: The Mahalla Festival

In 2015, the Searching Traces workshop produced a documentary, 'In the dark times', in Istanbul. The film was screened at the Pera Museum with only some of the filmmakers present. During this year, many Syrians travelled illegally abroad. Most of them risked their lives by crossing the Mediterranean. The Diyalog Association founded the Mahalla Festival 2017 in Istanbul as a travelling event to work internationally on strategies to promote sustainable communication structures through the arts and to empower vulnerable groups.

Searching Traces at Mahalla Malta

Illegal migration to Malta comes mainly from African countries. The workshop Searching Traces started in March 2018 on the premises of the Sudanese migrant association in Hamrun. The instructors Thomas Büsch and Sabine Küper-Büsch involved the NGO President Mohamed Ibrahim as a participant and co-lecturer. During a six-month period, a group of Sudanese, Eritrean and Venezuelan migrants and Maltese nationals worked together in three film workshops.

Motives of belonging

Most migrants face extreme difficulties during their boat trips. When brainstorming ideas for film themes, it was agreed that the sea should be the unifying motif. As was the case with Syrians in Istanbul, documentary style films about migrants' experiences around their journey were not preferred. The collaborative shooting of the film *Map of the Mediterranean* helped the participants to bond among themselves. A great deal of sharing of personal experiences had accompanied the development of the content had been accompanied by. A poem by Antoine Cassar, a contemporary strong voice in the Maltese literary scene, is about the shape of the Mediterranean Sea and the history of its

Figure 13.3: *Map of the Mediterranean*, 2018.

people, including ancient and contemporary migrations. A sensitive subjective camera operated by Mohammed Ibrahim follows Maltese teacher Heidi de Carlo as she recites the poem while strolling along Golden Beach, one of Malta's most visited coastal spots. The shooting was done collectively. Similar to the film *Beyond the Station* in Istanbul, everyone in the workshop identified with this film.

Artistic dialogues and community context

The Searching Traces workshops in Malta leading up to the festival were an important means of connecting members of the community and their specific themes. Collaboration with the local art scene and a close and intense engagement with the history, landscape and stories of the archipelago, its geography and unique language became a focus for the Mahalla Festival in Malta, providing a context for dialogues and sustained communication structures between the different groups. A collection of films was later screened at the Rima and the Mahalla Festival in Valletta and the University of Malta. Two museums, galleries and independent art spaces in different locations connected to diverse audiences. Fifty artists from thirty countries took part and shaped fourteen events in six venues. The festival showed artistic works addressing issues of migration and its causes as well as environmental, social and political issues from Malta and other countries and started up an international network to collaborate on art practices that contribute to the communication of ideas about migration amongst members of communities and serve to raise awareness of international conflicts, social justice and sustainable development policies.

Mahalla Murmuration

In the summer 2020, the Searching Traces workshop moved to Zoom meetings due to lockdowns. Emerging filmmakers from different locations were able to meet. Some of the Syrians involved in the first workshop in 2014 rejoined from the Netherlands and Canada, as well as participants from Malta. The Anna Lindh Foundation's network joined in 2021 with NGO activists from Northern EU countries. Participants from Gaziantep in Turkey and Syria became involved and created a direct line to regions experiencing an ongoing crisis. The first joint film project was produced in Malta. In *Taxi Malta*, directed by Eritrean activist Major Sium and Maltese artist Martina Camilleri, intellectuals in Malta spoke about the realities of past and present migration in Sium's taxi. The film was followed by a discussion at Malta's centre for creativity and art, Spazju Kreattiv, in Valletta.

In 2021, the theme for the Mahalla Festival was developed in the Searching Traces workshop by participants from three continents: Murmuration is a formation of travelling birds performed to protect themselves from cold, hunger and disorientation during long-distance flights. Mahalla Murmuration presented 30 artists from twelve countries in

Figure 13.4: *Taxi Malta*, 2021.

Istanbul. Despite pandemic restrictions, 1500 people visited the twelve events while 200,000 people followed on social media platforms.

Prospects

Forced migration continues to be a global reality. The COVID-19 pandemic caused barriers to movement worldwide and unexpectedly opened new possibilities for connecting on virtual platforms due to new habits of online communication. The Searching Traces workshops built an international network around the Mahalla Festival in the past seven years. These experiences helped to form the guiding principles for future work.

The local context and the disposition of newcomers are naturally shaping the direction of collaboration and the content that is developed. In contrast with Syrians in Istanbul, the intention of migrant participants in Malta focused on the desire for more inclusion. They were mainly concerned about their ability to connect to the Maltese context. The involvement of central figures like Sudanese Mohammed Ibrahim and Eritrean Major Sium, spokesperson of the Eritrean community, were essential avenues for local discourse.

Collaborative art projects between professionals and emerging artists from different cultural backgrounds generate synergies and can form new narratives by questioning power structures and repetitions of them in discourses. In this sense, they provide elements to build the dynamics for sustainable development to promote inclusion, and involvement of susceptible groups and serve information flow. Dissidents from crisis regions are a crucial source of information about global conflicts. The festival works on structures that facilitate collaborative and co-creative activities, which benefit newcomers and host communities alike.

The current global pandemic provides opportunities to generate new narratives about ways of living with others, while the field of arts and culture provides important tools and intersections for doing so. Topics like racism, diversity and multiculturalism, the dysfunctions of globalization, the transformation of urban spaces and the possibilities and borders of the digital metaverse provide fascinating new areas for all kinds of artistic disciplines and future festivals.

Note

1. These names are pseudonyms.

References

Di Carlo, H., & Ibrahim, M. (2018). *Map of the Mediterranean.* http://streetwalking.inenart.eu/archives/4538

Fares, M., & Halabi, B. (2014). *Beyond the Station.* http://streetwalking.inenart.eu/archives/2979

Franco Granovel, M., Adger, W. N., Safra de Campos, R., Boyd, E., Carr, E. R., Fábos, A., ... Siddiqui, T. (2021). The migration-sustainability paradox: transformations in mobile worlds. *Current Opinion in Environmental Sustainability, 49,* 98–109. https://doi.org/10.1016/j.cosust.2021.03.013

Küper-Büsch, S., & Büsch, T. (2020). Facilitating cross-cultural dialogue through film, art and culture: Searching Traces and the Mahalla Festival. In F. Baban & K. Rygiel (Eds.), *Fostering pluralism through solidarity activism in Europe* (pp. 189–216). New York, NY: Springer.

Mahalla Festival. http://mahalla.inenart.eu/

Searching Traces. *Methodology.* http://streetwalking.inenart.eu/archives/category/one-single-take

Sium, M., & Camilleri, M. (2021). *Taxi Malta.* https://www.kreattivita.org/en/event/taxi-malta/

Chapter 14

Participatory Art With Trees: A Pedagogical Approach

Maria Huhmarniemi

In Finland's city of Rovaniemi, cut-down trees have caused distress and a vibrant discussion among residents. While some people see mature trees as old friends, others think they are worthless. Consequently, many trees that people feel connected to have been lost. In spring 2020, along with four other residents, I produced a municipal initiative to better practice safeguarding biodiversity and mature trees in urban and suburban forests. We also set up a social media group called 'Friends of Trees: For the Nearby Forests of Rovaniemi'. Some artists joined the group and called for artistic actions that would draw attention to trees and create an understanding of their value. Following this joint agenda, trees and the human connection with them have been at the core of my artistic work since 2020. The approach is influenced by posthuman theories and artist-researchers and educators who aim to collaborate with more-than-human nature (Huhmarniemi, 2021; Van Borek, 2021; Ylirisku, 2021).

My artistic research was carried out at the University of Lapland and supported by the international research project 'Acting on the Margins: Arts as Social Sculpture' (AMASS), funded by the European Union. AMASS promotes art that educates society and introduces new perspectives for the future. I designed the *Encounter-a-tree* installation as a part of the so-called Soft Power Art testbed of the AMASS research. The Soft Power Art testbed focused on how the arts can be used to mitigate societal challenges by addressing policy issues head-on. The testbed was carried out by nine artists working in Lapland through participatory art. The overall aim was to target issues of environmental policies and the development of behaviour regarding attitudes towards activism, civic engagement and inclusion. All of these aspects were part of the *Encounter-a-tree* installation, with the aim of including a more-than-human quality to the sense of community and decolonizing the arts for cultural sustainability in the Arctic region. I followed the approach of arts-based action research (Jokela & Huhmarniemi, 2018) and documented the artistic work to share it.

In this chapter, I consider how contemporary artistic practices contribute to the strengthening of local communities and sustainability initiatives. I briefly describe a participatory artwork called *Powers of Nature* and the installation *Encounter-a-tree* (Figures 14.1–14.3). The *Powers of Nature* was a collaboration between human participants and trees in a forest. It was designed by four artists: druid Francis Joy (England/Finland), painter Smaranda Sabina Moldovan (Romania), dancer Hugo Peña (Chile/Germany) and me as a community artist (Finland). The workshop was part of the International Socially Engaged Art Symposium (ISEAS) organized in Finnish Lapland in August 2020.

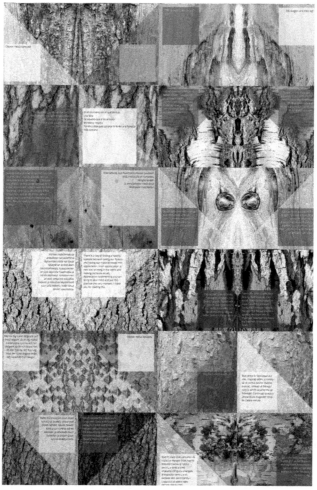

Figure 14.1: Detail of wallposters for the artwork *Encounter-a-tree*, 2021, by Maria Huhmarniemi and co-artists Francis Joy, Misha del Val, Hugo Peña, Amir Abdi, Tanja Koistinen, Raisa Raekallio, and Smaranda Moldovan.

Due to the COVID-19 crisis, Moldovan could only attend the workshop online, and Joy, Peña and I carried out the activities with local trees and members of a village community. In this chapter, I present my experience of the workshop as participatory art. The *Encounter-a-tree* installation followed the workshop and was presented for the first time in the 'ISEAS: Conversation' exhibition at Rovaniemi Art Museum in the summer 2021, curated by the head of ISEAS, Katja Juhola. *Encounter-a-tree* was presented to the residents of Rovaniemi and fulfilled my goal of promoting respect for trees in my hometown.

Figure 14.2: Detail of the artwork *Encounter-a-tree*, 2020, by Maria Huhmarniemi and co-artists Francis Joy, Misha del Val, Hugo Peña, Amir Abdi, Tanja Koistinen, Raisa Raekallio and Smaranda Moldovan.

Informal transformative education and new genre Arctic art

My research on participatory art with trees is informed by participatory aesthetics (Matarasso, 2019) and transformative education (Lin & Oxford, 2011). The participatory art presented in this chapter aimed to enhance participants' sense of unity with other humans and more-than-humans and thus to influence values towards an ecological turn in behaviour and a reduction in consumerism. This approach draws on posthumanistic theories that encourage recognition of the agency of other-than-human parts of nature. Posthumanist discourses are increasingly influencing arts and art pedagogies (Rousell & Fell, 2018; Ylirisku, 2021).

Strong human–nature connectedness is typical in northern communities throughout the Arctic region. Animals, forests and rock formations, for example, are considered to be alive and to have spiritual agency. For example, there is a belief in a female forest spirit and in the forest itself as an active agent. The well-known concept of 'forest cover' (*metsänpeitto*) in Finnish folklore reinforces the danger of getting lost in a forest and follows the belief in forests' agency in misguiding humans (Kuusela, 2020). The participatory art with trees presented in this chapter is partly based on traditional Finnish and Swedish views of trees and forests as active agents.

While working in Lapland and being active in the cultural politics of Arctic regions, my artistic production is rooted in the aim of decolonizing the arts from western dualism. I like to question the distinction between arts and spirituality, in addition to viewing arts, crafts and ecoculture as interwoven. The concept of 'Arctic arts' (Huhmarniemi & Jokela,

Figure 14.3: Posing for the 'ISEAS: Conversation' exhibition with an active member of the community 'Friends of Trees: For the Nearby Forests of Rovaniemi'. Photo: Marko Junttila, 2021.

2020) has been used in exhibitions and publications by members of the Arctic Sustainable Arts and Design network at the University of the Arctic. The concept itself is political since it draws attention to the value of arts and cultural production in the Arctic region and differentiates them from western arts as an effort at decolonization. Moreover, Arctic artists often participate in environmental and political discussions through art. The concept of a new genre of Arctic art defines contemporary artistic interventions that integrate themselves into ecoculture and include activism (Jokela, Huhmarniemi, Beer, & Soloviova, 2021).

Powers of Nature participatory art

The *Powers of Nature* participatory art project took place in a mature pine tree forest in Äkäslompolo village in Lapland. We invited participants through open calls and personal invitations, and they came from nearby villages. Each activity began with participants introducing themselves to the forest. In the second phase of the workshop, Francis Joy helped the participants strengthen their connection to trees through subtle awareness. Joy presented different ways to approach and communicate with trees using feelings, touch and sensations in the body and hands to sense the trees' energy fields. Some of the practices and techniques that Joy shared with the group are common to druids, while others he developed himself.

After the practices guided by Joy, participants were led into a creative dance and bodily dialogue together and with trees, encouraged by team member Hugo Peña. This happened by observing the form of the trees and following them in bodily movements. Each participant danced first with one tree, then with more trees and finally with human participants. Dancing together aimed to strengthen a sense of community equally among humans and trees.

The reflection was continued by working with clay, in one workshop by painting clay on rocks and in the second by forming a piece of clay. The painting with clay on rocks and forming pieces of clay were guided by me and implemented as an arts-based method to reflect on the encounters with the trees, other humans and the powers of nature. The participants had the opportunity to transform some of their emotions, experiences and topics for dialogue with the trees into visual images and forms. After focusing on the clay in their hands, the participants talked about their experiences. Some of them were emotionally moved: they cried and described the experience as special. For some participants, forming clay enhanced their sense of connectedness with trees.

> As I sat on the soft ground with the lump of clay in my hands, leaning on a tree, I noticed a sense of some kind of realm that I was connected with, that I had entered. I actually felt a strong presence of an ancient tree, some kind of 'Mother tree' with huge roots and a massive presence. I made the sculpture out of clay just by listening and being open to this Mother tree and I moulded the clay very directly.
> (Participant's reflection after the workshop, given by an e-mail message)

Encounter-a-tree installation

After the experiences in the *Powers of Nature*, I continued my work in AMASS to research how arts can be used to mitigate societal challenges. Researchers report a growing number of depressed and lonely people in Finland, worsened by the coronavirus pandemic. Part of the population is depressed by eco-anxiety, while others feel hatred for those who demand climate actions and the protection of nature. Social difficulties and restrictions have led Finns to spend time in forests. Thus, I was motivated to carry out research on enhancing a sense of connectedness with trees.

The *Encounter-a-tree* installation encouraged audience members to slow down, focus on trees, encounter the powers of nature and open up their senses in a forest. The installation was designed conceptually and visually by me, and the guidelines were given by me, Joy and Peña, who were facilitating *Powers of Nature* and five of the participants of it: artists Misha del Val, Amir Abdi, Tanja Koistinen, Raisa Raekallio and Smaranda Moldovan. Some guidelines gave straightforward guides such as 'Find a tree you feel drawn to. Sit and place the base of your spine against its trunk where it meets the earth'. Some guidelines were poetic, such as 'May the forest be with you!' The guidelines for encountering trees given by participants showed that a multi-level and spiritual relationship with trees had occurred in the *Powers of Nature*. For example, the work with clay was transformed into a guideline for experiencing communication with a tree (Figure 14.2).

Encounter-a-tree installation consists of a large-scale poster on a wall and shareable cards that visitors to the exhibition can take along to forests and urban parks. It is also presented as an Instagram artwork at the account @encounteratree. Sharable cards and the use of Instagram helped the artwork to reach a wider public. The artwork has about 35 different guidelines and sixteen different languages. Some guidelines are translated into many languages and others into a few. The use of multiple languages underscored the willingness to educate and share with other humans regardless of their cultural and linguistic backgrounds. A similar undertone is visible in other artistic productions created in the Soft Power Art testbed in the AMASS research (Huhmarniemi, 2021; Miettinen & Sarantou, 2021) and demonstrates the appearance of a new genre of Arctic art as insights and arguments from the North for the globe.

Reflections

The *Powers of Nature* participatory art and *Encounter-a-tree* artworks highlighted the value of trees and forests, as was my intention, based on discussions in the social media community 'Friends of Trees: For the Nearby Forests of Rovaniemi' (Figure 14.3). The focus was on both supporting individuals and strengthening the sense of belonging amongst human communities and more-than-humans.

While the examples presented in this chapter focused on personal relations with trees, forest maintenance in Finland is also discussed at the national and European political levels in relation to protecting biodiversity and forests as carbon sinks. Finland and neighbouring Sweden are Europe's most heavily forested countries. They are also the countries that oppose the regulation of forestry in the European Union and demand rights for clear cutting to meet the needs of the pulp industry. Views on forest policy split Nordic lawmakers in the European Parliament (Kurmayer, 2021), not just Finns.

This presentation of *Powers of Nature* and *Encounter-a-tree* illustrated one way for the artist to engage in environmental and cultural politics and to contribute to the strengthening of communities. Based on feedback from the audience, scaling the artwork by shareable cards and social media was successful. Cards were shared very fast, and many other local artists told me that they are also collaborating with trees or hoping to do so in the future. Further research is needed to evaluate the impact of arts on local and global communities.

Acknowledgements

The AMASS project has received funding from the European Union's Horizon 2020 research and innovation programme under the Marie Skłodowska-Curie grant agreement no. 870621.

References

Huhmarniemi, M. (2021). Forest talks to us – Art and coping with forest disputes. *ART Education VISUAL Journal IMAG*, 2021(11). https://www.insea.org/wp-content/uploads/2021/08/IMAG_11_HUHMARNIEMI.pdf

Huhmarniemi, M., & Jokela, T. (2020). Arctic art and material culture: Northern knowledge and cultural resilience in the northernmost Europe. In L. Heininen, H. Exner-Pirot, & J. Barnes (Eds.), *Arctic yearbook 2020: Climate change and the Arctic: Global origins, regional responsibilities?* Akureyri: Arctic Portal. https://arcticyearbook.com/

Jokela, T., & Huhmarniemi, M. (2018). Art-based action research in the development work of arts and art education. In G. Coutts, E. Härkönen, M. Huhmarniemi, & T. Jokela (Eds), *The lure of Lapland: A handbook of Arctic art and design* (pp. 9–23). Lapland: University of Lapland. https://lauda.ulapland.fi/handle/10024/63653

Jokela, T., Huhmarniemi, M., Beer, R., & Soloviova, A. (2021). Mapping new genre Arctic art. In L. Heininen, H. Exner-Pirot, & J. Barnes (Eds.), *Arctic yearbook 2021: Defining and mapping sovereignties, policies and perceptions*. Akureyri: Arctic Portal. https://arcticyearbook.com/

Kurmayer, N. J. (2021). Forest policy splits Nordic lawmakers in the European Parliament. September 20. https://www.euractiv.com/section/climate-environment/news/forest-policy-splits-nordic-lawmakers-in-the-european-parliament/

Kuusela, T. (2020). Spirited away by the female forest spirit in Swedish folk belief. *Folklore*, 131(2), 159–179. https://doi.org/10.1080/0015587X.2019.1701280

Lin, J., & Oxford, R. (2011). *Transformative eco-education for human and planetary survival*. Charlotte, NC: Information AGE Publishing.

Matarasso, F. (2019). *A restless art: How participation won, and why it matters*. Lisbon: Calouste Gulbenkian Foundation.

Miettinen, S., & Sarantou, M. (2021). Five salmon and two fish (viisi lohta ja kaksi kalaa). In R. Vella & M. Sarantou (Eds.), *Documents of socially engaged art* (pp. 36–46). Canterbury: Insea Publications.

Rousell, D., & Fell, F. (2018). Becoming a work of art: Collaboration, materiality and posthumanism in visual arts education. *International Journal of Education through Art, 14*(1), 91–110. https://doi.org/10.1386/eta.14.1.91_1

Ylirisku, H. (2021). *Reorienting environmental art education*. Espoo: Aalto University. http://urn.fi/URN:ISBN:978-952-64-0245-1

Van Borek, S. (2021). Water as artist-collaborator: Posthumanism and reconciliation in relational media arts-based education. *Reconceptualizing Educational Research Methodology, 12*(1). https://doi.org/10.7577/rerm.4247

Chapter 15

'Ngen' Ancient Spirits of the Woods: Art-Based Environmental Education in Chiloé Archipelago

Francisco Schwember, Felipe Palma, Antonia Condeza-Marmentini and Guillermo Marini

Context and project

The Chiloé Archipelago is one of a kind. Where the American continent fractures into the southernmost territories of Chile, and the Andes Mountain range pushes the last threads of habitable land into the Pacific Ocean, a collection of islands emerges as one of nature's richer and more beautiful and severe environments.

The archipelago, composed of the *Isla Grande de Chiloé* ('Big Island of Chiloé') and approximately 40 smaller islands, constitutes what has come to be known as a *maritory* or *searitory*: this is a water-based geographical area with human settlements usually along the coast, where the ocean acts more like a communication venue than an obstacle or frontier.

Chiloé was originally inhabited by Veliches, Mapuche-Huilliche and Chonos peoples and the oldest human remains date from between 5000 and 6000 years ago. During the sixteenth century, the Spanish Colony integrated this area into its empire, activating a slow process of racial mixtures that eventually bloomed into a peculiar *mestizo* culture, characterized by extreme isolation, a creative lifestyle that had to deal with an environment of harsh austerity and the coexistence of indigenous and occidental ways of living.

Throughout almost three centuries of colonial presence, such coexistence was key to producing artworks like the Churches of Chiloé inscribed into the United National Educational, Scientific and Cultural Organization's (UNESCO) World Heritage sites in 2000. These churches represent a unique example of outstanding ecclesiastical wooden architecture and bring together knowledge and practices of the Jesuit 'Circular Mission'[1] as well as the woodworking abilities of sailors, fishers and farmers.

Among the different traditions that reveal the spiritual values of these Indigenous-European communities, the *minga* has a significant role that may shed light on today's complex socio-environmental challenges. According to Obando (2015), *minga* is a word of Andean origin that refers to a particular type of communitarian agricultural work where benefits are shared among the entire tribe.

In Chiloé, this practice expands into all types of gratuitous collaborative tasks. Perhaps the most archetypical of these, and still in use today, is pushing a house across the country – sometimes with the help of oxen – to relocate an entire family. Figure 15.1 helps to show that a *minga* entails the collective development and preservation of ways of living and knowing that have historically survived up to our days while promoting human and more-than-human models of transformational power.

Art, Sustainability and Learning Communities

Figure 15.1: Minga in Chiloé. © Giovanna Bacchiddu.

As an interdisciplinary team that brings together visual arts, geography, anthropology and education, we recognize ourselves as engaged in the practice and the value of the *minga* in the quest to find alternative paths to overcome current civilizational crises. With this inspiration, we set out to work with children from the Chiloé Archipelago. As we developed a pedagogical approach based on the relational turn (DeLanda, 2006; Mesle, 2008), we put into play how we understand and enact our situation in the world, with a view to re-signifying and projecting possible and desirable futures for all.

Strategically, we partnered with Chiloé's CECREA Centre,[2] one of the regional informal education initiatives the Chilean State has activated throughout the nation in recent years. There, during a weekly collaboration dynamic with local teachers and artists, we crafted an interdisciplinary methodology that aims to re-visit and unveil the knowledge local communities possess about their territory – after millenary coevolution with nature – and that is threatened today by the accelerated materialist practices imposed by neoliberalism. Provocatively, we co-designed a work process that allows children to evoke ancient ways of knowing and to project new ones through the artistic creation of a Ngen.

The Ngen is a spirit of the Mapuche–Huilliche cosmovision, known as the force, owner or protector of a place (Di Giminiani & González Gálvez, 2018). It may manifest in zoomorphic, phytomorphic or anthropomorphic forms, as well as embody fire, water or wind. Traditionally, the Ngen must authorize the intervention or use of a place and demands restitution if nature suffers any change or damage. For instance, if someone needs wood to make a fire and eat a fish, both the Ngen that guards the wood and the one protecting the river will be pleased to receive a piece of corn, bread or even coins in return (Grebe, 1993).

Through children's voices, we realized the everyday presence of Ngen in people's lives on the island. These insights from more-than-human interactions allowed children to explore and recover powerful experiences of respect and reciprocity.

Methodology

We began by searching for the Ngen through a series of activities co-designed with teachers and artists from Chiloe's CECREA Centre in the city of Castro. Inspired by the *minga* tradition, we met in weekly working sessions focused on understanding, investigating and recreating the more-than-human guardian spirits children found around their homes and daily lives. Considering that the entire project took place during the 2019 COVID-19 pandemic and many participants experienced strict quarantines, our meetings combined virtual, hybrid and face-to-face interaction, in which careful listening and observation of the territory became a trigger for collaborative artistic creation.

This research-creation (Haseman, 2006) invited children to explore their territory using a 'multimodal micro-ethnography' strategy. We refer to *ethnography* in the sense that all activities were based on careful and extended consideration of more-than-human beings that inhabit Chiloé; *micro* inasmuch they implied a brief and focalized exercise; and *multimodal* because we promoted the study of more-than-human beings through a variety of register formats (visual, audio, textual, etc.) in a sensory and creative fashion.

To carry out this exploration within a pandemic situation, children received in their homes an 'ethnographic toolbox' consisting of different scale Chiloé maps, compasses, fieldwork notebooks, binoculars, hand lenses, pencils, paper, tempera and crayons, among other elements aimed at looking out for the archipelago's Ngen. Figure 15.2 provides a general view of the toolbox each child worked with.

In the first place, children interviewed their elders in search of ancient Ngen stories. Later, they received an introduction to the principles of scientific naturalism, birdwatching and botany. With these sets of knowledge as guidelines, they invited their parents to join the exploration of woods, rivers and coastlines, looking for the guarding spirits of nature that may dwell within a bird, an old tree or a cascade, among others.

Children identified and recorded on their 'ethnographic toolkit' those places and moments where a Ngen might live. By collecting objects, visual images and sounds, they had the opportunity to expand their comprehension of the existence of more-than-human beings that dwell in the area.

Once we were all back in virtual space, children showed the materials gathered during exploration, commenting on them and discussing their experiences. Based on those conversations, children began drawing and crafting their own power masks that impersonate a new Ngen of their own selection, choosing its main abilities and

Figure 15.2: Ethnographic toolbox. © Rosario Ateaga.

re-interpreting its supernatural dominion. For instance, some children chose the capacity to fly and observe nature from above; others decided to grow in strength and become a family-protection Ngen, and others opted for the power to clean and renew Chiloe's water courses and coasts. Figure 15.3 gives a glimpse of the actual homework during the project.

During our last virtual session, children presented their Ngen masks and described them as if projecting their desires on this figure. They told us what the Ngen could do, emphasizing in all cases a deep awareness of the values of care and restoration. Finally, we took pictures of each girl and boy with their power masks, protecting their personal identities as well as recognizing their original achievements of creation and care. As an example, Figure 15.4 shows a new Ngen which holds the power to clean water and resuscitate plants.

'Ngen' Ancient Spirits of the Woods

Figure 15.3: Boy painting blue dolphins on Isla Grande map. © Rosario Ateaga.

Restorative powers: Water, healing and death

This research-creation *minga* was a collaborative exercise of intersubjective resignification between students, teachers and artists based on concerns and desires that we all recognized as shared. Despite the geographical distance, and in favour of the different experiences we had throughout the project, we developed a working method that implied perceptual, descriptive, investigative, creative and critical dimensions. All in all, we came to realize how our world is always a place that is shared with more-than-human beings, with whom we coexist through different modes of living and knowing.

Along this journey, adults were confronted by children and their creations and urged to expand the limits of possibility and the definition of action. In exploring and creating the world of the Ngen, the ancient spirits of the archipelago, we were all invited to re-signify our own lives. Through the deployment of their millenarian and actual powers, we also found spaces for poetry to express our fears and desires for the future.

In this sense, we identified the fear of death as a constitutive element of childhood, which particularly today, is amplified by the uncertainty regarding the future of our planet. According to children's accounts, the violence of catastrophic discourses concerning the future clouds the hope for action, obscuring the comprehension of territory-based opportunities and the proactive organization of possible futures.

Figure 15.4: Girl impersonating a Ngen © Rosario Ateaga.

However, the overlap between fiction and reality, magic and social science, art and pandemic has something valuable to teach: children endowed their new Ngen with powers capable of restoring life to human beings, animals and plants, in a clear shift towards the extension of the community outside the limits established by rationalist languages and modern epistemic frames.

For instance, among the powers of the new Ngen, the restorative energy of water could confront death. This image of healing is present in the vision of children, and it seems a fundamental metaphor for building possible futures for all. Here, life and death coexist in a contemporary-mythical narration that our modern world wants to replace by the idea of productivity, reinforced by concepts such as 'human or natural resources', 'pristine nature', 'environment' or even the apparently well-intentioned 'recycling'. These concepts stand in the way of learning to re-value *natures*, plural as those articulated on physical, symbolic and metaphysical levels.

We acknowledge the need to integrate diverse ways of knowing as a key to re-interpret possible futures that address all 'earth beings' (De la Cadena, 2015) by means of true 'experiencing' (Mancilla Garcia, Hertz, & Schlüter, 2020) through the reconstruction of the languages, concepts, ethics and practices of care. In the case of Chiloé Ngen, indigenous traditional knowledge is crucial in envisioning a 'more-than-human world' (Panelli, 2010). In fact, they may help rearticulate social relationships given transformative projects with active political commitment (Stengers, 2010).

As we project possible futures through new collaborative work, we claim that it is possible to re-signify human–nature relationships. From the perspective of art-based environmental education, this entails broadening the comprehension and practice of contemporary art, integrating Indigenous art, popular art forms and symbols of restoration and transformation in a conscious effort to prevent epistemic injustice (Fricker, 2007). Accordingly, it is our honest expectation that this project will spur other forms of creation and relevant knowledge that open learning opportunities of cultural pertinence.

What remains are spaces for questions that necessarily require situated answers. Can we continue to educate using epistemic constructions that propose monological and normative understandings of nature circumscribed to the world of objects while disregarding other emerging values? Are we willing and prepared to admit within our pedagogical practices the expression of fears related to the human and more-than-human losses we suffer? What types of context-based educational experiences may generate transversal and meaningful learning in adults and children? We have open questions, and we will keep them open, emphasizing the need to create new processes of cultural recognition and recreation in each and every place where education is building pathways to better ways of living.

Notes

1. The Jesuits used a circulating system in their evangelization of the area: religious groups made annual tours, staying for a few days at the islands where churches were erected in collaboration with local communities. During the rest of the year, a specially trained layperson attended the spiritual needs of the inhabitants (UNESCO, 2021).
2. CECREA: Centres for artistic creation for children and youth where 'they can lead their learning processes and extend knowledge and understanding in new and unforeseen directions, favouring the discovery of new phenomena, new problems, new questions and answers, without necessarily conforming to the answers that others have pointed out' (Consejo Nacional de la Cultura y las Artes [National Council for Culture and the Arts], 2016).

References

Becker, H. (2007). *Telling about society*. Chicago, IL: The University of Chicago Press.

Consejo Nacional de la Cultura y las Artes [National Council for Culture and the Arts]. (2016). Management plan for CECREA Castro (Chiloé). http://www.cecrea.cl/wp-content/uploads/2016/05/PLAN-DE-GESTION-CECREA-CASTRO.pdf

Contreras, M. J. (2013). La práctica como investigación: nuevas metodologías para la academia Latinoamericana. *Poesis, 21–22*, 71–86. https://doi.org/10.22409/poiesis.1421-22.71-86

de la Cadena, M. (2015). *Earth beings: Ecologies of practice across Andean worlds*. Durham, NC: Duke University Press.

DeLanda, M. (2006). *A new philosophy of society: Assemblage theory and social complexity*. London: Continuum.

Di Giminiani, P., & González Gálvez, M. (2018). Who owns the water? The relation as unfinished objectivation in the Mapuche lived world. *Anthropological Forum, 28*(3), 199–216. https://doi.org/10.1080/00664677.2018.1495060

Fricker, M. (2007). *Epistemic injustice: Power and the ethics of knowing*. Oxford: Oxford University Press.

Grebe, M. (1993). El subsistema de los ngen en la religiosidad Mapuche. *Revista Chilena de Antropología, 12*, 45–64. https://revistadeantropologia.uchile.cl/index.php/RCA/article/view/17587

Haseman, B. (2006). Manifesto for performative research. Media International Australia incorporating culture and policy. *Quarterly Journal of Media Research and Resources, 118*(2), 98–106. https://doi.org/10.1177/1329878X0611800113

Mancilla Garcia, M., Hertz, T., & Schlüter, M. (2020). Towards a process epistemology for the analysis of social-ecological systems. *Environmental Values, 29*(2), 221–239. https://doi.org/10.3389/fsoc.2021.724751

Marres, N., Guggenheim, M., & Wilkie, A. (2018). *Inventing the social*. Manchester: Mattering Press.

Mesle, C. R. (2008). *Process-relational philosophy: An introduction to Alfred North Whitehead*. West Conshohocken, PA: Templeton Foundation Press.

Obando, J. C. (2015). La minga: un instrumento vivo para el desarrollo comunitario. *Revista de Sociología-Universidad de Nariño, 4*, 82–100. https://revistas.udenar.edu.co/index.php/revsoci/issue/view/381

Panelli, R. (2010). More-than-human social geographies: Posthuman and other possibilities. *Progress in Human Geography, 34*(1), 79–87. https://doi.org/10.1177/0309132509105007

Stengers, I. (2010). *Cosmopolitics I*. Minneapolis, MN: University of Minnesota Press.

United National Educational, Scientific and Cultural Organization [UNESCO]. (2021) *Churches of Chiloé*. https://whc.unesco.org/en/list/971

Chapter 16

Trash to Treasure: Sustaining and Preserving the Krobo Bead Culture Through Community Learning

Felix Amofa Gyebi

Introduction

The ideas in this chapter are guided by a collaborative smartphone documentary film with the working title *Trash to Treasure*, currently at the post-production stage. The film seeks to document an African Krobo community where beads represent the passing phases of life from birth till death. For centuries, the Krobo have recycled old glass bottles into beads that are adorned as necklaces, anklets, bracelets and waist beads. The knowledge and craft of recycled glass bead production have been transferred from generation to generation. The documentary, which is in four parts and online, captures the creative lifestyle of the innovative Krobo people in Ghana who are known for recycling old glass bottles into traditional beads.

More than just the making of a documentary, the film project is part of a larger research project which fits into the category of practice-led research. The overall project has some explicit research objectives, which are:

- to identify how collaborative smartphone filmmaking can give the Krobo community a voice,
- to identify the key features that define smartphone documentaries produced in Africa and,
- to document how *Trash to Treasure* can contribute to preserving the bead culture of the Krobo people.

This chapter is specifically guided by the first of the three objectives. The chapter is structured in three sections. The first section begins with a discussion of practice-led research, which is primarily centred on the creative processes and new media. The section concludes with a brief overview of a short documentary film. The second section considers editing practices with a focus on collaborative editing practices for community projects and community learning. The third section covers discussions about community learning and considers the influence of this learning on community-driven projects. The section concludes by advocating for the need to embark on and replicate collaborative documentary practices in underprivileged African communities through community learning to offer a voice to these communities.

Editing towards collaborative storytelling and community learning

In this section, I seek to discuss the evolution of collaborative editing practices in documentary films. The discussion begins by outlining intuition as an editing approach or concept suited for the artefact *Trash to Treasure*. In addition, the section also discusses the disconnect between filming and editing, which hinders collaborative creative practices. Finally, in this section, I consider adopting verité and evidentiary techniques (Bricca, 2017) with 'pop-in' moments by arranging into sequence the creative lifestyle of the ordinary Krobo person through collaboration. The Krobo community has been noted for recycling glass bottles and the like into fashionable beads for centuries. The use of these beads reflects a facet of their daily lives. The need to find innovative ways to documenting this unique lifestyle of the Krobo people is crucial. However, very little attention has been paid to this vibrant traditional industry in academia. As a bead maker and a researcher, I am motivated by this gap in knowledge to produce a documentary film by working with and for the Krobo people.

The art of filmmaking is generally perceived as a collaborative process compared to other forms of art (Aufderheide et al., 2016). I am inspired by this collaborative culture examined through the concept of editing while producing the collaborative smartphone documentary titled *Trash to Treasure*.

The persistent dynamic technological revolution has led to innovative means of producing documentaries for audiences both locally and internationally. These new opportunities come with a flexible approach to putting shots together by defying structured editing rules. Walter Murch, a renowned American editor, in an interview with Michael Wohl better explains these phenomena: 'Film editing is now something almost everyone can do at a simple level and enjoy it, but to take it to a higher level requires the same dedication and persistence that any art form does' (Wohl, 2002, p. 435).

The substance of this quote cannot be overemphasized since editing is generally perceived to be the bedrock of the art of film, as affirmed by Sergei Eisenstein and Lev Kuleshov (Baranowski & Hecht, 2017). Orpen (2003) devised a comprehensive approach to editing, where she opened up a discourse on 'expressive dimensions of film editing' (p. 3) other than the 'connective aspect' (p. 3), which is generally read in editing manuals and schools. She concedes, however, that sometimes the two distinct approaches can be merged, as was evident in *À bout de souffle* (Godard, 1960), where the rules of continuity were broken, which led to self-expressivity commonly referred to as intuition. Holt (2015) explains intuition as a seamless dichotomy between the creative process of the editor and cognitive response. Holt (2015) states that intuition can be conceptualized as an idea but has the ability to directly impact or shape the holistic experience of audiences. In her work, Holt mentions that: 'As a concept intuition has always been something of an enigma and in terms of editing reasons, it is so hard for editors to determine where exactly this fountain of knowledge comes from' (Holt, 2015, p. 26).

According to Lebow (2008), there was relatively less attention paid to audio-visual research before 2008. However, there has been an improvement in subsequent years. There exists limited literature on editing and the few that exist are generally grouped under three divisions which are reflected in textbooks or handbooks of editors, interviews with film editors and sometimes periodic compilation of transcripts (Orpen, 2003). Additionally,

Coover (2012) believes that filming and editing are inseparable but more often than not editing is sidelined in the narrative of filmmaking. In recent times, there has been a change in the status quo which has brought renowned editors to the fore. These new intuitive practices clearly define the key features of editing collaborative smartphone documentary films. Consciously adhering to this intuition facilitates effective collaboration and participation. In the end, consensus editing of the footage generated in the field leads to a satisfactory piece that all stakeholders accept. In my study, this feat was achieved through the use of smartphones by participants to capture community-generated content, which generally addresses my first research objective of working as a team with the Krobo community to produce the smartphone documentary film *Trash to Treasure*.

As the researcher and editor of this film, my role is comparable to the creative author who puts together text to form a creative literary piece. As an editor, I compiled shots generated by the community to tell the story in sequence by moving beyond the narrative structure of the film. In this regard, I am inspired to compose an art form from static and motion pictures interwoven with sound to generate a story as I engage with the audience as part of the production. This emotional journey fuses the elements of picture, motion and sound in addition to the artistic or visual representation displayed (Orpen, 2003).

Before the execution of this project, I had the opportunity to work with and research the Krobo community for over ten years. I am now well equipped, resourced and better placed to explore the knowledge garnered over the years in the community to produce *Trash to Treasure*.

Trash to Treasure: An Open Space New Media Documentary practice

This study is framed around the theory of practice-led research. This method offers a flexible field to integrate theory and practice and break the restrictive traditional boundaries of creative practices. Scott Brook and Paul Magee have raised concerns about the viability of practice-led research in academia, which has seen no significant transformation over the years (Brook & Magee, 2012). These concerns, among others, include the lack of consensus on creative arts programmes among practitioners in the creative arts fraternity. However, Josie Arnold argues firmly against this assertion and proposes that practice-led research generates new educational models that have a tremendous impact on creative people (Arnold, 2012). In as much as *Trash to Treasure* fills a knowledge gap through the creative processes, it affords 'new models of knowledge to the academy and [will] enrich the artistic practices of the practitioners themselves' (Arnold, 2012, p. 9). Zimmermann and De Michiel (2017) define collaborative projects in deprived communities, designing encounters and polyphonic collaborations as forms of Open Space New Media Documentary. This model is adopted in the current project as 'in Open Space Documentary, technologies meet places and people' (p. 1) for community-oriented projects.

Art, Sustainability and Learning Communities

Figure 16.1: An 'Open Space' in Upper Manya Krobo District in Ghana.

Community learning through collaborative smartphone filmmaking workshops

In recent times, smartphone filmmaking (Schleser, 2010, 2012, 2018) has evolved as an active tool to give voice to the voiceless. This came about through a series of participatory video research methods, which have proven to be impactful in effecting change among local communities.

The collaborative approach employed throughout this practice-led research makes it suitable to apply the Verité and Evidentiary editing techniques (Bricca, 2017). The word Verité denotes a sense of cinematic truth (Rouch, 1974). This occurs through a series of observational scenes demonstrating spontaneous behaviour on screen. In Verité editing, characters simultaneously interact in scenes without a break in the flow of dialogue. This smooth flow ignites a sense of belief among members of the audience that the interaction among characters in the scene did happened.

A two-day filmmaking workshop was organized for community members that was scheduled in two parts. The first part introduced the participants to some basic smartphone filmmaking skills. Here, the participants were exposed to mobile filming and editing apps, including Filmic Pro, Adobe Rush and Open Camera, to mention a few. During this session, participants observed and learnt the technicalities involved in smartphone filmmaking amidst intermittent discussions through questions raised.

After this session, participants were asked to apply this new skill to capture shots around them, adhering to the three-part story structure of beginning, middle and end. The second part allowed participants to apply the skills learnt to film and subsequently meet as a team to edit. Overall, the workshop had four objectives: training, participants applying skills, collaborative editing and feedback as a form of evaluation.

Figure 16.2: Researcher engaging with participants (learners), photographed by Felix Gyebi.

Figure 16.3: A cross-section of participants at a smartphone filmmaking workshop in the Krobo community.

Community participation, which is the hallmark of impacting and sharing knowledge, comes with challenges that lead to the ineffective involvement by community members if not well addressed. Aryeh-Adjei (2021) states that the foremost challenge is the lack of

Figure 16.4: A participant filming with a smartphone during the workshop.

stakeholder engagement before implementation. Bella et al. (2021) corroborate this but further suggest the need to diversify approaches aimed at improving the livelihoods of deprived communities through investment in modern but affordable technological tools to achieve desired results from learners.

After the workshop, participants were equipped with skills in smartphone filmmaking and they were able to apply to capture and document stories about their daily lives. In *Trash to Treasure*, participants (the Krobo people) narrated their own stories. This is interlaced with household activities (mainly the craft of bead making) that demonstrate to viewers the ideas behind what is being said. In addition to breaking the status quo of applying conventional means of knowledge sharing and transfer, this study was generally facilitated by content generated by the community as a novel form of providing learners with adult literacy skills, irrespective of status or rank in society, thereby leveraging active participation in community-generated projects.

References

Arnold, J. (2012). Practice led research: Creative activity, academic debate, and intellectual rigour. *Higher Education Studies, 2*(2), 9–24.

Aryeh-Adjei, A. (2021). Community participation in school management in Ghana. *Journal of Interdisciplinary Studies in Education*, *10*(SI), 79–95. https://www.ojed.org/index.php/jise/article/view/2873

Aufderheide, P., Larry, E., Bill, G., Lindsay, G., Larry, K., Brigid, M., Chris, P., Maggie, B. S., & Russell, W. II. (2016). *The new storytellers: Documentary filmmaking in the 21st century*. Cannes: The International Association of Film and Television Schools (Centre International de Liaison des Ecoles de Cinéma et de Télévision – CILECT).

Baranowski, A. M., & Hecht, H. (2017). The auditory Kuleshov effect: Multisensory integration in movie editing. *Perception*, *46*(5), 624–631. https://doi.org/10.1177/0301006616682754

Bella, B.O ,Peter, K., Susan, K. (2021). Effects of instructional materials used at the community learning resource centers on adult learners' participation in community development activities in Nyamira North Sub-county Kenya. *International Journal of Education and Literacy Studies*, *9*, 15. https://doi.org/10.7575/aiac.ijels.v.9n.1p.15

Bricca, J.ACE. (2017). *Documentary editing: Principles & practice*. Milton Park: Taylor & Francis.

Brook, S., & Magee, P. (2012). Postscript [Special issue website series]. *TEXT*, *14*. http://www.textjournal.com.au/speciss/issue14/content.htm

Coover, R. (2012). Visual research and the new documentary. *Studies in Documentary Film*, *6*, 203–214. https://doi.org/10.1386/sdf.6.2.203_1

Godard, J. L. (1960). *À bout de souffle* [Film]. Les Films Impéria.

Gyebi Amofa, F. (Forthcoming). *Trash to Treasure* [Film].

Holt, J. (2015). *The 'art of editing': Creative practice and pedagogy* (Ph.D. thesis). Hawthorn: Swinburne University of Technology.

Lebow, A. (2008). AVPhD: Supervising in the dark. *Journal of Media Practice*, *9*(3), 201–213. https://doi.org/10.1386/jmpr.9.3.201_1

Orpen, V. (2003). *Film editing: The art of the expressive* (Vol. 16). UK: Wallflower Press.

Rouch, J. (1974). The camera and man. *Studies in Visual Communication*, *1*(1), 37–44. https://repository.upenn.edu/svc/vol1/iss1/6.

Schleser, M. (2011). *Mobile-mentary. Mobile documentaries in the contemporary mediascape*. Sarbruecken: Lambert Academic Publishing.

Schleser, M. (2012). Collaborative mobile phone filmmaking. In E. J. Milne, C. Mitchell, & N. de Lange (Eds.), *Handbook of participatory video* (pp. 397–411). Lanham, MD: AltaMira Press.

Schleser, M. (2018). Smart smart (phone) filmmakers >> Smart (political) actions. In M. Bohr & B. Sliwinska (Eds.), *The evolution of the image: Political action and the digital self* (pp. 113–123). London: Routledge.

Schleser, M. R. C. (2010). *Mobile-mentory mobile documentaries in the mediascape* (Ph.D. thesis). Westminster: School of Media, Arts and Design, University of Westminster. https://westminsterresearch.westminster.ac.uk.

Wohl, M. (2002). Editing techniques with Final Cut Pro (CD-ROM included). *Reference and Research Book News*, *17*(1), 435.

Zimmermann, P. R., & De Michiel, H. (2017). *Open space new media documentary : A toolkit for theory and practice*. Milton: Routledge.

Chapter 17

Changing Climate, Changing Communities

Stephanie H. Danker, Shafkat Khan and Katie L. Feilen

Climate change education and communication often follow typical scientific communication, focusing on explaining facts and refuting misconceptions (Dudo & Besley, 2016). However, traditional science communication does not lead to active engagement and action by the public (Lesen, Rogan, & Blum, 2016). In general, climate change outreach, education and conversations are more effective when combined with a relatable, humanistic narrative (O'Neil & Nicholson-Cole, 2009). In this regard, integrating art into climate change education and community actions has enormous potential for making climate change communication and education more relatable, understandable and emotionally appealing to community members, students and diverse audiences (Burke, Ockwell, & Whitmarsh, 2018; Lesen et al., 2016).

Art education can be a tool to explore the places people live; thinking globally while creating and discussing art in a more local context may cultivate empathetic connections (Lai & Ball, 2002). Artists' and art educators' responses to environmental conflicts and exploitation of natural resources can play a meaningful role in communities by fostering cultural resilience, impacting values, enhancing hope and campaigning with art (Huhmarniemi, 2021). Art-based resources which culminate in a community event can open dialogue and connect stakeholders across generations, organizations and institutions.

When teachers, students and community members engage together to integrate local issues into educational activities, teaching and learning can become dynamic for both young people and adults (Smith & Sobel, 2010). The concept design we used for our exhibitions and community events emphasized art as a call to action, referring to Lawton et al.'s (2019) goals of community-based art education: '**C**onnect, collaborate and create through **a**rt-based activity that is asset-centred; **L**isten to the stories of others to **L**earn and build more inclusive and equitable communities and practices' (p. 3). We focused attention on these goals throughout the different stages of our work together. Place-based art education provides an opportunity for art and environmental educators to come together to create powerful experiences for students and community members by bringing self and community into dialogue with the place (Blandy & Hoffman, 1993; Inwood, 2008).

Participatory, place-based community art can be a powerful tool as the community, rather than being the passive receiver of an artist's vision, is able to actively create art and engage in affective dialogue around difficult topics such as climate change (Burke et al., 2018). Integrating art and other humanities-based approaches in climate change communication can thus provide the crucial personal and local narrative context otherwise missing from climate change discussions.

Learning communities and events

Using the CALL to action goals of community-based art education (Lawton et al., 2019), various learning communities connected and collaborated to host community art exhibitions entitled 'Changing Climate, Changing Communities' in Oxford, Ohio, USA, in 2019 and 2020. Oxford is a town of 21,000 people and the home to Miami University. The community art exhibition allowed community members to listen and learn about climate change in a place-based context during the exhibition openings, while others processed their affective connection to climate change and place through artistic expression. The Oxford Community Arts Centre (OCAC) hosted the exhibitions during their 2nd Friday Art event and throughout the sequential months.

Stakeholders with varying degrees of involvement within learning communities collaborated to host the 'Changing Climate, Changing Communities' initiatives. The core organizing group consisted of five Miami University faculty members: three were part of the Department of Biology that taught a professional master's programme (Project *Dragonfly*) focused on social and ecological changes, one was based in the Department of Media, Journalism and Film, and one from the Department of Art (Art Education) with expertise in art integration and community engagement. Intending to engage the broader Oxford community in conversation on climate change through artistic, affective and place-based methods, the faculty learning community collaborated with the OCAC to host a community art exhibition on climate change.

As a cultural and community centre in Oxford, Ohio, the OCAC connected the faculty learning community with key collaborators at Talawanda Middle School (a secondary school in Oxford, Ohio, USA) and other community organizations interested in sustainability and climate change issues. We connected more learning communities and built additional collaboration by distributing the 'Changing Climate, Changing Communities' call for art in November 2019 to the community members, additional local school districts and various departments within Miami University, including the Departments of Art and Biology. The 2019 call for art was intentionally created to invite the local community to learn and reflect collectively and updated in 2020 to reflect on the place-based effects of climate change in this region.

Additionally, the faculty learning community curated climate change lesson plans on a website to share educational resources with teachers and artists. Miami University students in our courses created the following resources for inclusion: *Introduction to Art Education* students created art-integrated lesson plans connected with illustrated children's books; *Art Across the Curriculum* students curated a selection of contemporary artists whose work centres on climate change; the master's level course offered through Project *Dragonfly*, *Climate Change*, created scientific lesson plans with an emphasis on issues impacting the Midwest region of the United States.

Talawanda Middle School became a key learning community that collaborated with the Miami faculty learning community. A science teacher from the school created a learning community outside her science classrooms. Selected students, called the Climate Change Student Ambassadors, met with Miami University faculty to learn how climate change impacted Ohio and then shared the knowledge with other students in the school. In the science classes, the students communicated their understanding of climate change through artistic expression in response to the call for art. Additionally, the science teacher collaborated with the art teacher to bring climate change lessons into the art classroom. Art students made etchings showcasing animals that climate change is impacting.

The 2019 art show featured 100 pieces of contributed art, 80 from the Talawanda Middle School, ten from undergraduate students at Miami University and ten from community members. The students and community members expressed their emotions and viewpoints on climate change through drawings, paintings, murals and an interactive book series.

To further address the CALL to action goals, the 2nd Friday opening exhibition of 'Changing Climate, Changing Communities' featured ten community partners working on climate change issues. The community partners included the local city government (Oxford City Council), environmental non-profits and community groups (Three Valley Conservation Trust, 1 World 1 Change, Take 3 Oxford, Climate Action Oxford, Hefner Museum of Natural History, Oxford Empty Bowls and League of Women's Voters Oxford), and local businesses that supported climate change initiatives (Oxford Coffee Company, Moon Co-Op). Each organization featured information and activities that demonstrated their mission, the way that their mission is connected to climate change, and actions community members can do to make a difference in climate change, such as writing to elected local representatives, composting food and reducing plastic consumption. Visitors to the exhibit were invited to create a 'flag' expressing their feelings towards climate change; the flags were added to the exhibition (Figure 17.1). By featuring art from the local school, university students and community members, many diverse voices within the community were empowered to share their perspectives on climate change with their communities.

In 2020, we hosted the second 'Changing Climate, Changing Communities' art exhibition, which opened on 14 February. Through the second iteration of the art show, we collaborated and connected with additional learning communities. These include connecting the art initiative with the local primary school (Kramer Elementary) and continuing the relationship with Talawanda Middle School. Additionally, the Miami University faculty learning community members connected with their professional graduate student communities, including additional K-12 school learning communities within a 100-mile radius of Oxford, Ohio and the Cincinnati, Ohio and Northern Kentucky artistic community.

The second exhibition featured 192 pieces of art: 50 pieces from community members, including professional artists, and 142 pieces of student art from school learning communities. Similar to the first year, the event featured opportunities to listen, learn and connect with community partners, including Miami University's Hefner Museum of Natural History, League of Women's Voters Oxford, Zero Waste Oxford, Climate Action Oxford and the City of Oxford. Community members hosted three interactive art and engagement

Art, Sustainability and Learning Communities

Figure 17.1: Participatory art created by attendees at the opening of the 'Changing Climate, Changing Communities' art exhibition in Oxford, Ohio, 2019.

activity stations, including creating Earth Valentines, writing pledges and designing Zines focused on environmental art.

As a part of the month-long exhibition programming, Miami University Professor of Art Roscoe Wilson collaborated with the learning community to present an artist talk entitled 'Spill/87 Days Project: The Dilemma of Consumerism and Waste in Contemporary Society' at the OCAC on 20 February 2020 (Figure 17.2). For more information about the artist, see roscoewilson.com. The talk was co-sponsored with the Miami University Department of Art's Contemporary Art Forum lecture series. It engaged university students from both Oxford and Regionals campuses, along with community members, and brought them together off-campus. While students were off-campus, they were able to view the community art exhibition, further connecting the distinct populations and perspectives.

Formal evaluation of impact

We surveyed the participants of the art show using a twelve questions mixed-methods survey designed to assess attendees' attitudes and motivation to change behaviours related to climate change after attending the opening of the 'Changing Climate, Changing Communities' exhibition (IRB: 03191e Miami University; Feilen, Sullivan, Danker, & Khan,

Figure 17.2: 'Backyard Superfund' (2017). Woodcut by Roscoe Wilson (edition of 4), 38 inches × 24 inches (printed by Evil Prints in St. Louis, MO). Image courtesy of Roscoe Wilson.

2022). The participants increased their emotional connection to climate change issues, and many participants reported positive feelings (free response words included: motivated, inspired, encouraged) after seeing the exhibition. Most participants (66 per cent in 2019; 72 per cent in 2020) responded that the art was the most impactful part of the exhibition event.

Conclusion

In both years of the exhibition, we were excited to see the community participation and collaboration in creating the art and discussing the environmental themes the artwork represented, especially in a local context. Our efforts in motivating community learning met a deep desire identified by our community to discuss the environmental changes the community is experiencing and is expected to undergo. Our community's interest in discussing climate change tracks with different communities around the United States and the globe in tackling climate change challenges (American Association for the Advancement of Science, 2019). We believe that learning communities, addressing the CALL to action goals, can form an affective understanding of complex climate change issues facing them through art-based collaborations and discussions.

Our community art-based collaborations engaged the greater community at various scales, from learning communities of students taking climate change conversations home to community organizations providing diverse ideas and voices suited to the community's aptitude on this topic. Such diversity of voices discussing community-wide climate change effects is necessary for building community resilience to climate change.

In our work, art education and engagement played a central role in motivating community-scale conversations around topics and ideas that can seem too complex, abstract and distant. From our experience, we see art educators' tremendous role in driving community conversations and learning on climate change topics by collaborating with experts from other fields. Similarly, our approach can be instrumental in motivating affective engagement with a wide range of environmental challenges, from water resource use to environmental injustice.

References

American Association for the Advancement of Science. (2019). Stories of community response to climate change. In *How We Respond: Community Responses to Climate Change*. https://howwerespond.aaas.org/. Accessed on 20 December 2021.

Blandy, D., & Hoffman, E. (1993). Toward an art education of place. *Studies in Art Education, 35*(1), 22–33.

Burke, M., Ockwell, D., & Whitmarsh, L. (2018). Participatory arts and affective engagement with climate change: The missing link in achieving climate compatible behaviour change? *Global Environmental Change, 49*, 95–105. https://doi.org/10.1016/j.gloenvcha.2018.02.007

Dudo, A., & Besley, J. C. (2016). Scientists' prioritization of communication objectives for public engagement. *PLoS One, 11*(2), e0148867. https://doi.org/10.1371/journal.pone.0148867

Feilen, K. L., Sullivan, A., Danker, S. H., & Khan, S. (2022). Climate change community art exhibition changes attitudes towards climate change. Department of Biology, Miami University.

Huhmarniemi, M. (2021). Art-based events for conflicted communities: Engaging and educating through art. *International Journal of Education Through Art, 17*(2), 271–280.

Inwood, H. J. (2008). At the crossroads: Situating place-based art education. *Canadian Journal of Environmental Education, 13*(1), 29–41.

Lai, A., & Ball, E. L. (2002). Home is where the art is: Exploring the places people live through art education. *Studies in Art Education, 44*(1), 47–66.

Lawton, P. H., Walker, M. A., & Green, M. (2019). *Community-based art education across the lifespan: Finding common ground*. New York, NY: Teachers College Press.

Lesen, A. E., Rogan, A., & Blum, M. J. (2016). Science communication through art: Objectives, challenges, and outcomes. *Trends in Ecology & Evolution, 31*(9), 657–660. https://doi.org/10.1016/j.tree.2016.06.004

O'Neill, S., & Nicholson-Cole, S. (2009). Fear won't do it: Promoting positive engagement with climate change through visual and iconic representations. *Science Communication, 30*(3), 355–379. https://doi.org/10.1177/1075547008329201

Smith, G. A., & Sobel, D. (2010). *Sociocultural, political and historical studies in education: Place- and community-based education in schools*. Florence, SC: Routledge.

Chapter 18

Reclaiming the Street: The Expanded Garden

Eva Marín Peinado

According to the geographer Nogué (2014), today's society faces an ongoing landscape conflict, especially in peri-urban areas. There is a demand for harmonious landscapes that include a certain ideal of beauty and nature versus the need to assimilate new territories for the economic and social development of the metropolis in a globalized world that has reached its limit in terms of sustainability.

However, the idea of limitation posed by climate change over recent decades does not seem to have been applied to the endless urbanization of the outskirts of major European capitals. On the contrary, land consumerism has taken over public space in the periphery of cities such as Barcelona, causing, as Sala (2012) points out, the appearance of unpleasant, diffuse and chaotic landscapes. Furthermore, this use of concrete throughout the land has occurred hastily and, in many cases, without providing sufficient green areas in high-density neighbourhoods. As new studies point out, this directly affects the inhabitants' health (Barboza et al., 2021).

To trigger a more balanced and greener landscape on the periphery, we need to change landscape policies in a participative and socially consensual manner, as Nogué (2007) proposes. However, we also urgently need to bring into focus the damage we are inflicting and rethink periphery areas as a space for change. In this process of challenging urban development, art can play an active role. It can question the damage and proposes alternative and more responsible ways of relating with the periphery.

Looking for nature and freedom through art in the periphery

Several contemporary Spanish artists draw attention to the conflict of life in the periphery. Such artists depict abandoned plots in suburban areas as spaces for connecting with nature, freedom and change.

Xavier Ribas, a Spanish artist and lecturer at the University of Brighton, has portrayed the need for nature that people in Barcelona's outskirts experience in his *Sundays* series (1994–97). The images show families at lots around Barcelona on the weekend having picnics, playing and having fun, as though they are unaware of the desolation around them. The author shows the inhabitants of these areas making use of the territory beyond the pre-established norms by occupying unurbanized and degraded spaces. This appropriation of the land depicts an expression of freedom and hope. It is as though the periphery, despite being the favourite haunt of disorganized capitalism, could simultaneously become the place to overcome it. Alternatively, it feels like the narrow green spaces between the concrete could become a small crack where the system might fracture.

Lara Almarcegui, a Spanish artist based in the Netherlands, also proposes an escape from the control that the city exerts through artistic investigations of wastelands awaiting construction. Representative of Almarcegui's work is her 'wasteland guides', which she has undertaken in several cities around the world. In contrast to the typical tourist guide, she creates alternative guides in which she explains the characteristics of each plot in terms of property, land data and also vegetation (Almarcegui, 2015). These guides refer to land not yet conquered by concrete – autonomous areas in which we can find nature searching for a way back. While Ribas photographs actions that have already taken place on the abandoned lots, Almarcegui opens wastelands to the public, inviting people to use them as a public, shareable good.

Constructing responses through care and community

My own project, *The Expanded Garden* (2017), connects with this type of research and vindication of the periphery. This project puts a spotlight on an elderly woman's strategy for creating beauty and community through the seizing of public space in a town on the outskirts of Barcelona. *The Expanded Garden* (Figures 18.1–18.4) is a video installation comprising an essayistic video projection and three plants placed on a pedestal, representing the small gesture of freedom by an inhabitant of this town, Maria Rosa Clastre. More than ten years ago, this woman decided to decorate her street with patio plants. This seemingly innocent action was, in fact, transgressive, as it violated municipal regulations prohibiting the placing of objects in urban spaces.

This piece connects Maria Rosa's innocent action in her town to the worldwide Green Guerrilla movement, which aims to create green living spaces in urban environments. According to The Spatial Agency (n.d.), the term 'guerrilla gardening' was coined by artist Liz Christy, the founder of the Green Guerrilla movement. She lived and worked in New York in the 1970s, when many parts of the city experienced a massive lack of public investment due to the economic crisis. The city was full of vacant and abandoned lots. Christy, who lived at the time in Manhattan's Lower East Side, saw the potential of growing plants in the abandoned lots to combat urban decay. Liz Christy and the original band of Green Guerrillas decided to throw 'seed green-aids' over the fences of vacant lots and into disused tree planters on the busy New York City streets to revitalize these underused spaces. Today, the work of Liz Christy has spread throughout the city, and there are more than 600 community gardens in New York City where citizen gardeners grow food for their families and neighbours. Importantly, they connect city kids to the earth. They also give the elderly cool green spaces to spend hot summer days. In other words, they allow people to create a sense of community and return to nature in an urban environment.

Thus, *The Expanded Garden* (2017) presents the story of Liz Christy in New York, creating a parallelism with the story of Rosa Maria Clastre, as if the biographies of both

Figure 18.1: *The Expanded Garden* (2017). Installation view, solo exhibition *Landscapes, Persistence and Affections*, at Can Manyé, Art and Creation Space, Alella, Barcelona. 2020. Courtesy of the artist.

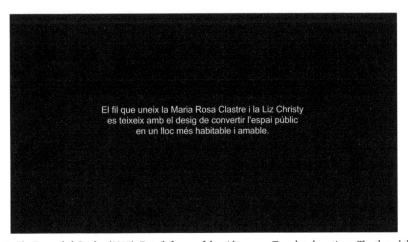

Figure 18.2: *The Expanded Garden* (2017). Detail, frame of the video essay. Translated captions: The thread that unites Maria Rosa Clastre and Liz Christy is woven with the desire to turn the public space into a more liveable and friendly place. Courtesy of the artist.

women of a similar age but such different backgrounds could touch via an imaginary thread stretching between two continents. The narration of the video essay uses fragments of an interview with Maria Rosa Clastre, in which she explains what led her to carry out this street occupation with her plants. This story alternates and intersects

Figure 18.3: *The Expanded Garden* (2017). *Note.* Installation view with the video projection and the plants Maria Rosa Clastre gave to Eva Marín. Courtesy of the artist.

Figure 18.4: *The Expanded Garden* (2017). *Note.* Detail, final frame that shows Maria Rosa Clastre's plants in front of her house. Courtesy of the artist.

with Christy's and the artist's voice, which appears as written text in white font against a black background.

The idea of a landscape conflict in the periphery is brought to life in the video essay with the narration of Maria Rosa Clastre. One of the most meaningful and touching moments is when Clastre describes memories of her childhood landscape, when her surroundings were more connected to nature. These memories lead her to expand her intimate world of plants to the public space when her landlord asks her to remove them from her patio. She also explains how much she loves the plants. She speaks of the joy they bring her and how she wants to share their beauty with everyone by putting them on the street.

Maria Rosa's voice represents a generation of women that has been made invisible by society. These older women have traditionally borne the brunt of childrearing and household chores. The same care they invested in their homes and families is shown in this video, yet devoted to plants. Maria Rosa nurtures and loves her plants as if they were family members. The piece also tries to reclaim caring for plants as a way to unleash Maria Rosa's need to recreate a more natural environment on the streets of the peripheral urban space she inhabits. This act, born out of nostalgia and pure affection, has created a sense of community, as happened with the Green Guerrilla movement. As she recalls during the interview, putting plants on the street caused a chain reaction as more people in the old part of the town started to do the same. Furthermore, the town council turned a blind eye. Thus, this personal and innocent act has become global and political, despite never being the intention.

Trying to emulate the kind of care Maria Rosa Clastre shows for her plants, the footage of the video essay pays close attention to details through a careful gaze. The camera attempts to care for the protagonist as much as she cares for the plants. For instance, her entire face does not appear at any point in a single frame. We only see fragments of her flowered attire, her hands, her eyes, her jewellery and macro views of the plants on the street, as if the camera were caressing her and the plants. Towards the end of the video, the frame opens, and we finally see a general view of the street with the plants placed in front of Maria Rosa's home, but without her, putting the humble plants centre stage. At the end of the interview used for the piece, Maria Rosa Clastre gave me some plants to take care of, as she had too many and lacked the energy to look after them all herself. Significantly, the installation in the gallery features these plants placed on a base. The video narration explains that these plants are now in front of my house, emulating Maria Rosa Clastre's action.

As Liz Christy did with the Green Guerrillas in New York, transforming abandoned lots into community gardens, the expansion of Maria Rosa's own garden into the street has become a political act of rethinking the public space. It challenges those who decide about policies on the public space and questions the lack of nature in peripheries. It is, therefore, an artistic action with no intention of being so, a political action without the will to be one. This small act of rebellion also creates a community, as her action has been taken up by her neighbours and even accepted by the local government.

Women and caring as a transformative action

Paradoxically, in an unequal decision-making system that obstructs women from reaching the positions they are entitled to, what *The Expanded Garden* (2017) project proposes is that women are those who can provide the methodologies needed to address the challenges that unsustainability and urban destruction force us to face. In a periphery conquered by concrete, love for a landscape linked to nature becomes an indispensable tool for society. Caring for the family and the community – tasks traditionally considered feminine – are revolutionary when applied to the landscape. Feminizing the landscape as a community good and transferring this love for it to new generations is crucial to bring about the cultural change needed to face the major challenge of transforming the planet into a more liveable place. As Puleo (2012) put it, we need all those qualities marginalized as feminine such as compassion and emotional connection to start to treat the planet and the different species living on it with the respect they deserve.

Taking plants from our homes and putting them on the street may not change the course of climate change, but it certainly disrupts our gaze in a periphery lacking green areas. In urban and suburban areas, actions like Maria Rosa Clastre's, in a more domestic scope, and Liz Christy's, as the founder of a global movement, can become levers of change towards a more conscious and responsible vision of our territories.

Moreover, because love becomes political when directed at the landscape, understanding our responsibility in our neighbourhood can lead us to be responsible citizens of the world. In this sense, art and women can be instrumental in proposing utopian horizons for the socioeconomic and cultural transformation necessary to achieve ecological equality and justice. This will allow us to live more fairly with the planet and each other.

References

Almarcegui, L. (2015). Descampados, demoliciones y ruinas (Wastelands, demolitions and ruins). In T. Blanch (Ed.), *Topografías invisibles (Invisible topographies)* (pp. 32–53). Barcelona: Universidad de Barcelona Edicions.

Barboza, E. P., Cirach, M., Khomenko, S., Lungman, T., Mueller, N., Barrera-Gómez, J., ... Nieuwenhuijsen, M. (2021). Green space and mortality in European cities: A health impact assessment study. *Lancet Planetary Health*, 5(10), e718–e730. https://doi.org/10.1016/S2542-5196(21)00229-1

Nogué i Font, J. (2014). Sentido del lugar, paisaje y conflict (Sense of place, landscape and conflict). *Geopolítica(s)*, 5(2), 155–163. http://dx.doi.org/10.5209/rev_GEOP.2014.v5.n2.48842

Nogué i Font, J. (2007). Territories without discourse, landscapes without imaginary. Challenges and dilemmas. *Ería*, (73–74), 373–382.

Puleo, A. (2014, November). Feminismo y ecología (Feminism and ecology). *Mujeres en Red (Women in Network)*. http://www.mujeresenred.net/spip.php?article2060

Sala, P. (2012). Perifèries urbanes. L'experiència dels catàlegs de paisatge de Catalunya (Urban peripheries. The experience of the Catalan landscape catalogues). In J. Nogué, L. Puigbert, G. Bretcha, & À. Losantos (Eds.), *Franges. Els paisatges de la perifèria (Plecs de Paisatge; Reflexions; 3). Observatori del Paisatge de Catalunya (Fringes. The landscapes of the periphery [Landscape Folds; Reflections; 3]).* Spain: The Landscape Observatory of Catalonia.

Spatial Agency. (n.d.). *Guerrilla gardening.* In database. https://www.spatialagency.net/database/guerrilla.gardening

Chapter 19

Diffractive Methodology as a Posthuman Approach to Engage With Human Equity Through Socially Engaged Artistic Practice

Susan (Susie) Lachal

Introduction

Socially engaged artistic practice, combined with critical posthuman methodologies, can generate more equitable relations. In turn, these relations can support transitions towards increased human equity. This chapter outlines an example of socially engaged artistic practice (social practice), which relationally engaged a group of participants (co-workers) across two cultures in Australia and Cambodia to develop understandings of human equity through the education system in Kampong Thom, Cambodia, from 2017 to 2019.

Artmaking is part of my everyday experience, and the example of social practice described here emerged from ongoing relations with the people of Kampong Thom and a decision to undertake a Ph.D. in the School of Art at RMIT University in Naarm/Melbourne, Australia. I have been embedded in the Kampong Thom education community for seventeen years as a volunteer, primarily with Teachers Across Borders Australia Inc., coordinating annual conferences of workshops for Cambodian teachers, teacher trainees and principals in pedagogy and content (in alignment with the Cambodian national curriculum). Cambodia is considered one of the least developed countries, and Kampong Thom is one of its poorest provinces. Also, 'ending learning poverty' allows for the building of 'human capital' thereby increasing human equity (World Bank, 2019).

A critical posthuman position argues for a more equitable state for all things. Following this critical position, things are identified as all living and non-living entities. What emerges from the relational engagements among things are new things. For example, my social practice invites humans to be attentive to the world around them and, through lived experience, open up to new understandings of human equity. In this context, the co-workers and attentiveness are things that are relationally engaged. One of the new things to emerge was an increased understanding of human equity. Researchers in higher education, Karin Murris and Vivienne Bozalek (2019), suggest that a diffractive method allows two or more things to be articulated with and through one another. The things involved in diffraction are affected by and affect each other, allowing for new things to emerge, which lead to 'unpredictable and creative provocations and becomings' (Murris & Bozalek, 2019, p. 9).

A posthuman understanding of sustainability suggests that all things are interdependent within an entanglement. An entanglement involves an array of things that are relationally engaged from which new things emerge. A diffractive method allows the artist to understand and unravel what emerges from the interdependence of things in an entanglement. Influenced by Karen Barad (2014), I define a diffractive method as a cross-disciplinary, non-representational and practice-led method that includes reading one thing with and through another to encourage new things to emerge.

Human equity and environmental justice are two components through which a more sustainable planet can be achieved. For the purposes of this research, human equity is defined as all humans being attributed equal value whereby colonial, racial and gendered frameworks are challenged. Of equal importance is environmental justice, defined here as all things living and non-living being attributed value. The ongoing project for posthuman relations advocates for the reduction of anthropocentrism. Srinivasan and Kasturirangan (2017) define anthropocentrism as the 'superiority of humans over all other' things (p. 126). According to philosopher and eco-feminist, Val Plumwood, humans in western cultural traditions tend toward anthropocentrism. They have developed 'conceptions of themselves as belonging to a superior sphere apart [...] from nature and ecology' (Plumwood, 2002, p. 99).

This chapter focuses on social practice that addresses human equity. This instance of social practice entangled with critical posthuman theory to design and test two diffractive methods: attentiveness and mapping. Attentiveness activated the co-workers and mapping was designed to analyze the social practice.

I developed attentiveness as a method having been influenced by the philosopher, Isabelle Stengers' call for engaging in the '*art* of paying attention' (Stengers & Goffey, 2015, p. 62). And in turn by van Dooren, Kirksey, and Münster (2016) through their exploration of cultivating an art of attentiveness. Attentiveness is defined as a deliberate and conscious engagement with the subject's internal senses, emotions, external observations, responses and interactions.

Mapping as a method is used to understand the co-workers' perceptions of human equity as a key analytical and creative tool. This manifests as a sculptural mapping work. This practical mapping allows me to think with and through the theory in a tactile and physical way to determine what emerges. Inspiration for developing mapping as a method arose from Rick Dolpijn and Iris van der Tuins' research with cartographies (2012).

Attentiveness

Attentiveness is an opening up to and an awareness of surroundings and things. It is a deliberate and conscious engagement that can be observational, responsive and interactive. As a method, attentiveness diffracted the co-workers' experiences to allow for the emergence of new understandings of human equity. As the artist, I was also attentive to the co-workers' new understandings and the emergent impacts they had within the social practice.

The social practice involved a group of Australian co-workers from a Naarm/Melbourne-based private company that specialized in project management in the construction industry.[1] Two pairs of Australian co-workers were self-selected from the company to travel to Cambodia for one week. It was understood that each pair would share their project management knowledge with a group of Cambodian educators from the local planning department of the Provincial of Education and provide funds to build a rural school. The Cambodian co-workers comprised two English-speaking translators (Thy and Narith), the principal of the school to be built and the six members of the planning department.[2] Through the developing relations, the Australians, Cambodians and I (as an artist) emerged as one group of co-workers.

I took each pair of Australian co-workers to Kampong Thom to visit the school construction site and meet the planning department to share knowledge across four sessions. In addition, we travelled to five rural schools. Narith was the principal at one of these schools (see Figures 19.1 and 19.2).

The social practice was interdisciplinary: undertaken within a framework of humanitarian aid using ethnographic methods such as video interviews, video footage of activities and field notes. The purpose of the video interviews was twofold: to activate co-workers' attentiveness to their immediate experiences of human inequity, and for me as the artist to understand what they were experiencing. The Australian co-workers were interviewed in pairs. The first interview was in Cambodia prior to meeting the Cambodian co-workers. Three further interviews were conducted in Cambodia. Two more interviews were conducted two weeks and six months after their return to Australia. The co-workers were given the questions prior to the interviews. Thy and Narith were also interviewed at the conclusion of the social practice. In total, fourteen interviews were conducted. In hindsight, I would have interviewed all of the Cambodian co-workers throughout the social practice.

To discern what was happening in the social practice, I made a twelve-minute video from the field notes and video footage of the interviews and activities. It was through the interviews that co-worker attentiveness emerged as having agency, leading to a reconfiguring of co-worker understandings and the decision by them to fundraise and construct a second school building. As the artist, my attentiveness allowed for an analysis of what had occurred

Figure 19.1: Construction site visit – Jess Ryper, Ho Sivuthy, Erik Alarcon, January 2018. Image by Susan Lachal.

Figure 19.2: Sharing project management knowledge – Em Watkinson, Pete Smith, Bun Boroith, Moeurn Rithy, Sot Pisey, Bun Hong, April 2018. Image by Susan Lachal.

in Cambodia through the video making. This was a further diffraction that involved a theoretical engagement by reading and thinking through philosopher Karen Barad's theories in *Meeting the Universe Halfway* (2007) with the physical process of making the video.

The Australian and Cambodian co-workers relationally engaged with one another to understand that they shared a common goal: to alter human equity for a population in need. Co-worker knowledge was generated through relational engagements resulting in the understanding that together it was possible to construct a school and share project management skills. What emerged from the diffractive method of attentiveness was collaboration across the group of co-workers and an enactment of responsibility to fundraise and project manage a second building. In turn this social practice had a material impact in both Australia and Cambodia.

From the Australian co-workers' perspective, this social practice became the Australian company's major corporate responsibility project for two years. The interviews indicated that the co-workers believed that the activities undertaken led to the company becoming an employer of choice within construction project management in Naarm/Melbourne.

The United Nations' Sustainable Development Goal Number 4 – Quality Education is the premise for this social practice (United Nations Statistics Division, n.d.). According to their data, 'children living in rural areas and in the poorest households are consistently more disadvantaged in term(s) of educational participation and outcomes than their urban, wealthier peers' (United Nations Statistics Division, n.d.). The construction of two schools in Kampong Thom offered improved learning conditions for teachers and students. Not only was there a doubling in the student numbers at the two schools, but the quality of education had the capacity to improve. Subsequently, this increased the prospect of more families escaping the poverty cycle. In addition, the Cambodian co-workers reported that the workshops on project management equipped the planning department to 'roll out the national school buildings survey' more effectively. These changes resulted in improved human equity for students from Kampong Thom now and into the future.

Mapping

At the completion of the social practice, I used sculptural techniques and materials to undertake mapping as a diffractive method that was creative and performative. This enabled analysis of the social practice. While mapping was representational in form it was also diffractive in practice, allowing for reading critical posthuman theory with and through the social practice. Applying the diffractive method of mapping allowed for the emergence of new knowledge: that attentiveness (also a diffractive method) can be deployed as a framework for research in social practice. The potential is the capacity for a subject's reconfiguring of their understandings in a transition toward greater human equity (in this case the co-workers including me as the artist).

The *Mesh of Entanglements II* was mapping that took the form of a three-dimensional installation constructed from strings and discs. Its purpose was to trace the entanglements that emerged from the interviews, field notes and video footage, read with and through the relevant critical posthuman theory. A spreadsheet of the things that constituted the social practice entanglements was developed. Each wooden disc had the name of a thing written on it, for example, co-worker, Cambodian students, interviews, poverty, human equity, second school building. They were then suspended at three different heights, not in a hierarchy, but rather to indicate whether a thing was a concept being communicated, a thing of the social practice or a thing that had emerged. (see Figure 19.3) I sat with the installation, tracing the entanglements with my eyes and mind, attempting to understand what shimmered through and emerged. I later transposed my thinking to a conceptual map that documented the tracing of entanglements. (see Figure 19.4)

While making *Mesh of Entanglements II*, I engaged in continuous toggling backwards and forwards between artistic practice, posthuman theories and my writing. *Mesh of Entanglements II* generated three 'states of being' for a subject to think more equitably.

The first 'state of being' is the development of the subject as attentive and open to the conditions of the world of which they are a part. Through activating attentiveness, the subject becomes embedded in the world around them and open to experiences they might previously have ignored. It was through the interviews by reliving relational engagements that the co-workers experienced heightened attentiveness and their understandings of human equity were brought into sharper focus.

The second is the development of an account for and understanding of the past, present and future as entangled. The possible subject position of acknowledging past experiences and thinking forward with affirmative ethics toward enhancement for all necessitates action in the present.

Art, Sustainability and Learning Communities

Figure 19.3: *Mesh of Entanglements II* – mapping as creative practice, August 2019. Image by Susan Lachal.

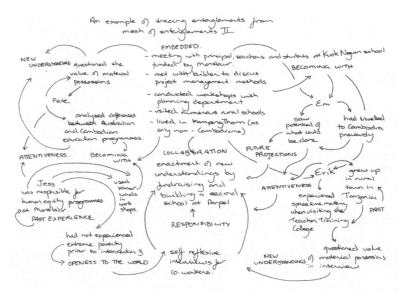

Figure 19.4: Tracing the entanglements that emerge from mapping, February 2019. Image by Susan Lachal.

And the third 'state of being' is the development of responsible action framed by affirmative ethics. Relations of responsibility become visible through the mapping and tracing of entanglements of past human activity and affirmative future planning. According to Braidotti, '[a]ffirmative ethics builds on radical relationality, aiming at empowerment' (Braidotti, 2019, p. 165). Braidotti's affirmative ethics as ready for action provides the subject with a framework for Barad's actions of responsibility to be enacted (Barad, 2007).

These three 'states of being' have the potential to encourage a subject to alter equity by acting in the present. Mapping was generative for determining the contribution made by the social practice.

Action in the world

I worked in the world through creative practice developing and testing new methods that attempted to generate new knowledge for world-making. This research project has adapted Barad's theory by designing and testing two diffractive methods: attentiveness and mapping. (Barad, 2007, 2014). The diffractive method of attentiveness became the catalyst for co-worker collaboration, encouraging emergent responsibility toward an instance of human equity. This materialized as the action to fundraise and project manage the construction of a second building. By acting collaboratively and in a responsible manner, humans can choose to act to alter the circumstances for millions of humans affected by colonial, racial and gendered frameworks to encourage greater human equity. As an artist, I used the diffractive method of attentiveness to understand what occurred within the social practice through the interviews and video making. Finally, by diffracting the diffraction (i.e., to return to what emerged from the diffraction of attentiveness and diffract this through the second diffractive method of mapping), further analysis emerged from the social practice: three 'states of being' for a subject to act and alter human equity.[3]

Diffractive methods offer the artist a framework grounded in posthuman thinking that encourages analysis of the participants' experience, the artist's experience and an understanding of what the social practice has achieved. Additionally, Barad suggests that a diffractive method assists in 'understanding the world from within and as part of it' (Barad, 2007, p. 88). Diffractive methods offer the artist opportunities to think through and with the world in which we live.

Artists can tender opportunities for human equity and environmental justice and thereby contribute to the ongoing sustainability of the planet. It is my hope that the artist/reader will adapt, design and test their own diffractive methods to help understand what is happening in their creative practice and what they can do to enact transitions towards a more equitable and sustainable planet.[4]

Acknowledgement

I would like to acknowledge the Wurundjeri Woi Wurrung and Boon Wurrung (Bunurong) people, who are the traditional custodians of the lands and waters on which I live and create. I pay my respects to the Elders past, present and emerging of the Kulin nations around Naarm/Melbourne and recognize their continued connection to Country that has never been ceded. I am open to their ancient knowledge systems and what they choose to share.

Notes

1. I was a silent director of the company but well known to the co-workers as the life partner of the managing director. I acknowledged the possibility of unequal power relations and was unable to eliminate them.
2. The two translators (Thy and Narith) were paid. Thy was paid for project management services to build the schools in Cambodia. The remaining co-workers were not paid for their participation. Thy, Narith and I have been co-workers for seventeen years across three not-for-profit organizations in an ongoing capacity.
3. For more detail on diffracting the diffraction refer to Barad's paper 'Diffracting diffraction: Cutting together-apart' and Murris and Bozaleks' paper 'Diffracting diffractive readings of texts as methodology: Some propositions'.
4. This chapter is a distillation of research undertaken for a Ph.D. in the School of Art at RMIT University, Naarm/Melbourne, Australia. The digital book containing the dissertation can be accessed on my website www.susielachal.com.

References

Barad, K. (2007). *Meeting the universe halfway: Quantum physics and the entanglement of matter and meaning*. Durham, NC: Duke University Press.
Barad, K. (2014). Diffracting diffraction: Cutting together-apart. *Parallax, 20*(3), 168–187. https://doi.org/10.1080/13534645.2014.927623
Braidotti, R. (2019). *Posthuman knowledges*. Cambridge: Polity Press.
Dolphijn, R., & van der Tuin, I. (2012). *New materialism: Interviews & cartographies*. Ann Arbor, MI: Open Humanities Press.
Murris, K., & Bozalek, V. (2019). Diffracting diffractive readings of texts as methodology: Some propositions. *Educational Philosophy and Theory, 51*(14), 1504–1517. https://doi.org/10.1080/00131857.2019.1570843
Plumwood, V. (2002). *Environmental culture: The ecological crisis of reason*. New York, NY: Routledge.
Srinivasan, K., & Kasturirangan, R. (2016). Political ecology, development, and human exceptionalism. *Geoforum, 75*, 125–128. https://doi.org/10.1016/j.geoforum.2016.07.011
Stengers, I., & Goffey, A. (2015). *In catastrophic times: Resisting the coming barbarism*. London: Open Humanities Press.

United Nations Statistics Division. (n.d.). SDG Indicators. https://unstats.un.org/sdgs/report/2022/Goal-04/

van Dooren, T., Kirksey, E., & Münster, U. (2016). Multispecies studies. *Environmental Humanities, 8*(1), 1–23. https://doi.org/10.1215/22011919-3527695

World Bank. (2019, November 8). *Ending learning poverty: A target to galvanize action on literacy.* https://www.worldbank.org/en/news/immersive-story/2019/11/06/a-learning-target-for-a-learning-revolution

Chapter 20

Inviting Teacher Candidates in Art Education to Become Global Agents for Sustainability

Kazuyo Nakamura and Anita Sinner

This chapter presents an international arts-based approach to advance the United Nations' (UN's) sustainable development goals (SDGs) through pre-service teacher education. The UN adopted the 2030 agenda for sustainable development to overcome the world's most pressing challenges (United Nations, 2015). To be effective in shaping our world into a more just, peaceful, tolerant, inclusive and sustainable one, pre-service teacher education has been called on for transformational change in objectives, content and methods. Vella, Caruana, and Zammit (2021) highlighted this need for change and for art educators' responsibility towards resolving global issues by reconstructing the learning experience invested in art for furthering sustainability. Addressing this global agenda, art educators have begun to reconceptualize education for teacher candidates in a way aimed at infusing it with principles of sustainable development (Pavlou & Kadji-Beltran, 2021). Effective approaches have been sought to empower teacher candidates to become proactive contributors to sustainable development. Our art-based approach discussed in this chapter results from an international collaboration with two undergraduate classes in 2021 at Concordia University in Canada and Hiroshima University in Japan. We demonstrate the effectiveness and challenges of implementing this approach through case study research.

Activating international collaborations

Our universities are officially committed to the 2030 agenda and are promoting partnerships and research collaborations to advance the SDGs. At Hiroshima University, the class is part of the pre-service teacher education programme designed for students to acquire their licence to teach in elementary schools, and, at Concordia, the Community Art Education class is designed for artist-teachers. The semesters of the two universities follow different schedules. This collaboration overlapped for six weeks during January and February 2021.

We initiated this transnational collaboration as a pilot study to familiarize teacher candidates with global perspectives for education through art guided by the UN's SDGs. None of the candidates had any learning experience that involved interactive learning with foreign universities in this manner. Thus, we began with an introductory level objective: to help candidates develop their own perspectives to frame their global actions for sustainability.

The context of the collaboration was designed with three core learning dimensions to enhance teachers' competencies across the globe (e.g. Longview Foundation, 2008). The first pertained to knowledge of the interdependency of world events and issues and involved the study of the UN's 2030 agenda (United Nations, 2015) for sustainable development in relation to the candidates' lives. This introduced the history of the 2030 agenda with relevant documents in relation to art education (e.g. United Nations Educational, Scientific and Cultural Organization, 2016). A study log was assigned to candidates in which they could file the photos and notes that they collected regarding the SDGs in daily life.

The second dimension was aimed at enhancing candidates' global competencies through art. Referring to a framework proposed by Pavlou and Kadji-Beltran (2021), we designed our pilot to place art at the heart of learning how to think and act as a global citizen in favour of sustainable development.

This learning involved the following processes: (1) creating a pre-image of self-identity as an educator in advance of collaboration, (2) working collaboratively as part of an international team to create a vision statement for sustainable development, (3) creating a post-image of self-identity to make one's new perspective explicit and (4) participating in an online exhibition related to individual and collective expressions that address a more sustainable world for the public (see Figure 20.1).

The third core dimension was to acquire pedagogical skills and nourish the commitment to helping students become responsible global citizens. From perspectives acquired through international learning, candidates were encouraged to create an art unit based on the SDGs. Our students were invited to take leadership roles within their assigned teams, to meet online as frequently as possible (using a communication platform such as Microsoft Teams) and to seek ways to implement the SDGs in their teaching practice locally. Due to the pandemic, this implementation varied based on location.

By implementing art-based international collaborative online learning, we intended to explore the potential of artistic practices and art education to help teacher candidates become oriented towards social activism and to think and act as global agents to advance sustainability as part of an international learning community. We believe that the power of art prompted the experience of transforming the self, with both the creator and the

Figure 20.1: Concordia University and Hiroshima University Partnership Online Art Exhibition 2021. © 2021 Kunstmatrix.

viewer gaining a broadened perspective that opened spaces for a shift in attitude and an increase in knowledge, as articulated by Jackson (1998), an educational philosopher. As Dewey (1934/2003) pointed out, art as a universal mode of language that enables us to share values of life through imagination that transcends different races and nations to create inner bonds between human beings and thus to create a more humane community. Our approach utilized this art-related power.

To determine the effectiveness of this approach and improve the concepts and practices involved, we conducted case study research. Three teacher candidates from each university (a total of both cohorts = 37 students) volunteered to participate in a conversation regarding the project. We also collected artwork and written documents that the participants produced during the course. The interview questions were structured with our three core learning dimensions in mind: (1) new perspectives for becoming a global agent through education for sustainable development (e.g. Do the SDGs inform how you envision your future art curriculum and instructional delivery?), (2) the process of arts-based collaborative online international learning (e.g. Can you talk about the process of developing a collaboration as a team? What strategies did you employ as an artist and teacher?) and (3) assessment of international learning (e.g. What recommendations do you have for improving future activities related to international learning?).

In analyzing a multitude of data, the artwork proved to be key in gaining an empathetic understanding because of the expressive qualities of student experiences (Eisner, 2006). We not only examined the aesthetic dimensions unique to each participant but also searched for meaning that emerged from the repetition of phenomena for the participants. Coding was used to classify visual and written texts to identify patterns within these conditions. Efforts were made to achieve the validity of interpretation by using multiple methods, such as interviews, document reviews and cross-checking performed by two researchers (Stake, 1995).

Motoki and Clayton: Sharing emergent perspectives

All six participants offered unique perspectives from which to become global agents. Their emergent perspectives included the teacher's role as a facilitator to transform consciousness, effective growth and the development of the sustainable world, the value of intercultural empathy, the importance of creating common ground to bring together those who have different viewpoints to work towards a shared goal, teachers' public responsibility and power to have a global impact regarding the UN SDGs, teachers' mindfulness of each learner's voice, and the power of collaboration to accomplish a significant task. In this case, we share reflections by Motoki and Clayton. The formation of each perspective was triggered when the participants encountered experiences that they found meaningful in regard to both personal growth and professional development while working with international team members to explore their vision for a more sustainable world.

Motoki Wada described how he, together with his team comprising two Japanese and two Canadian teacher candidates, created a collaged image on the theme of SDG #12, responsible consumption and production. As a team, they exchanged ideas via e-mail and chat platforms and agreed on the direction to take as well as the means of production. Subsequently, they proceeded to co-produce their image with the use of an online application, Canva, working in real-time despite the fourteen-hour time difference between Canada and Japan. Through teamwork, Wada built his confidence in interacting and collaborating with those who spoke a different language and lived in a foreign country. He expressed that this process enhanced his ability to create new relationships with people he had never met before. Prior to this collaboration, the pre-image of his self-identity as an educator revolved around creating new methods and/or materials the use of which is effective in teaching. This image radically changed after collaboration and came to embody a significant transformation. Wada stated,

> I [have] come to realize that the mission of the teaching profession is to connect people and nurture them so that they can live in society, and that I should aim to facilitate children so that they can build networks and co-operate with each other by themselves.

His post-image of self-identity was entitled 'Making Common Things Closer to People' (see Figure 20.2).

Wada bridged the gap between the Canadian and Japanese members by listening to the views on both sides, identifying common points and working together in a mutual direction. The final work, as shown in Figure 20.2, expresses Wada's newly acquired perspective:

> Straight, curved, and polygonal bands represent an individual's daily life. At first glance, it seems that many people have nothing to do with each other. However, there are common points of contact or intersection. The bubble placed where one kind of band meets another kind represents my image of the teacher I want to become. The teacher facilitates building the relationship between people by creating a space where people interact with each other, become aware of their relationships, and gain a new viewpoint for thinking.

Clayton Ross, a Canadian participant, also underwent a significant transformation in terms of his perspective by realizing the value of building co-operation and connection with people through engaging in a transnational collaborative project. He was among the few students across our classes who continued to contact team members and maintain friendships with them even after the course ended. Ross and two Japanese members used the online media Photopea for collaboration.

In working with Japanese members, Ross experienced cultural differences, noting that the Japanese were more reserved and hesitant about expressing their ideas. In response, he sought to facilitate conversation and made deliberate efforts to help them speak out by asking direct as well as open-ended questions. He believed that the team successfully co-produced the concept of design and, as a result, collaborated well as a team. Before the

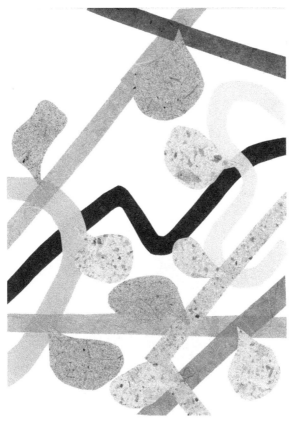

Figure 20.2: 'Making Common Things Closer to People' collage, Japanese paper, Motoki Wada. © 2021 Motoki Wada.

collaborative project began, he identified his role as one of leadership as an artist-teacher. As seen in his post-image (Figure 20.3), his orientation changed dramatically, and he began attaching much value to collaboration.

The figure at the base of the image represents Ross as a teacher, lifting the second figure, representing the learner, to reach a new goal. Clayton states the following:

> The goal (key) is too high for either of us to reach alone; however, we are able to retrieve the key together. The fact that my figure is at the bottom and the learner is on the top symbolises the fact that I do not want the key for myself, but rather, want the learner to take the key/achievement for [themself].

Drawing on these two examples, we consider how the transformation of the teacher candidates' perspectives was facilitated by a series of pedagogic moments. For example,

Figure 20.3: 'Education Cultivates Resolve' photograph. Photo-editing, Clayton Ross. © 2021 Clayton Ross.

students realized commonalities in the lifestyles of people from Canada and Japan, such as what undergraduate students do during after-school hours. These commonalities were discovered through the exchange of their study logs or informal conversation, and this prompted them to develop a sense of affinity together. Second, successful communication was key. The Japanese teacher candidates were not fluent in English, and, in general, all of the participants struggled with the language barrier in the beginning. However, both the Japanese and Canadian participants overcame this problem using visuals as communication tools and finding online translation media. The third aspect was the successful creation of a common vision for sustainable development that was acceptable to all members with different viewpoints joining together to achieve progress in collaboration. Finally, the achievement of a goal through teamwork made them feel rewarded, recognize the value in international exposure and appreciate how their art education perspectives shifted towards effective change.

Concluding remarks

Core global competencies acquired through this pilot included an understanding of the interdependency of global issues specified in the SDGs, empathetic communication, innovative thinking and adaptability. These competencies were gained when the participants interacted with the unfamiliar, including new subject matter, encountering unexpected situations with different viewpoints and then resolving to understand each other more fully. Learning together in this way generated a sense of global citizenship. Canadian and Japanese members of each team expressed their shared interpretations of the SDGs by actively exchanging ideas with fellow members and transforming local understandings into transnational ones.

The international collaboration project immersed the participants in a situation in which they had to co-operate with each other to achieve a goal and/or find commonalities to build upon to further develop their work. Transnational topics and universal modes of communication helped build empathetic communication among team members. This extended to innovative thinking through brainstorming activities and exchanging ideas regarding the aims of the SDGs. Adapting to barriers such as language and time differences, the teams improvised in the moment by coming up with ideas and sourcing images that matched individual directions to help create a collective space. Some students brought strong art backgrounds, while others brought more classroom teaching experience, both from different international contexts. By finding common ground with each other as well as developing mutual understanding, they kept all voices alive in the process.

This case study demonstrates that such activities are both practical and productive in terms of learning to teach, providing teacher candidates with opportunities for educative interaction beyond geographical borders, where the use of the visual arts facilitates dialogue and transforms perspectives towards thinking and acting as global agents. The study also indicates that, at the pre-service stage, it is important to have students engage in and achieve successful experiences of international collaboration to accomplish a shared goal. This type of experience will prompt them to form proactive attitudes towards contributing to sustainable development both locally and globally.

References

Dewey, J. (2003). Art as experience. In L. Hickman (Ed.), *The collected works of John Dewey, 1882–1953: The later works of John Dewey, 1925–1953* (Vol. 10). Toronto: InteLex. (Original work published 1934)

Eisner, E. (2006). Does arts-based research have a future? *Studies in Art Education, 48*(1), 9–18.

Jackson, P. (1998). *John Dewey and the lessons of art*. London: Yale University Press.

Longview Foundation. (2008). *Teacher preparation for the global age: The imperative for change*. http://www.longviewfdn.org/122/teacher-preparation-for-the-global-age.html

Pavlou, V., & Kadji-Beltran, K. (2021). Enhancing arts education with education for sustainable development competences: A proposed framework for visual arts education educators. In E. Wagner, C. Svendler Nielsen, L. Veloso, A. Suominen, & N. Pachova (Eds.), *Arts, sustainability and education* (pp. 217–235). New York, NY: Springer.

Stake, R. E. (1995). *The art of case study research*. London: Sage.

United Nations Educational, Scientific and Cultural Organization. (2016). *Schools in action: Global citizens for sustainable development: A guide for teachers*. https://www.gcedclearinghouse.org/resources/schools-action-global-citizens-sustainable-development-guide-teachers

United Nations. (2015). *Transforming our world: The 2030 agenda for sustainable development*. https://sdgs.un.org/2030agenda

Vella, R., Caruana, C., & Zammit, C. (2021). It's about time: Re-imagining present and future times in art, education and sustainable development. In E. Wagner, C. Svendler Nielsen, L. Veloso, A. Suominen, & N. Pachova (Eds.), *Arts, sustainability and education* (pp. 115–129). New York, NY: Springer.

Chapter 21

Social Sculpture Perspective: Re-Sculpting or De-Sculpting Citizenship by Shaping Art as a Vehicle for Social Change

Ana María Marqués Ibáñez

Introduction

The notion of social sculpture was first defined by Joseph Beuys in the 1970s to describe a concept that demonstrates the value of art as an approach towards social transformation. Social sculpture requires the participation of the social sphere to create the final work (Leo, Balla, Cantwell, & Tate 2020), fostering collective action among people by means of a process can change the participants' social values. Regarding the creative process, it is fundamental to consider what Beuys referred to as 'invisible materials' related to thoughts, invented or processed images, and discourse since these are the means by which we understand our environment and shape social sculpture (Beuys in Tisdall, 1979; Sacks, 2016, 2017, 2018). What Beuys referred to as dead zones were not physical residues but rather spaces void of thought based on prejudices and a lack of awareness of social issues. Drawing from Goethe's approach to science and Rudolf Steiner's ideas about social art, Beuys established a procedure for exploring participatory experiences, analyzing how reality is perceived through consciousness (Lachman, 2003; Steiner, 2013). Beuys saw everyone as artists and potential agents of social transformation and believed that the innovative artistic process of social sculpture invited citizens to explore their potential to enact social change (Adam, 1992; Beuys & Harlan, 2007).

Indeed, it is precisely these acts of participation in social sculpture processes that shape relationships between individuals and constitute the final piece, whether transient or long-lasting. Before commencing the tree-planting phase of the *7000 Oaks* project – Beuys's most emblematic work – workshops were held to foster interaction between participants. This piece is an example of social mobilization through which a collaborative and collective sculpture was created by group members (Antliff, 2014; Beuys, 1998). Although *7000 Oaks* is often associated with ecological art, based on the perception of tree-planting as a form of environmental protection, the artist aimed to change thinking rather than to save the environment (Gyorody, 2014; Quigley, 2020).

Social sculpture from the perspective of contemporary art

This section examines the terms *social practice, socially engaged practice* (Saldanha & Balsa, 2021; Vella & Sarantou, 2021) and *community art* (Jokela & Coutts, 2019) and publications related to social sculpture in contemporary art (Bacharach, Fjærestad, & Neil, 2016) as a basis for exploring artists who operate along similar lines to Beuys's philosophy, albeit without the necessary involvement of the general public.

Although *socially engaged practice* and *community art* both exist in cultural and intellectual spheres (Martegani, Kasper, & Drew, 2020), their difference lies at the institutional level since *community art* takes place outside museums, schools and community institutions, while *socially engaged practice* originates in dedicated art spaces.

The field of social sculpture has been researched by prominent social sculpture practitioners and thinkers such as Johannes Stuettgen and Shelley Sacks, and commentators Volker Harlan and Wolfgang Zumdick. One of the first socially engaged art projects was Martha Rosler's *If you lived here* (1989) in New York – a work involving artists and urban planners that highlighted the social issue of affordable housing in the United States. Meanwhile, Shelley Sacks collaborated with Beuys and created social sculpture projects (Sacks, 2011), such as *Exchange Values* (1996), which enabled participants to experience and analyze the exploitation of banana farmers in the Caribbean (Cook, 2000; Exchange Values, 2016). This installation included twenty 'listening stations' and a huge round table covered in banana skins, providing a space for engaging with the farmers' voices on the 'listening stations' and exploring new ideas to create a better future. The public's participation in a 'connective aesthetic practice' was an essential component of this piece with a view to building a common aesthetic through a process intended to overcome numbness while expanding the boundaries of art and empowering participants to engage with the challenges of their environment. Other social sculpture projects created by Sacks include *Landing Strip for Souls* (2000), *University of the Trees* (2005) (see Figure 21.1) and *Earth Forum* (2011) (see Figure 21.2). These works share common features as interdisciplinary

Figure 21.1: *University of the Trees* (2005), Shelley Sacks. Courtesy of the artist. *Note*: *University of Trees* (photograph) by Shelley Sacks (2005). SSRU (http://www.social-sculpture.org/university-of-the-trees-as-part-of-the-field-of-social-sculpture/).

Figure 21.2: *Earth Forum* (2011), Shelley Sacks. Courtesy of the artist. *Note: Earth Forum* (photograph) by Shelley Sacks (2011). SSRU (http://www.social-sculpture.org/earth-forum-at-occupy-democracy/).

and expanded artistic practices and experiences that examine the relationship between imaginative thinking (Quigley, 2020) and building a more democratic and ecologically sustainable system (Sacks, 2017). The sharing of experiences in these social sculpture connective practices promotes community thinking and enables people to become agents of social change (Sacks, 2018).

Contemporary artist Ai Weiwei's work (Sculpture As Social Practice, 2019) explores issues associated with human rights. Following the 2008 earthquake in Sichuan, the sculptor brought together volunteers to compile information on the names of children who had died when their schools collapsed. Other examples of artistic practices associated with Beuys's philosophy (Zumdick, 2019) were presented by the *Social Sculpture Research Unit* include *Agents of Change* (2006–07) and *Basic Income Network and Film* (2013).

Educational art practices through social sculpture

The design of the projects discussed in this section was initially conceived as a part of the art education part of the *Practicum I* course taken by students of the early childhood and primary education degrees at the University of La Laguna in Tenerife, as a means of creating and enriching activities for their subsequent application in school classrooms.

Three educational art practices based on social sculpture were conducted: a displacement project, a social education methodology project and an experimental collaborative drawing project. These projects were designed for individual or group work and comprised a review of the relevant theory, the presentation of case studies in the classroom and an examination of works by social sculpture artists. According to the ideas of Sholette, Bass, and Social Practice Queens (2018) and Helguera (2011), these artistic practices should be focused on the school, the local community and the surrounding environment. As such, before starting the projects, examples of community art and socially engaged art (both of which differ from the concept of social sculpture) were presented and discussed in class to enrich the artistic vision of the students.

Displacement project

This project is centred around Marcel Duchamp's concept of the *readymade*, a concept also used by Beuys to define his social sculpture work, whereby an element from any context can be turned into art by displacing and displaying it as such and forcing the spectator to think. While this project did not employ Duchamp's concept of distancing whereby a found object is exhibited as a work of art, the objects were decontextualized and used as elements for reflection and creation.

The following instructions were given to students: create a project based on the concept of the *readymade*. An everyday object or action is displaced in such a way that its new location provokes interesting social responses or perceptions.

The concept of found art was employed to adapt this activity for use in primary and early childhood classrooms, taking an icon related to ecology as the basis for representation through drawing and real objects (see Figure 21.3).

Social education methodology project

Certain learning approaches are based on introspection and individual knowledge. In social practice projects, these assumptions are challenged to transform forms of learning into social action. This project employs a social education methodology based on the idea that all social projects are created in groups within the community, whereby concepts of art must be explored and acquired through group communication rather than on an individual basis.

The following instructions were given to students: choose an individual activity from your past educational experience related to any subject area. Transform this individual activity to involve other people whereby issues are solved, and the group acquires knowledge.

Knolling photography (a photograph taken from above of a group of objects) was employed to adapt this activity to the educational context as a vehicle to learn about colour and ecology simultaneously. A symbol of ecology was selected – in this case,

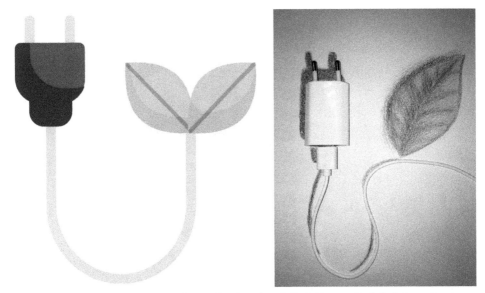

Figure 21.3: Icon and composition. Found art and ecology (2021). Keyla Fiesenig. Bachelor's degree in primary education.

the sun – and a group of students created a knolling photograph by arranging found objects in the colour spectrum of the rainbow. Figure 21.4 shows an example created individually due to COVID-19 restrictions. This activity offered multiple opportunities for group work by assigning different colours, shapes and areas to different students. Collective reflection was encouraged through dialogue among the students while arranging the objects.

Experimental collaborative drawing project

Finally, in the collaborative drawing activity, the students work in groups to create a piece of art associated with an ecological theme while learning about different concepts of drawing, tonal ranges and composition. The aim is for the students to undergo a transformation through socially enriched artistic experiences. Collective reflection and creation of social sculptures make artistic actions multidimensional and effective in re-sculpting and de-sculpting citizenship by implementing the arts as a tool for social change. In Figure 21.5, a collaborative drawing related to a social issue – in this case, ecology – was created as a group activity. This activity is inspired by the *exquisite corpse* technique used by the Dadaists and Surrealists, albeit in this case with greater conceptual coherence and a more collaborative approach.

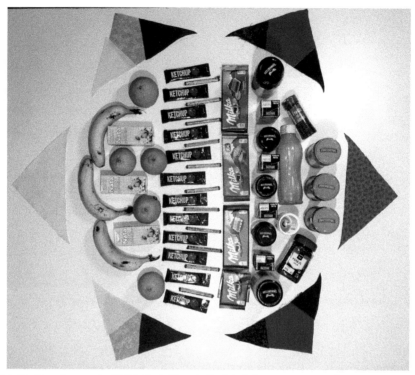

Figure 21.4: Knolling photography (2021). Keyla Fiesenig. Bachelor's degree in primary education.

The following instructions were given to students: each participant should create a drawing related to a topic previously selected by the group, such as environmental protection, on a medium of predetermined dimensions. The lines were extended to enable the next participant to continue the drawing. Finally, the individual drawings were joined together to form a final composition. In this example, the pieces fit together like a jigsaw puzzle to help students learn about sustainability.

Conclusion

Social art methodologies are wholly dependent on multidisciplinary group participation (Bishop, 2006) as this dynamic generates collective thinking that transcends individual skills. In the educational context, such practices offer future teachers the opportunity to act as agents of social change. The activities presented are open and flexible in terms of approach and technique and, therefore, are suitable for development and adaptation to different types of learning content. Effective implementation of these activities relies on

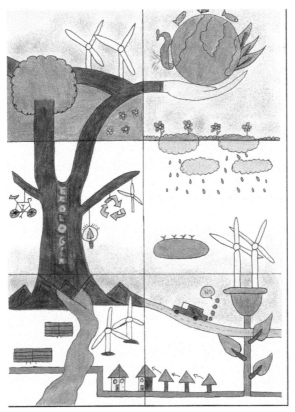

Figure 21.5: Collaborative learning (2022). Crisbel Casañas Padrón. Master's degree in early childhood education.

selecting appropriate topics and approaches to suit the target group, considering factors such as age, diversity, interests and context.

Although these social sculpture art projects are intended as educational practices, they can also be implemented in community art contexts by adapting the objectives, formats and techniques used. Although collective creativity and reflection are the main points of focus in the classroom context, these activities also have additional benefits when extended to the broader community, such as dialogue between different generations and interaction and collaboration among citizens. Accordingly, the results of such projects can be highly enriching when there is generational and social diversity among participants working together outside traditional learning environments, such as the teacher–student classroom setting, which is characterized by generational – and hence experiential – uniformity of learners and acquired skills and competencies.

References

Adam, D. (1992). Joseph Beuys: Pioneer of a radical ecology. *Art Journal, 51*(2), 26–34. https://doi.org/10.2307/777391, https://www.jstor.org/stable/777391

Antliff, A. (2014). *Joseph Beuys*. London: Phaidon Press.

Bacharach, S., Fjærestad, S. B., & Neil, J. (2016). *Collaborative art in the twenty-first century*. London: Routledge.

Beuys, J. (1998). *Social sculpture, invisible sculpture, alternative society, free international university. In conversation with Eddy Devolder*. Gerpinnes Tandem DL.

Beuys, J., & Harlan. V. (2007). *What is art? Conversation with Joseph Beuys*. West Hoathly: Clairview Books.

Bishop, C. (2006). *Participation (Documents of contemporary art)*. London: Whitechapel Gallery.

Cook, I. (2000). Cultural geographies in practice: Social sculpture and connective aesthetics: Shelley Sacks's Exchange values. *Ecumene, 7*(3), 337–343. https://doi.org/10.1177/096746080000700306

Exchange Values. (2016), *Exchange Values – On the Table*. http://exchange-values.org/story-of-the-project/on-the-table-2007/

Gyorody, A. (2014). The medium and the message: Art and politics in the work of Joseph Beuys. *Sixties: A Journal of History, Politics & Culture, 7*(2), 117–137. https://doi.org/10.1080/17541328.2015.1043800

Helguera, P. (2011). *Education for socially engaged art: A materials and techniques handbook*. New York, NY: Jorge Pinto Books.

Jokela, T., & Coutts, G. (Eds.). (2019). *Relate North: Collaborative art, design and education. Arctic sustainable arts and design (ASAD)*. Columbus, OH: Insea Publications. https://doi.org/10.24981/2019-2

Lachman, G. (2003). *A secret history of conciousness*. London: Lindisfarne Book.

Leo, G., Balla, D., Cantwell, A., & Tate, B. (2020). Regulating engagement through dissent. In M. McDermont, T. Cole, J. Newman, & A. Piccini (Eds.), *Imagining regulation differently: Co-creating regulation for engagement* (pp. 145–166). Bristol: University of Bristol.

Martegani, M., Kasper, J., & Drew, E. (2020). *More art in the public eye*. Durham, NC: Duke University Press.

Quigley, G. (2020). Finding the golden thread: Why we need social sculpture. In D. Curtis (Ed.), *Using the visual and performing arts to encourage pro-environmental behaviour* (pp. 113–126). Cambridge, MA: Cambridge Scholars Publishing.

Sacks, S. (2011). Social sculptures and new organs of perception. New practices and new pedagogy for a humane and ecologically viable future. In C. M. Lern Hayes & V. Walters (Eds.), *Beuysian legaciess in Ireland and beyond*. Berlin: Lit Verlag.

Sacks, S. (2017). Contemporary social sculpture and the field of transformation. In J. Kettel (Ed.), *Übergangsformen von Kunst und Pädagogik in der Kulturellen Bildung-Künstlerische Kunstpädagogik im Kontext*. Oberhausen: Athena Verlag.

Sacks, S. (2018). Sustainability without the I-sense is nonsense: Inner technologies for a viable future and the inner dimension of sustainability. In O. Parody & K. Tamm (Eds.), *Personal sustainability exploring the far side of sustainable development* (pp. 171–188). London: Routledge.

Saldanha, A., & Balsa, R. (Eds.). (2021). Invisibilidades. Revista Ibero-Americana de Pesquisa em Educação, cultura e artes. In *Arte como Escultura Social*. Rede Ibero-Americana de Educação Artística APECV – Associação de Professores de Expressão e Comunicação Visual (Vol. 1, no. 15, pp. 1–105). https://doi.org/10.24981/16470508.15

Sculpture As Social Practice. (2019). https://somethingcurated.com/2019/10/30/sculpture-as-social-practice/

Sholette, G., Bass, C., & Social Practice Queens. (2018). *Art as social action: An introduction to the principles and practices of teaching social practice art*. New York, NY: Allworth Press.

Social Sculpture Research Unit (SSRU). (2021). http://www.social-sculpture.org/

Steiner, R. (2013). *The social future: Culture, equality and the economy*. Hudson, NY: Steiner Books.

Tisdall, C. (1979). *Joseph Beuys*. New York, NY: Solomon R. Guggenheim Museums, Thames and Hudson.

Vella, R., & Sarantou, M. (2021). *Documents of socially engaged art* (1st ed.). Columbus, OH: Insea Publications. https://doi.org/10.24981/2021-DSEA, https://www.insea.org/wp-content/uploads/2021/12/DocumentsOfSociallyEngagedArt_web.pdf

Zumdick, W. (2019). Social sculpture and education: Schiller, Steiner, Beuys & Sacks. In. V. D. Rijke (Ed.), *Art and soul: Rudolf Steiner, interdisciplinary art and education* (pp. 97–115). New York, NY: Springer Nature.

Contributors

Thomas Büsch (MA Visual Communication, Kunsthochschule Kassel, 1986) formed a part of the organizational team for art events such as the documenta IX in Kassel between 1989 and 1997 and took part in several international exhibitions as an artist and a curator. In 1998, Thomas Büsch moved to Istanbul as an artist-in-residence funded by the Berlin Senate and began teaching in the Department of Visual Communication at Istanbul Bilgi University. Since 2002, he has been producing documentaries with his wife Sabine Küper-Büsch and has developed a curriculum to teach short-film production using the single-shot technique to diverse groups. Thomas Büsch has served and acts as a consultant for several artists in residency programmes from Germany, Austria and Switzerland in Istanbul. The artist, filmmaker and curator brings his diverse expertise to the organization and virtual presentation of the Mahalla Festival and other platforms of the Diyalog association.

Vincent Caruana's mission in life is to inspire people to take action for a better self and a better world. In 2014, he obtained his Ph.D., focusing on education for sustainability and the social economy, through four case studies, in Egypt, Malta, Italy and Palestine. Vince is currently a full-time lecturer and researcher at CEER – Malta's University Centre for Environmental Education and Research. He is active in the social and development scene locally and at a European level and is an established mentor, trainer and evaluator for various organizations.

Antonia Condeza-Marmentini is a Chilean geographer, with a Ph.D. in education from the Pontificia Universidad Católica de Chile. She is currently a faculty member in the School of Education at Alberto Hurtado University and a director of the 'Transformative Education Project' focused on the development of teacher training programmes in the Anthropocene context. Her areas of interest link Latinoamerican studies to socio-ecological issues. Based on a complex thinking approach, affective turn and decoloniality, her research is focused on the configuration processes of complex environmental knowledge at schools.

Stephanie H. Danker, Ph.D., is committed to creating integrated learning experiences with students and colleagues, and dedicated to expanding awareness, critical thinking and empathy through experiences with art. She is an associate professor of art education and a coordinator of the Pre-Art Therapy programme at Miami University (Ohio). She earned her Ph.D. in art education from the University of Illinois at Urbana-Champaign. Regarding this work, she is deeply grateful for her co-authors and colleagues from both the university and the local community, who are devoted to climate change education and the belief that art can impact social change.

Katie L. Feilen, Ph.D., is an engaged scientist, educator and conservation biologist. She studies how ecological systems respond to changes. She also engages communities in conversations about climate change through art and works to increase science engagement to broad audiences. She received an MA and Ph.D. in anthropology (biological) from the University of California – Davis and is an assistant teaching professor at Miami University.

Felix Amofa Gyebi (B.A., Dip., MPhil.) is a mixed-media artist and an educator with vested interest in the use of mobile media. He is currently a Ph.D. candidate and an Adobe Digital Coach at Swinburne University in Australia. He is passionate about Emerging Media and Smartphone Filmmaking. As a co-producer at MINA, he has contributed in diverse ways on committees during its annual global smartphone conferences. He was part of the production team that worked on a recent documentary project known as the OPERA project (https://opera.eclc.org.au/). The project captures personal stories about how old people in the Eastern part of Melbourne in Australia enjoy and live independent lifestyles even as they advance in age. Felix explores community engagement through storytelling for social change. His current project *Trash to Treasure* (https://spark.adobe.com/page/IT13uQptuAaa1/) explores collaborative smartphone documentary practice among the Krobo community of Ghana. He looks forward to building relationships and sharing experiences with members of the smartphone filmmaking community across the world who have keen interest in giving a voice to marginalised communities.

Emese Hall is a senior lecturer in art and design education at the School of Education, University of Exeter, UK. Previously a primary and early years teacher, she has worked within teacher education since 2005. Her research interests include teachers' professional learning and environmental art education. She is a member of the International Society for Education through Art (InSEA) and the (UK) National Society for Education in Art and Design (NSEAD), until recently, holding the position of NSEAD Vice President (January 2018–December 2021). She was a co-editor (with Nigel Meager) of the Pedagogy Volume of the *International Encyclopedia of Art and Design Education* (Wiley-Blackwell, 2019); a subject lead for Primary Art, Craft and Design for Oak National Academy (October 2020–March 2021); a member of the (UK) National Expert Subject Advisory Group for Art and Design Education; and (UK) South West Regional Network co-ordinator for the Cambridge Primary Review Trust.

Maria Huhmarniemi (DA) is an artist–researcher–teacher in the University of Lapland and a docent at the University of the Eastern Finland, in the field of social pedagogy, especially community-based art education. She is a senior research fellow for the AMASS (*Acting on the Margins: Arts as Social Sculpture*) H2020-funded research project. Her post-doctoral research focuses on arts-based methods in environmental conflict mediation, creative tourism and transformative education. She has over 30 peer reviewed research publications and she had participated a number of group and joint exhibitions as an installation artists and artists-researcher.

Martha Ioannidou has a doctorate in art history and is a museologist, senior assistant professor at the School of Primary Education, Faculty of Education, Aristotle University of Thessaloniki (AUTH) and a member of the Centre of Pedagogical Research and Praxis – CPRP. Her BA, Certificate, MA and Doctorate are in art history and theory (Aristotle University of Thessaloniki, Universities of Cambridge and Essex), and she also holds a PGD in Museum Studies (University of Leicester). In December 2006, she attended the Foundation Course successfully in Art Therapy (BAAT, London). She has worked in museums in England and Greece and since 2000, before coming to the Faculty of Education, held academic posts at universities in Greece and abroad. Her research interests and publications focus on art history, learning through the arts, arts education and multicultural – museum education, visual art education and sustainable development.

Bob Jickling is a long-time Yukon resident and professor emeritus at Lakehead University. His interests include environmental philosophy; environmental, experiential and outdoor education; and philosophy of education. His current research includes what he calls Wild Pedagogies – an attempt to find openings for radical re-visioning of education. His most recent collaborative books include *Wild Pedagogies: Touchstones for Re-Negotiating Education and the Environment in the Anthropocene* (2018) and *Environmental Ethics: A Sourcebook for Educators* (2021). As a lifelong wilderness traveler, much of his inspiration is derived from the landscape of his home in Canada's Yukon.

Chrysanthi Kadji-Beltran is an associate professor at Frederick University (education for sustainable development), vice chairperson of the Department of Education. She received her Ph.D. (environmental education) and M.Sc. (science education) in educational sciences from the Institute of Educational Sciences, University of Warwick. She graduated from the programme BEd in primary education at the Aristoteles University of Thessaloniki with honours and obtained with honours her teaching diploma by the Cyprus Pedagogical Academy. She worked as a post-doctoral researcher at Zurich University, Institute of Environmental Sciences (currently institute of evolutionary biology). She teaches education for the environment and sustainable development in undergraduate and postgraduate programmes and coordinates the masters programme MSc in education for sustainable development and social change. Her current research focuses on ESD competences, quality education and transformative ESD in teacher education and university education.

Shafkat Khan is a conservation ecologist with training in forests and climate change. He received his Ph.D. from the Odum School of Ecology, University of Georgia. During his time with Project Dragonfly, an interdisciplinary conservation program at Miami University, Shafkat gained a deep appreciation for the connection between participatory education and community-based conservation. He has taught field courses in tropical biology, traditional ecological knowledge and religion-based conservation in Guyana, Baja California of Mexico, and Western Ghats of India. Informed by his experience and the need to address conservation problems through different lenses, Shafkat sees art-based engagement to be a central piece for promoting community conversations on climate change and other environmental challenges. Shafkat currently serves as the director of Conservation for the Detroit Zoological Society.

Sabine Küper-Büsch (MA political science, Hamburg University, 1992) has published several books and articles on politics, art and culture in Turkey and the Middle East and produces documentary films together with her husband Thomas Büsch. The Istanbul-based filmmaker has organized art events related to political conflicts in cooperation with local and international organizations since 2006. She curated and published several exhibitions and publications on political cartoons between 2006 and 2017. These activities responded to the crisis related to cartoons of the prophet Muhammad published in a Danish newspaper in 2005 and were able to serve as a platform for peaceful dialogue on the hot topic. Together with her husband Thomas Büsch, she participated three times in the parallel event programme of the Istanbul Art Biennale as a curator of mobilizing art events to strengthen the civil society. One of them was the first edition of the Mahalla Festival in 2017.

Susan (Susie) Lachal is an artist and a change agent for human equity working in Naarm/Melbourne Australia and Kampong Thom Cambodia. Her artistic practice reconsiders ways to act and become with things in the world, by encouraging greater human equity and environmental justice. Susie's Ph.D. examined how socially engaged art practice can develop enhanced attention to the entangled relations between humans and non-human things. What emerged was new methodology for socially engaged artistic practice to engage with critical posthuman concepts. She continues to make object-based art focusing on environmental justice while her social practice relationally engages with human equity in Cambodia. https://www.susielachal.com/

Costas Mantzalos was trained in the visual arts in the United Kingdom. He also registered for a higher research degree and investigated the survey of post-modern graphic arts in Cyprus. His first academic post was in 1989, while in 1991, he was appointed as a head of the department. He is currently the dean of the School of Arts, Communication and Cultural Studies at Frederick University. Parallel to his academic career, he has been involved in numerous international art and design consultations. Since 1996, he has been the cofounder of the TWO|FOUR|TWO art group, with architect Constantinos Kounnis. The group lives and believes in art as an evolutionary institution which changes in time and mutates with the passing of time; however, like democracy, it remains a supreme power vested in the people and characterized by the recognition of equality of opinions and voices. The group has had an active involvement in the international art scene.

Eva Marín Peinado is an artist, researcher and lecturer. She investigates the tensions etched in the landscape and specifically the periphery as a place of ecological destruction, exploring how people living in such areas attempt to recover a sense of nature. Her practice takes the form of audio-visual installations, videos, photographs, writing and presentations. She holds a Ph.D. in fine arts from the University of Barcelona (2017). Her thesis, entitled 'The institutionalized landscape versus the invisible landscape: A critical approach through artistic practice', received the Special Doctoral Award from the university. Her work has been shown in galleries and museums in and around Barcelona, including Senda, Can Manyé, Can Palauet and Arts Santa Mònica. She is undertaking a long-term artist residency at Roca Umbert, Fàbrica de les Arts and has been involved in environmental and feminist activism since her youth. https://www.evamarin.net/theexpandedgarden

Guillermo Marini has a BA in philosophy from Pontificia Universidad Católica Argentina (2002), EdM in arts in education from Harvard University (2007) and a Ph.D. in philosophy and education from Columbia University (2012). His teaching and research deals with relationships between everyday aesthetics and the experience of students, teachers and administrators in schools, for instance, the association between certain school spaces and specific temporal practices, and the comprehension of what 'nature' stands for on school grounds. At present, he is involved in a three-year study aimed at exploring a common language among those who build and inhabit schools. He has published in *ARQ, Studies in Philosophy and Education, Journal of Philosophy of Education, Journal of Aesthetic Education, Visual Ethnography, Visual Communication, International Journal of Education Through Art, Educação e Sociedade*, and *Trans/Form/Ação*. Currently, he is an associate professor at the School of Education, Pontificia Universidad Católica de Chile. https://uc-cl.academia.edu/GuillermoMarini

Ana María Marqués Ibáñez completed her Ph.D. at the Faculty of Fine Arts at the University of Granada and currently works as a permanent teacher at the Faculty of Education and the Faculty of Fine Arts at the University of La Laguna, Tenerife. Her doctorate analyzed the ability of images to communicate in classical Italian literary texts such as the Divine Comedy with a visual comparison of illustrations and visual representations in Dante's work.

Currently, she teaches on the teaching degrees in early childhood and primary education, master's degree in teaching and in certain areas in fine arts. She focuses on the dissemination of contemporary art and its relationship with the field of art education. Her current research focuses on the creation of teaching materials related to visual culture.

Soula Mitakidou is a professor emerita of Aristotle University of Thessaloniki, where she served at the School of Primary Education. She received her BA from the English Department of Aristotle University of Thessaloniki, her MA from McGill University of Montreal, Canada and after completing her Ph.D. coursework at Kent State University, USA, she was awarded her doctorate degree from the School of Early Childhood Education of Aristotle of Thessaloniki, Greece. Her teaching experience covers a wide age range from preschool to graduate school students. She has also worked extensively with teachers in in-service workshops. Her research interests and publications focus on the many aspects of diversity, including the education of children from vulnerable social groups and in particular, the teaching of Greek as a second language for language minority children, cross-cultural/inclusive education and literacy development through children's literature.

Kazuyo Nakamura is a professor of art education and curriculum studies and serves as a chair of the Curriculum and Instruction Department at Hiroshima University, Japan. Her research focuses on a historical study of John Dewey's philosophy of art and aesthetic education for children. She is a director of John Dewey Society of Japan and serves also as a director of Japanese Association of Art Education. Her recent book publications include *The Handbook of Art Education* (Sangensha) and *Living Histories: Global Conversations in Art Education* (Intellect).

Felipe Palma is an assistant professor in the School of Anthropology at Pontificia Universidad Católica de Chile. He is the director of the Visual Anthropology Lab (LAV-UC) and a researcher of Center of Intercultural and Indigenous Research (CIIR) at the same institution. He completed his Ph.D. in visual sociology at Goldsmiths, University of London, and his undergraduate studies at Pontificia Universidad Católica de Chile. His research interests lie in an interdisciplinary approach to understanding and exploring the social world using visual, sensory and other experimental media.

Victoria Pavlou is a professor of visual arts education at the Education Department of Frederick University, Cyprus. Her teaching and research focus on initial and continuous professional development of generalist teachers in art education and on children's learning preferences, motivation and creative potential. Her professional passions include changing attitudes, building confidence and connecting art with real-life issues. She has experiences in numerous European-funded projects as a partner and/or external evaluator. She is the coordinator of the CARE (Visual art education in new times: Connecting Art with REal life issues, 2019–22) and the CARESS (Critical ARts Education for Sustainable Societies, 2022–24) European-funded projects. She is a member of InSEA (serving for several years in the ERC InSEA council – elected and co-opted) and an editorial board member of the *International Journal of Education through Art*.

Margerita Pulè is an artist, curator, researcher and cultural manager, with a master's degree in fine arts from the University of Malta. She is a founder–director of Unfinished Art Space, an independent and nomadic space showing contemporary art in Malta, through which she engages in an open, collaborative and symbiotic curatorial practice. She is also a founder–member of the Magna Żmien Foundation, which digitizes twentieth century analogue home archives, forming a community archive accessible to researchers and artists. She was a researcher on the Horizon 2020 project Acting on the Margins; Arts as Social Sculpture (2020–23), measuring the impacts of socially engaged art practice, and previously was an editor of ArtPaper, Malta's quarterly art publication.

Recent curatorial projects include The Ordinary Lives of Women (co-curation, 2022, Spazju Kreattiv), Past Continuous (solo show, Alex Urso, 2021, ŻiguŻajg Festival), Debatable Land(s), Strangers in a Strange Land (group show, 2020, MUŻA) and Daily Bread (co-curation, 2019, Gabriel Caruana Foundation).

Maren Richter is an Austrian curator and researcher. Currently she works remotely in Namibia for WIBCA (Windhoek International Biennial of Contemporary Art) as a consultant and curator. Her work is characterized by aspects of artistic practice as a forum for expressions and concerns, forms and methods of sharing experiences, stories and (local) knowledge. Her work is engaged with the 'performative' as a way of producing collaborative modes and models of and for caring. She aims to look into the potentiality of the diversity of encounters, which art can advocate. From 2016 to 2018, she was a curator for visual arts for the European Capital of Culture, Valletta2018. She is the co-initiator of 'Grammar of Urgencies', a research-based collaborative project. In 2013, she co-curated the Maldives Pavilion 'Portable Nation' at the 55th Venice Biennial, which was designed as an 'eco-aesthetical' space for international exchange. Recent exhibitions: *Debatable Land(s)* (2020, 2021), *Hasenleiten Revue* (2020), *This Land is Your Land* (2019), *Dal-Baħar Madwarha* (2018) and *Fleeting Territories* (2017).

Francisco Schwember is a Chilean artist and researcher. He has a Ph.D. in educational sciences from the Pontificia Universidad Católica de Chile. He teaches at the School of Art and the MA in cultural heritage programme at the same institution and coordinates the Minga Nómade project, a platform focused on generating transdisciplinary and collaborative experiences based on indigenous communities' ancestral knowledge. His work focuses on the relationship between art, education, heritage and indigenous communities from a transdisciplinary approach and an action-research methodology. Francisco Schwember has taken part in over 70 art exhibition projects and is the author of the books Journeys Through the Invisible Knowledge, Class Lessons and Contemporary Chilean Painting: Practice and Displacements from the UC School of Art.

Anita Sinner is a professor of art education at The University of British Columbia, Vancouver, Canada. Her research interests include artwork scholarship, international art education, historical perspectives and community education. She works extensively with stories as pedagogic pivots with particular emphasis on creative nonfiction, and diverse forms of arts research in relation to curriculum studies and social and cultural issues in education. Recent books include *Provoking the Field: International Perspectives on Visual Arts PhDs in Education* (Intellect) and the companion text, *Visually Provoking: Dissertations in Art Education* (Lapland).

Chris Turner has spent a major part of his professional career in education. Currently, he is an honorary lecturer at the University of Exeter and an associate fellow of the Centre for Climate Change and Sustainability Education at University College London. As the principal of a community college for over 20 years, he witnessed the power of the arts in engaging children, young people and adults in collaborative and transdisciplinary learning experiences. Chris has a first degree in zoology, an MA in educational leadership and a Doctorate doctorate in Education education from the University of Exeter. His research and writing interests are in the aesthetics and ecology of education from which he has developed the theoretical concepts of aesthoecology. He is a member of the Creativity and Emergent Educational Futures Network, an affiliate of the Global Systems Institute at the University of Exeter and he has lectured widely on aesthoecology, educational leadership and community education. He is a member of the Philosophy of Education Society of Great Britain, a Fellow fellow of the Royal Society of Arts, a fellow of the Linnean Society of London and, in 2001, was awarded an OBE for services to education.

Raphael Vella is a professor of art education at the Faculty of Education, University of Malta. Apart from coordinating postgraduate degrees in art education and social practice arts and critical education, he is involved in research projects related to sustainability and art, the impact of socially engaged arts, and arts education in Malta. His research interests include art and art education in the Mediterranean region and issues of identity in contemporary artistic practice and pedagogies. His publications include *Artist-Teachers in Context: International Dialogues* (Sense, 2016), *Art – Ethics – Education*, co-edited with C.-P. Buschkühle and D. Atkinson (2020, Brill/Sense) and *Documents of Socially Engaged Art*, co-edited with M. Sarantou (2021, InSEA). He is also active as an artist and a curator. His artistic work has been shown in many exhibitions in different countries, including Malta, Germany, France, the United Kingdom, Argentina, the United States, Canada, Japan and New Zealand.

Contributors

Ernst Wagner studied painting, sculpture and teaching at the Art Academy in Munich. Later he read for a Ph.D. in art history at the Ludwigs Maximilian University of Munich. Today he researches and teaches mainly in international networks, currently at the University of Munich and at the UNESCO Chair in Arts and Culture in Education, University of Erlangen-Nuremberg, where he coordinates the European section of the project 'Exploring Visual Cultures' (www.explore-vc.org). His main areas of interest are arts education and sustainable development (in a broad sense); international and transcultural pedagogy; transnational artistic projects.

Milton Keynes UK
Ingram Content Group UK Ltd.
UKHW052125240124
436640UK00002B/32